W9-CES-588

SECOND EDITION

The Writer's Handbook

REVIEWER/CONSULTANTS

John B. Karls
Milwaukee Public Schools

Ronald Szymanski
Milwaukee Public Schools

National Textbook Company
a division of *NTC Publishing Group* • Lincolnwood, Illinois USA

ACKNOWLEDGMENTS

From "The Life and Death of Vaudeville" in MUCH ADO ABOUT ME by Fred Allen. Published by Little, Brown and Company; copyright 1956 by Portland Hoffa Allen (pseudonym for Mary Portland Sullivan)./ From "As I Walked Out One Evening"; Copyright 1940 and renewed 1968 by W. H. Auden. Reprinted from COLLECTED SHORTER POEMS 1927–1957, by W. H. Auden, by permission of Random House, Inc. and Faber and Faber, Inc./ From TEACHER IN AMERICA by Jacques Barzun. Published by Little, Brown and Company in association with The Atlantic Monthly Press./ Mildred R. Bennett, THE WORLD OF WILLA CATHER, New Edition with Notes and Index. Copyright © 1961 by the University of Nebraska Press. Reprinted by permission./ "A Sunny Garden" by Norbert Blei. Copyright by Norbert Blei and used by permission./ "Driving to Town Late to Mail a Letter" by Robert Bly. Reprinted from SILENCE IN THE SNOWY FIELDS, Wesleyan University Press, 1962. Copyright © 1962 by Robert Bly, with his permission./ From A MAN FOR ALL SEASONS by Robert Bolt. Published by Random House, Inc.; copyright 1960 by Robert Bolt./ From SILENT SPRING by Rachel Carson. Published by Houghton Mifflin Company; copyright 1962 by Rachel L. Carson./ From "City bike paths: less than primrose" by John Conroy in The Chicago Guide, June, 1974; copyright 1974 by WFMT, Inc./ From 1974 CONSUMER BUYING GUIDE. Published by Publications International, Ltd.; copyright 1974 Publications International, Ltd./ "Me" by Danny in I HEARD A SCREAM IN THE STREET, edited by Nancy Larrick. Published by M. Evans and Company, Inc./ From "Attorney for the Defense" by Clarence Darrow in Esquire Magazine, October, 1973. Reprinted by permission of Esquire Magazine © 1936 by Esquire, Inc./ From "Poof! The Magic Castle" by Angela Rocco DeCarlo in the Chicago Tribune, May 19, 1974; copyright 1974 Angela Rocco DeCarlo./ From "What's Wrong with American Medicine?" by Donald Drake in A.D.; copyright 1972 A.D. Used by permission./ "Sonnet" by Alfred A. Duckett in

(ACKNOWLEDGMENTS continued on page 255.)

1995 Printing

This edition first published in 1990 by National Textbook Company, a division of NTC Publishing Group.
© Copyright 1990, 1975 by NTC Publishing Group, 4255 West Touhy Avenue,
Lincolnwood (Chicago), Illinois 60646-1975 U.S.A. Originally published by
Laidlaw Brothers, Publishers. All rights reserved. No part of this book may be
reproduced, stored in a retrieval system, or transmitted in any form or by any
means, electronic, mechanical, photocopying, recording or otherwise, without
the prior permission of NTC Publishing Group.
Library of Congress Card Catalog Number 89-61659
Manufactured in the United States of America.

5 4 3 2 1 BC 9 8 7 6 5

Contents

How to Use This Book

Whatever kind of writing you do—practical, creative, or some of both—this book can help you solve the writing problems you are bound to encounter. Make no mistake about it, transforming a blank sheet of paper into an effective and interesting written communication poses problems. What do you say? How do you say it? What form do you use? What rules do you follow? How is an essay different from a research report? A business letter from a friendly letter? How do you write a summary? A poem? A story?

The Writer's Handbook is designed to help you solve problems at each stage of the writing process—before you write, as you write, and after you have completed your first draft. To make finding solutions to your writing problems as easy as possible, *The Writer's Handbook* is divided into three major sections.

Writer's Glossary

This first section of the handbook is made up of alphabetically arranged terms and topics important to writers and writing. In it you will find brief definitions, explanations, and examples. At the same time this glossary acts as an index for the rest of the book. Remember, when you need a solution to a writing problem, look in the Glossary first. There you'll find a quick answer, a direction to other parts of the book, or both. For example, suppose you are in a class and the term *central idea* comes up. You're not sure what it means or how it relates to tomorrow's assignment. Look under **C** in the Writer's Glossary.

central idea

The main point developed in a paragraph or in a series of paragraphs is called the central idea. Often expressed in a **topic sentence**, the central idea helps the writer select and arrange details. Every sentence in a paragraph should be related to a central idea. However, you may sometimes use several paragraphs to develop a single idea.

(*See also* **coherence**; **unity**; WRITER'S GUIDE, page 194.)

Terms in heavy type—like **topic sentence**, **coherence**, and **unity**—are related to the term you looked up, and they too have explanations in the Writer's Glossary. If the term you've looked up is also discussed in the Writer's Guide, page numbers will direct you to additional information there.

Writer's Guide

The Writer's Glossary provides answers to the question, What is it? The Writer's Guide provides answers to the question, How do I use it? For example, the Glossary tells you what *conflict* is. The Guide tells you how to use conflict in writing a story.

Because the act of writing is a process that progresses through three stages—prewriting, writing, and revision—the Guide has three divisions, Before You Write, While You Write, and After You Write. A special section gives advice for writing The Research Paper.

Because the kind of writing you do is determined by your purpose, While You Write offers advice for three different kinds of writing, Writing to Inform, Writing to Persuade, and Writing to Entertain.

Practice

The last section in *The Writer's Handbook* provides practice exercises you can use to clinch your understanding of some common problems in usage and mechanics. For example, after you've read the explanation of **its and it's** in the Glossary, you can try your hand at the exercise on page 247 to see if you can apply what you have learned.

Remember, the fastest way to find help for a writing problem is to look first in the Glossary. Now, pick a problem, and see how *The Writer's Handbook* can help you solve it.

Writer's
Glossary

A

a and an

A is used before words that begin with a consonant sound. *An* is used before words that begin with a vowel sound. Sound, not spelling, determines which to use.

a history	an honor
a red umbrella	an umbrella
a blanket	an orange blanket
a JFK supporter	an FDR appointee

abbreviations

In general, it is wise to avoid using abbreviations, other than widely accepted ones like *Mr.* and *a.m.* Some categories of frequently used abbreviations follow:

ACRONYMS   Words formed from abbreviations are called acronyms. Many acronyms, like *Core* (Congress of Racial Equality) and *scuba* (self-contained underwater breathing apparatus), are better known than the words they stand for.

AGENCIES AND ORGANIZATIONS   Abbreviations for names of agencies and organizations are frequently written without periods. Unlike acronyms, these abbreviations are pronounced not as words but as a series of letters. If you use such an abbreviation, be sure your reader understands its meaning.

IBM (International Business Machines) and ILGWU (International Ladies' Garment Workers' Union) submitted reports.

LATIN EXPRESSIONS   In formal writing, the following abbreviations for Latin expressions are often used:

cf.	*confer*	compare
e.g.	*exempli gratia*	for example
et al.	*et alii*	and others
etc.	*et cetera*	and other things
i.e.	*id est*	that is
vs.	*versus*	against

In informal writing, however, it is appropriate to use the English words for these Latin expressions. One exception is *versus* and its abbreviation *vs.*, both of which are frequently used in sportswriting.

(*See also* **a.m. and p.m.**; **b.c. and a.d.**; etc.)

TITLES WITH NAMES   Certain titles used before names are abbreviated. Such abbreviations are usually listed in the dictionary. But other titles are generally spelled out.

The committee was composed of Mr. Richards, Mrs. Garcia, Dr. Colby, and Ms. Stavros.

Professor Reeves, Senator Bianco, Rabbi Feldman, the Reverend Ralph Clark, and Mayor Thorslund attended.

(*See also* **period.**)

affect and effect

Although these words are often pronounced alike, they are different. *Affect* is always a verb and means "to produce a change" or "to influence."

The bad weather affected the number of shoppers, and the stores were less crowded than usual.

Effect is a noun meaning "result."

No one knows what the effect of the fuel shortage will be.

Effect is also used as a verb meaning "to bring about" or "to cause."

Trying to effect peaceful change is difficult.

agreement

When a word in a sentence has determined the form of another word, then both words are said to be in agreement. Look at the following sentence.

Janice works at the garage in her free time.

Because the subject *Janice* is singular and third person, the verb *works* is the singular, third-person form. Because the noun *Janice* is singular and refers to a woman, the pronoun *her* is the singular, feminine form. Thus, words in sentences may agree in NUMBER, PERSON, and GENDER.

(*See also* **everyone, anything, and somebody; his, her, ·and their; one and you; one of those who; several, each, and some; subject-verb agreement.**)

ain't

In informal speech *ain't* is sometimes used as a contraction for *am not, is not, are not, has not,* or *have not.*

Jamie **ain't** interested.

Ain't should be avoided in writing and in formal speech.

Jamie **isn't** interested.

allegory

A story in which the characters and events are meant to represent some social or moral idea is called an allegory. One of the best-known allegories is the biblical story of the Good Samaritan. On one level it is simply the story of a passerby who aids a man robbed and injured by thieves. On a second level, however, it is intended to illustrate the idea that one should help a stranger in need. *Aesop's Fables* and John Bunyan's *The Pilgrim's Progress* are famous allegories. In modern literature George Orwell's *Animal Farm,* William Golding's *Lord of the Flies,* and Ursula K. LeGuin's *A Wizard of Earthsea* are popular allegories.

alliteration

The repetition of a sound at the beginning of two or more words is called alliteration.

> Sticks and stones are hard on bones.
> Aimed with angry art,
> Words can sting like anything.
> But silence breaks the heart.
> —PHYLLIS McGINLEY

Alliteration is used in prose as well as in poetry to produce a musical effect and sometimes to bind key words together or give them emphasis.

> The law must be stable, but it must not stand still.
> —ROSCOE POUND

Perhaps the most common use of alliteration is in advertising, as headlines and slogans.

> Good things happen on a Honda
> Mayflower means moving

Alliteration should be used sparingly and carefully. In ordinary factual reports, it is usually inappropriate.

allusion

A brief, passing reference to history, literature, famous people, or events is called an allusion. It can be an effective way to pack a good deal of meaning into a very few words. For example, Sigmund Freud was once called "the Columbus of the mind." The writer could have said that Freud made discoveries about the human mind that forever altered the course of psychological knowledge. But the allusion was more compact and more suggestive.

almost and most

Almost means "nearly" or "just about." In informal speech *most* is sometimes used with this meaning. In formal speech and in writing, however, *almost* should be used.

> Almost everyone has finished.
> Almost all the supplies were in her pack.
> The movie is almost over.

alright

This variation of *all right* is being used more and more, especially in advertising. However, the two-word spelling, *all right*, is still preferred.

a.m. and p.m.

The abbreviations *a.m.* and *p.m.* stand for the Latin words *ante meridiem*, "before noon," and *post meridiem*, "after noon." They are used when the time is expressed in numerals.

> Nancy will arrive at 10 a.m.

When the minutes, as well as the hour, are expressed in figures, a colon separates the two.

> At 6:42 p.m. the bus pulled into the station.

Noon is occasionally expressed as *12 m.* Thus, midnight would be *12 p.m.* These abbreviations are used only with numerals and never as substitutes for the words *morning* and *afternoon*.

> The eclipse began exactly at 12:01 p.m.
> I'll look for you tomorrow afternoon.

(*See also* o'clock.)

ambiguity

A sentence that can be interpreted in more than one way is ambiguous. The following sentence, for example, has two possible meanings because the pronoun *she* could refer either to Sally or to Lisa.

Sally told Lisa that **she** was sure to win.

The sentence can mean either that Lisa was sure to win or that Sally was sure to win. A reader cannot be sure from the sentence itself which meaning is intended. Perhaps the surrounding sentences would provide a clue. But it would be better to rewrite this ambiguous sentence to give it a single, clear meaning. One good way to do this is to cast the sentence as a direct quotation.

Sally told Lisa, "You're sure to win."
Sally told Lisa, "I'm sure to win."

Like an unclear pronoun reference, a carelessly placed modifier may also make a sentence ambiguous.

Reggie said **often** Darnell was brilliant.

The previous sentence can mean either that Reggie made the statement often or that Darnell was brilliant often. In order to make the intended meaning clear, the sentence should be recast.

Reggie often said Darnell was brilliant.
Reggie said Darnell was often brilliant.

Sometimes a comparison that is not completely expressed may also make a sentence ambiguous.

Marty likes Nan **more than Lori.**

That sentence might mean that Marty likes Nan more than Lori likes Nan, or it might mean that Marty likes Nan more than Marty likes Lori. To make clear which meaning is intended, the sentence should be rewritten to express the comparison completely.

Marty likes Nan more than she likes Lori.
Marty likes Nan more than Lori does.

In revising what you write, be alert for ambiguity. Ambiguous sentences, once they are noticed, are usually not difficult to correct.

For practice see page 238.
(*See also* **squinting modifier; than I and than me.**)

among and between

Among is used only when more than two persons or things are involved; *between* is generally used when just two persons or things are involved.

Nina strolled **among** the exhibits at the fair.

Tom had to choose **between** living close to work and commuting.

Between is also used to refer to more than two items when they are being considered as separate units, not as a group.

Between the five of them, they managed to raise the money.

The new shopping center was midway **between** Langdon, Prairie Hills, **and** Port Rio.

Notice that *and,* not *or,* is used to join objects after *between.*

amount of and number of

These two phrases are used with two different kinds of nouns.

Nouns like *time, rain,* and *courage,* to which the question *how much?* may be applied, are MASS NOUNS. *Amount of* is used with mass nouns.

We only have a small **amount of** cream left.

A certain **amount of** honesty seems necessary.

Nouns like *days, inch,* and *performer,* to which the question *how many?* may be applied, are COUNT NOUNS. *Number of* is used with count nouns.

A large **number of** jockeys disagreed.

A **number of** the signatures were forged.

analogy

A **figure of speech** in which unlike items are compared at some length is called an analogy. An analogy differs from a **simile** or a **metaphor** in being longer and more fully developed. In the following paragraph the analogy is drawn between examinations in school and crucial events in life.

Examinations are not things that happen in school. They are a recurring feature of life, whether in the form of decisive interviews to pass, of important letters to write, or life-and-death diagnoses to make, or meetings to address, or girls to propose to. In most of these crises, you cannot bring your notes with you and must not leave your wits behind. The habit of passing examinations is therefore one to acquire early and to keep exercising even when there is a possibility of getting around it.   —JACQUES BARZUN

(*See also* WRITER'S GUIDE, page 132.)

analogy in persuasion

One of the methods of reasoning often used in **persuasion** is called analogy. In following this method, you argue that because two things are alike in several ways, they must also be alike in several other ways.

(*See also* **methods of development;** WRITER'S GUIDE, pages 152-155.)

anecdote

See WRITER'S GUIDE, pages 118-120.

antonyms

Pairs of words whose meanings are opposite are called antonyms. For example, *joy* and *sorrow* are antonyms, as are *good* and *bad, simple* and *complicated.*

(*See also* **synonyms.**)

apostrophe

This punctuation mark ⬚ is used to show possession, to indicate missing letters in contractions, and to form plurals:

INDICATING CONTRACTIONS   Shortened forms of words, contractions, are written with apostrophes to indicate that letters have been left out. Contractions are widely used in informal speaking and writing.

I⬚m = I am   they⬚ve = they have   won⬚t = will not

Notice that the contraction of *will not* is *won't.* A few contractions have more than one meaning, but the context of the sentence usually indicates which one is intended.

She'd gone by the time we got there. [she had gone]
I know she'd help us if she could. [she would help]

(*See also* **doesn't and don't; its and it's; let's; their, there, and they're.**)

INDICATING PLURALS   The apostrophe may be used to form the plural of a figure, a letter, a symbol, or a word when it is referred to as a word. In such instances, simply adding an *s* might be confusing, so *'s* is used.

The 3 ' s on this page of typing are all blurred.

Are there three *p* ' s *in Philippines?*

There are too many *anyway* ' s in this composition.

INDICATING POSSESSIVES   Singular nouns and indefinite words like *somebody* and *everyone* use *'s* to show possession. Plural nouns ending in *s* add just the apostrophe, and irregular plurals add *'s*.

Rover just ate the cat ' s dinner.

Somebody ' s bike is getting wet.

The boys ' room is a mess; ask them to clean it up.

The Stevenses ' house is being painted.

Children ' s toys are often fun for adults, too.

For practice see page 238.

argumentation
See persuasion.

article
A brief, factual prose composition, often including personal reaction and opinion, is called an article. An article is usually intended both to inform and to entertain. Feature stories and most essays that appear in magazines, Sunday supplements to newspapers, and other periodicals may be classified as articles.

(*See also* essay; feature story; WRITER's GUIDE, pages 161-168.)

as
When used as a connecting word between two sentence structures, *as* may have more than one meaning. It may, for example, refer to the manner in which an action is performed, meaning "the way."

Mimi sounded cheerful, as she usually does. [manner]

As may also refer to time, meaning "when" or "while," or to cause, meaning "because" or "since."

The play began as we walked to our seats. [time]
I didn't answer as I didn't hear the question. [cause]

Sometimes it is not clear whether *as* refers to time or to cause.

As I was going for a walk, Tom asked me to mail a letter for him.

To avoid such misunderstanding, use a more exact connecting word.

Because I was going for a walk, Tom asked me to mail a letter for him. [cause]
While I was going for a walk, Tom asked me to mail a letter for him. [time]

(*See also* **as if and as though; like and as.**)

as I and as me

See **than I and than me.**

as if and as though

In informal speaking and writing, *like* is often used for *as if* or *as though*.

It sounds like we can expect another test soon.

In formal usage, however, *as if* or *as though* should be used.

It sounds as though we can expect another test soon.

(*See also* **as; like and as.**)

at

In informal speech an unnecessary *at* is sometimes added to the end of a question beginning with *where*.

Where's Cookie at?

In writing and in formal speech, *at* is never used at the end of *where*-questions.

Where's Cookie?

audience

The readers for whom a composition is written are called the audience. The audience may be limited; in fact, it may be an audience of one. A letter applying for a job, for example, is usually addressed to a particular person. On the other hand, the audience may be fairly large but still specific—lawmakers who are urged in an editorial to pass a certain bill. Finally, the audience may be both large and general. This is the kind of audience many writers of popular fiction have in mind. The characteristics of a given audience have direct effects on the composition. Who the audience is will determine the writer's choice of words, details, and form. Not having a particular audience in mind usually results in uneven or foggy writing.

(*See also* WRITER'S GUIDE, pages 121, 141-146, 212-213.)

autobiography

An account of a person's life written by that person is called an autobiography. Autobiography frequently appears as a full-length book but may also take the form of an essay or autobiographical sketch. Book-length autobiographies include Margaret Mead's *Blackberry Winter: A Memoir*, Malcolm X's *Autobiography of Malcolm X*, and Ann Morrow Lindbergh's *Hour of Gold, Hour of Lead*. Autobiographical essays and sketches include Abraham Lincoln's "A Little Sketch" and N. Scott Momaday's "The Way to Rainy Mountain."

Fiction and poetry may also be based on autobiography. Autobiographical novels include James Joyce's *Portrait of the Artist as a Young Man* and Sylvia Plath's *The Bell Jar*.

(*See also* **biography**.)

B

bad and badly

The adjective *bad* is used to modify nouns. It is also used after the verb *be* and after linking verbs like *feel, sound,* and *look*.

That was a **bad** accident.

Your cough sounds **bad**.

They feel **bad** about the score.

The adverb *badly* is used to modify verbs.
The team played **badly.**

In informal speech, however, *badly* is often used as an adjective after *feel.*
They feel **badly** about the score.

Bad and *badly* have the same comparative and superlative forms—*worse* and *worst.*

balanced sentence
See sentence forms.

ballad
A poem that tells a usually tragic story, largely through **dialogue,** is called a ballad. Folk ballads were originally created to be sung or recited. Seldom written down, they were passed on orally from one generation to the next. In most cases, their authors are unknown. A **stanza** of a ballad consists of four lines whose end words rhyme *abcb.* The following is a stanza from a folk ballad entitled "The Demon Lover."

"O where have you been, my long, long love,   a
This long seven years and more?"   b
"O I'm come to seek my former vows   c
Ye granted me before."   b

Literary ballads are more modern poems written in the ballad form. These ballads may imitate the language and subject matter of folk ballads, or they may use modern language and subject matter. The following are two stanzas from a literary ballad entitled "As I Walked Out One Evening."

I'll love you, dear, I'll love you
Till China and Africa meet,
And the river jumps over the mountain
And the salmon sing in the street.

I'll love you till the ocean
Is folded and hung up to dry,
And the seven stars go squawking
Like geese about the sky.
—W. H. AUDEN

Other literary ballads include Samuel Taylor Coleridge's "The Rime of the Ancient Mariner," Ernest Thayer's "Casey at the Bat," and Alfred Noyes' "The Highwayman."

B.C. and A.D.

The abbreviations B.C. and A.D. are used to designate time before and time after the beginning of the Christian era. B.C. stands for "before Christ." A.D. stands for the Latin *anno Domini,* which means "in the year of the Lord." B.C. follows a specific date, and A.D. comes before one.

Augustus was emperor of Rome from 27 B.C. to A.D. 14.

When a century is referred to, rather than a specific date, it is written out and the abbreviation follows.

The Aztec pyramids in Mexico were built around the thirteenth century A.D.

between

See among and between.

between you and me

The pronouns *me, you, him, her, it, us,* and *them* are used after words like *between, against, for,* and *with.*

I made this cake for him and her.
Ken and Anne will compete against you and me.
Are you going with them or us?
Just between you and me, I don't like it.

bibliography

An alphabetical listing of books and other published materials on a particular subject is called a bibliography. A bibliography may stand by itself or accompany a report or research paper. In either case, the information provided in each entry of a bibliography is the same. A typical entry includes (1) the author's name, (2) the title, and (3) the facts of publication.

(*See also* footnote; research paper; WRITER'S GUIDE, pages 225-226, 230, 232, 234-235.)

biography

An account of a person's life prepared by someone else is called a biography. The traditional biography is book-length and covers its subject from birth to death. However, there are other, shorter forms of biography. Profiles and sketches of interesting and well-known people often appear in magazines. Moreover, print is not the only medium for biography—the stage and especially motion pictures have been used to portray lives. But whatever the medium or the length, the biographer should aim at fairness. Both favorable and unfavorable facts about a person's life should be presented. A biographical magazine sketch, later published in book form, is *Portrait of Hemingway,* by Lillian Ross. A traditional biography is Elizabeth Jenkins' *Elizabeth the Great.* Motion-picture biographies include *Wilson* and *Madame Curie.*

(*See also* autobiography.)

black and white

When used to designate race, the words *black* and *white* are usually not capitalized, nor is the term *black power.* However, *Black Muslim* and *Black Panther* are capitalized, because they refer to specific organizations.

The words *Afro-American, Negro,* and *Caucasian* are usually capitalized.

(*See also* capitalization.)

blank verse

Poetry written in blank verse has three characteristics: (1) each line has ten syllables; (2) the second, fourth, sixth, eighth, and tenth syllables of each line are stressed; and (3) the lines do not rhyme. The word *blank* refers to the ends of the lines which are left unrhymed. The epics of Milton and much of the plays of Shakespeare were written in blank verse. In modern times, Robert Frost has written skillfully in blank verse. The following lines of blank verse are from a well-known poem of Frost's, "Mending Wall." The stressed syllables are indicated.

Before I built a wall I'd ask to know
What I was walling in or walling out

—ROBERT FROST

brackets

This pair of marks [ ] is used to enclose material inserted in a quotation by someone other than the original writer or speaker.

> As Mark Schorer noted, "On second glance at these two women [Jane Austen and George Eliot], the contrast fades; they are not so different after all."

(*See also* WRITER'S GUIDE, page 219.)

bring and take

Bring indicates motion in the direction of the speaker.

> Would you **bring** me some Portuguese bread for supper?

Take indicates motion away from the speaker.

> Let's **take** Uncle Joe some Portuguese bread when we visit him.
> You'd better **take** your new sneakers to school and **bring** the old ones home.

business letter

Most often addressed to someone you do not know, or know well, the business letter is formal in language and style. If it cannot be typed, it should be written neatly in ink. It should come to the point quickly, but courteously, and be brief, but clear. A business letter has six parts: the heading, inside address, greeting, body, closing, and signature. Business letters include letters of application, letters ordering items such as records and books, letters asking for information, letters to editors of newspapers and magazines, and letters of complaint.

(*See also* **friendly letter.**)

C

can and may

In formal speech and in writing, *can* is used only to express ability. *May* is used to express permission or possibility.

We can walk home if the bus is late. [ability]
May I have another glass of milk? [permission]
It may snow again tonight. [possibility]

In informal speech and writing, however, *can* is often used to express ability or permission.

Can I have another glass of milk? [permission]

can't hardly

The word *hardly* is used to mean "just barely" or "almost never." It has the force of a negative and should not be combined with another negative word like *never, not,* or the contraction *n't.* So, instead of writing *we can't hardly understand,* you would write *we can hardly understand* or *we can't understand.*

(*See also* **double negative.**)

capitalization

Capital letters are used in a number of ways:

BEGINNING WORDS   The first word of a sentence, a quotation, or a line of traditional poetry is capitalized.

NORTH, SOUTH, EAST, AND WEST   When used to indicate direction, these words are not capitalized. But they are capitalized when used to indicate sections of the country.

Turn left at the lights and continue north for two miles.
Though reared in the East, she prefers living in the West.

PROPER NOUNS, WORDS DERIVED FROM THEM, AND I   Nouns which refer to a particular person, place, or thing, called proper nouns, are capitalized. This large group includes names of people, places, organizations, historical events and documents, buildings, political parties, religions, races, languages, countries, days, months, and holidays, and titles of courses in school. Words derived from proper nouns, like *American* from *America,* are capitalized. The pronoun *I* is also capitalized.

Although Carlos is Brazilian, he grew up in Canada.
The only science course I'm taking next September is Introductory Physics.
Much Chicano literature is written in a blend of Spanish and English.

In **Philadelphia** we visited **Independence Hall,** where the **Declaration of Independence** was adopted on **July 4, 1776.**

When a noun like *river* or *street* is part of a proper name, it is capitalized. But don't capitalize such a noun when it is used in the plural with two or more names.

Part of the boundary between Washington and Oregon is formed by the **Columbia River.**

The **Columbia** and **Missouri rivers** are two important waterways.

(*See also* **black and white.**)

TITLES OF PUBLICATIONS   Capitalize the first word and any important words in the title of a publication.

I Am the Darker Brother is an anthology of poetry; the title is a line from a poem by Langston Hughes called "I, Too, Sing America."

One of my favorite movies is *The Loneliness of the Long-Distance Runner;* someday, I'm going to read the book.

Did you know that the play *A Raisin in the Sun* is also a musical?

TITLES WITH NAMES   When used with a person's name, a title is usually capitalized, whether or not it is abbreviated. A title used as a form of address instead of as a person's name is also capitalized.

The panel members included **Mrs. Russo** and **Governor O'Brien.**

Would you comment, **Governor,** on the fuel shortage in your state?

We saw the **governor** in the Thanksgiving Day parade.

The word *president* is capitalized when it refers to the President of the United States.

We saw the **President** on television last night.

A title indicating a family relationship is capitalized when used with the name or when used alone in direct address.

I'd like you to meet **Aunt Madge.**

Do you know where my skates are, **Mom?**

My **aunt** is coming to visit next month.

(*See also* **abbreviations.**)

For practice see page 239.

card catalog

The cabinet containing alphabetically arranged cards for each book in a library is called the card catalog. Card catalogs are designed to help readers find out what books the library has and where each book is located.

Most books in the library are listed in the catalog on at least three cards. One is alphabetized by the author's last name, one by the first word in the book's title (excepting *a, an,* and *the*), and one by the book's subject. Fiction and poetry do not have subject cards. A book may be listed on more than three cards if it has more than one author or more than one subject.

Each card in the catalog gives the book's CALL NUMBER, which indicates its location in the library. Catalog cards may also show —in addition to the book's author, title, and subject—facts about the publication and the length of the book.

(*See also* WRITER'S GUIDE, pages 222-223, 224-225.)

cause and effect

Ideas for a sentence, a paragraph, or even an essay may be developed by arranging them in a pattern of cause and effect. Here, for example, is a sentence taken from a book of recipes:

> If the butter is left in the heated pan too long [cause], it will begin to smoke [effect].

In this sentence, a single cause is used to explain a single effect, or result. But both the order and the number of causes and effects will vary from one piece of writing to another. In the following paragraph, the writer begins with an effect. Then he lists a number of causes that produced this effect.

> The reasons for the overwhelming similarities . . . in American speech are found in the settlement history and social structure of the country. From the beginning, every American community was characterized by dialect mixture, having settlers from many parts of the British Isles. Most of the early settlers, too, were middle class . . .
>
> The frontier was another leveler of dialect differences, as it was of other social differences. The development of mass education and of means of transportation and communication . . . have familiarized people in one section with the way Americans in other sections talk. Nor must we forget national magazines, national advertising, and the nationally-distributed mail-order catalogue.
>
> —RAVEN I. McDAVID, JR.

Note that the writer began with the phrase *the reasons for.* This phrase and words like *because, since, so,* and *as a result* are signals of a cause-and-effect development.

(*See also* **methods of development**; WRITER'S GUIDE, pages 134-138, 149-152.)

central idea

The main point developed in a paragraph or in a series of paragraphs is called the central idea. Often expressed in a **topic sentence,** the central idea helps the writer select and arrange details. Every sentence in a paragraph should be related to a central idea. However, you may sometimes use several paragraphs to develop a single idea.

(*See also* **coherence; unity**; WRITER'S GUIDE, page 194.)

chronological order

The simplest and most common arrangement of details in writing is chronological. That is, details are arranged in the order of their happening. Signals to chronological order are words like *first, next, then,* and *finally.* Chronological order is an arrangement best suited to **narration.** But other types of writing may also use chronological order when a series of steps is being described. For example, the details in the following paragraph explaining a process are arranged chronologically:

> It is possible to improvise a casting rod from an empty Coke bottle and some fishing line. First, tie one end of your fishing line to the neck of the bottle, just under the lip. Then, wind the rest of the line about the "waist" of the bottle, leaving three or four feet of line free. To the free end, secure your sinker and hook. Then, bait the hook. Hold the bottle in one hand, the base pointed outward in the direction you want to make your cast. With the other hand begin swinging the end of the line in a circular motion around your head—faster and faster. When you release the end of the line, the rest of the line will unwind from the Coke bottle as if from a spinning reel. To draw in your line, simply turn the bottle and wind it up.

(*See also* **order of importance; spatial order**; WRITER'S GUIDE, pages 122, 197-198.)

cinquain

This verse form has five lines. In sequence, the lines have two, four, six, eight, and two syllables. The cinquain, like the **haiku,** focuses on a brief, sharp impression.

> These be
> Three silent things
> The falling snow . . . the hour
> Before the dawn . . . the mouth of one
> Just dead.
>
> —Adelaide Crapsey

classification and division

Two related methods for developing ideas in compositions are classification and division. Classification involves bringing together items that are similar and pointing out how they are related. Suppose, for example, you are writing about styling trends in modern automobiles. One way to develop your ideas would be to group together the different makes of automobiles according to their style features. Division, on the other hand, involves separating something into parts. For example, if you were reporting on a particular automobile, you might develop your ideas by writing about the car's braking ability, acceleration, fuel economy, handling, and turning radius. Which method of development you use will depend upon your subject and your purpose in writing about it.

(*See also* **methods of development;** Writer's Guide, pages 122-126, 143-146.)

cliché

An expression that has been used so often it has become stale and nearly meaningless is a cliché. Expressions like *an open-and-shut case, mad as a wet hen, nipped in the bud, the last straw,* and *sharp as a tack* are typical of the hundreds of clichés in English. Once colorful and forceful, expressions like these make writing dull and mark the writer as lazy or immature. An inexperienced writer may not always recognize a cliché. But even a beginner can avoid clichés by using simple, straightforward language and specific detail. For example, rather than write "Leon is a chip off the old block," it is better to write "Leon is just like

his father." Or, you can specify how Leon is like his father—
"Leon and his father both eat fruit on their cereal, root for the
Cubs, and fall asleep in front of the TV."

(*See also* WRITER'S GUIDE, page 213.)

climax

The moment of greatest tension and greatest interest in a story
or a play is its climax. In both drama and fiction, the climax is
the moment when the action reaches a turning point and moves
toward a conclusion.

(*See also* **plot.**)

close punctuation

See WRITER'S GUIDE, pages 219-220.

coherence

In writing, coherence means that ideas are arranged and presented in an order that makes sense. Coherence also means that
a reader can move easily and without confusion from one idea
to another. To achieve coherence, you may use a number of
linking elements to build bridges between sentences and between
paragraphs. Here are some of these elements:

CONNECTIVES   Words like *and, but, for,* and *however* are connectives. They are used to link words within sentences and
sentences within paragraphs.

He said no, **and** I can't blame him.

Millie agreed to sing. The committee, **however,** will be
unable to pay her.

PRONOUNS   Sentences within paragraphs can be linked by pronouns. But you should be sure that each pronoun has a definite,
clear referent. Too often the pronouns *this* and *that* are used
vaguely to refer to general ideas.

Mrs. Gardner showed Jim and me how to bait a hook.
We had been doing **it** wrong.

REPETITION   Sentences within paragraphs and paragraphs
within compositions can be linked by repetition. Overused,

repetition can be irritating. Used thoughtfully, it is one of the most effective ways you have of achieving coherence.

A nation, like a person, has a body—a body that must be fed and clothed and housed . . . A nation, like a person, has a mind—a mind that must be kept informed and alert . . .   —Franklin D. Roosevelt

SUMMARIZING PHRASES   What has gone first in a composition can be pulled together by a summarizing phrase and linked to what follows.

Jill speaks four languages. She has a degree in finance. She can do calculus in her head. All these skills make finding the right job difficult.

TRANSITIONAL ELEMENTS   Phrases like *as a result, in the first place, on the other hand, at the left,* and *instead of* are called transitional elements. They link sentences and paragraphs by pointing out relationships between them.

Dazzled by the rapidly rising market, even conservatives wanted in. Instead of selecting stocks, they bought anything that was for sale.

It is possible to write coherent sentences and paragraphs and still produce a composition lacking in coherence. For this reason, you must read over your whole composition—perhaps several times. Has an important step been left out? Has unrelated information been included? Does the composition reach a sensible conclusion? These are some of the questions you must ask in checking for coherence.

(*See also* **emphasis; unity;** WRITER'S GUIDE, pages 120, 139.)

collective nouns

Nouns like *group, committee, panel, team, band,* and *crew,* even when they are singular in form, refer to a collection of persons or things. They are called collective nouns. Such nouns usually take singular verbs and singular pronouns.

The crew is ready to give its final report.

Note that *crew* here is considered as one unit. If you wished to emphasize the several members making up the crew, then this word could be treated as plural. Or, you could rephrase the sentence to make the subject clearly plural.

The crew were upset by the resignation of their leader.
The crew members were upset by the resignation of their leader.

For practice see page 240.

(*See also* subject-verb agreement.)

colon

This mark [:] is used in a sentence to introduce a list that is not preceded by *for example* or *such as*.

> Lee recommended her three favorite novels[:] *Catch 22, Go Tell It on the Mountain,* and *Breakfast of Champions.*

A colon is not used, however, directly after a verb.

> Her three favorite novels are *Catch 22, Go Tell It on the Mountain,* and *Breakfast of Champions.*

A colon is used after a statement which is followed by an explanation.

> Shultz didn't care that the project failed[:] none of his money was involved.

A colon is used to introduce a long or formal quotation.

> Malcolm Crowley wrote of F. Scott Fitzgerald and the Jazz Age[:] "Fitzgerald not only represented the age but came to suspect that he had helped to create it, by setting forth a pattern of conduct that would be followed by persons a little younger than himself. That it was a dangerous pattern was something he recognized almost from the beginning."

A colon is used to separate hours from minutes when the time of day is expressed in figures.

> We'll meet you there at 7[:] 30.

A colon is used after the greeting in a **business letter.**

> Dear Ms. Yamato[:]

(*See also* a.m. and p.m.; quotation marks; Writer's Guide, page 216.)

comma

This mark [,] has a wide variety of uses within sentences:

SEPARATING SENTENCE PARTS   Commas are used to separate three or more items in a series.

> We all knew our hero was trusty ▢ loyal ▢ and brave.
> Skiing in the Alps ▢ surfing in the Pacific ▢ and sailing in the Caribbean all appeal to me.

Commas are not needed, however, if the items are joined by *and*.

> We all knew our hero was trusty **and** loyal **and** brave.

When two modifiers qualify a noun in exactly the same way, they are treated as a series and separated by a comma.

> The shy▢quiet gentleman clenched his fist.

A comma is usually used between sentence structures joined by a word like *and, but, for,* or *or*. If both sentence structures are short, the comma may be omitted.

> The professor finally arrived ▢ but most of her students had already left.
> Did the lights just flicker ▢ or was that my imagination?
> The earth shook and the sky burned. [No comma needed.]

A comma is used to separate the items in a date, an address, or a geographical name.

> On Tuesday ▢ May 21 ▢ we finally arrived in Yuba City ▢ California.

SETTING OFF PARTS OF LETTERS   A comma is used after the greeting in a **friendly letter** and after the closing in either a friendly letter or a **business letter**.

> Dear Fran ▢
> Cordially yours ▢

SETTING OFF SENTENCE PARTS   A comma is used to set off certain introductory elements from the rest of a sentence.

> When the timer rings ▢ take the cake out of the oven.
> Believing completely in his cause ▢ Sparky defended himself well.
> Because the meeting was almost over ▢ Sue decided to wait.
> Yes ▢ I think we will be able to help you.

A comma is usually used to set off a direct quotation from the rest of the sentence in which it appears. If the quotation is interrogative or exclamatory, then a question mark or exclamation point may be needed instead of a comma.

Rita asked [,] "Where are we going?"

"Where are we going [?] " asked Rita.

"Where [,] " asked Rita [,] "are we going?"

Commas are used to set off words in direct address.

Your essay [,] Eric [,] is very well written.

Have you seen the new *Sports Illustrated* [,] Penny?

Commas are used to set off interrupting elements.

That bill [,] as you know [,] is sure to be amended.

The play was [,] in my opinion [,] poorly directed.

Commas are used to set off words that provide added information but that are not essential to the meaning of a sentence. Such words are called NONRESTRICTIVE elements.

Ms. Verlo [,] who has been in Mexico City for a month [,] is arriving on the next flight. [*Who has been in Mexico City for a month* is not needed to identify *Ms. Verlo.*]

My best friend [,] Marcy [,] moved to Springfield. [*Marcy* tells the name of the *best friend,* but this fact is not needed to identify the person.]

Words that are essential to the meaning of the sentence in which they appear, RESTRICTIVE elements, are never set off with punctuation.

My friend Marcy moved to Springfield. [*Marcy* is needed to make clear which friend.]

(*See also* **quotation marks.**)

SHOWING WORD OMISSIONS   A comma is used to indicate the omission of a word or words.

Mr. Garvey ordered sea bass; his wife [,] filet of sole.

For practice see page 241.

(*See also* WRITER'S GUIDE, pages 216-219.)

comma fault

See **run-on sentence.**

comparison and contrast

Within a paragraph or a series of paragraphs, ideas may be developed by comparison or contrast. In a comparison, similarities between persons, objects, or ideas are listed; in a contrast, differences are listed. But even in listing differences, there is an assumed comparison. That is, the items being contrasted must have something in common. You would not, for example, contrast apples and mountains. In the following excerpt, the writer contrasts the service guarantees offered by manufacturers of color TV sets.

> There are other minor variations in the guarantees being offered by various manufacturers. Sears and Zenith, for example, will pay a service technician to come to your home to fix a 19-inch color set under its labor guarantee, whereas most other set makers require any set under the 21-inch size to be brought into the shop by the owner. . . .
>
> Another variation, offered by Hitachi, provides all the standard coverage plus a ten-year guarantee on transistors. . . . Sony has an unusual guarantee that actually provides less coverage. Sony television sets . . . are only guaranteed for labor charges for six months, half the standard term. Many dealers and distributors take it upon themselves, however, to extend the Sony guarantee to a full year.   —CONSUMER GUIDE

(*See also* **methods of development**; WRITER'S GUIDE, pages 130-132.)

compound subject

Two or more words functioning as a subject and joined by *and* take a plural verb form.

Martha and her brother are learning to play chess.

Two singular words joined by *or, either . . . or,* or *neither . . . nor* take a singular verb form.

Blue or purple is the color to use.

Either lacquer or varnish has been used on this table.

Neither Tom nor Carol wants to go.

A compound subject may have one word that is singular and another that is plural. The verb then agrees with the closer word.

Either the kittens or the dog has torn the rug.

Either the dog or the kittens have torn the rug.

It is sometimes better to avoid such constructions by rephrasing the sentence.

Either the dog has torn the rug or the kittens have.

For practice see page 241.

(*See also* **subject-verb agreement.**)

conflict

The problem that characters in a story must face is called the conflict. The conflict may be external. For example, a hero must overcome a villain or struggle through a blizzard to deliver badly needed medicine. Or the conflict may be internal. For example, a character must decide what to do about a friend who has committed a crime. The conflict is the spring that sets the characters in action. For this reason, the conflict usually appears early in fiction and drama. The actions of the characters are attempts to resolve the conflict. These actions make up a bulk of the story. When the conflict is resolved, the story ends.

(*See also* **plot;** WRITER'S GUIDE, pages 172-173, 175-176.)

contractions

See **apostrophe.**

could of and should of

In conversation, *could have* may often sound like *could of,* and *should have* like *should of.* If you trust your ear rather than your eye, you might mistakenly substitute *of* for *have.* In writing, *have,* not *of,* follows *could* and *should.*

Who else could have known?

couplet

Two lines of verse that form a unit because they are set off as a **stanza** or because they rhyme are called a couplet.

> The grizzly bear, whose potent hug
> Was feared by all, is now a rug.
> —ARTHUR GUITERMAN

D

dangling modifier

Words which qualify the meanings of other words are called MODIFIERS. A dangling modifier is one that seems to qualify a word or words that it cannot logically qualify. The modifier in the following sentence is dangling because it seems to qualify the word *idea*.

> **Walking along aimlessly,** a bright **idea** suddenly came to me.

Logically, ideas do not "walk along aimlessly." One way to revise a dangling modifier is to make it qualify the word it is supposed to qualify.

> **Walking along aimlessly,** I suddenly had a bright idea.

Sometimes a dangling modifier can also be rewritten as a sentence structure within a complete sentence.

> **While I was walking along aimlessly,** a bright idea suddenly came to me.

For practice see page 242.

dash

This mark ⊖ is used to set off explanatory material that stands in sharp contrast to the sentence in which it appears. If the element to be set off comes in the middle of the sentence, two dashes are used.

> The crowd ⊖ you should have been there ⊖ went wild.

> Amy Islander ⊖she used to be our baby-sitter ⊖is graduating from law school next month.

A dash can be used to show a sudden interruption or hesitation, especially in **dialogue.**

"As soon as Jenny gets here, we can ⸻ here she is now."

"You mean to say ⸻ " he began.

"I ⸻ I ⸻ I just can't believe that!"

A dash can be used to set off a list of items from a summarizing word group that begins *all* or *all these.*

Maggie, Lisa, Tanya, Omar, and Ray ⸻ all the cousins were there.

A dash can be used to mean "namely" or "in other words" before an explanation at the end of a sentence.

At that time there was only one person I couldn't get along with ⸻ my brother.

Dashes are meant to convey a special emphasis or contrast. Used too frequently, they lose their force.

(*See also* WRITER'S GUIDE, pages 216, 217-218.)

declarative sentence

See **sentence functions.**

definition

A brief statement giving the meaning of an unfamiliar word or phrase is called a definition. The term *definition* is also applied to a method for developing an entire composition. In using this method, you would explain your subject by defining it at length. For example, you might develop an essay about the generation gap by explaining what this phrase means to teenagers. Definition which goes beyond a brief statement of meaning is called EX-TENDED DEFINITION. Extended definition is used in developing a paragraph, a series of paragraphs, or even a whole composition.

(*See also* **methods of development;** WRITER'S GUIDE, pages 126-130, 145-149.)

denouement

The outcome of a story, or the resolution of the **conflict,** is called the denouement.

(*See also* **plot.**)

description

Writing that tells what some person, place, or thing looks, feels, smells, tastes, or sounds like is called description. Descriptive writing seldom runs to great length. Usually, it is only a part of some longer composition. For example, novels often contain descriptions of characters and scenes. But the bulk of any novel is given over to narrating events, not to describing physical appearances. Travel books and texts on art, history, and architecture probably contain the largest and purest examples of descriptive writing.

(*See also* WRITER'S GUIDE, pages 112-115, 178-181.)

dialect

Differences in pronunciation, vocabulary, and grammatical form tend to mark off the speech of one area from that of another area. These differences, based on geography, produce varieties of a given language called dialects. In the United States, there are three major dialect areas—northern, midland, and southern. Within each of these areas, there are also minor dialects. Everyone, then, speaks a dialect, whether aware of doing so or not. Moreover, one dialect is not necessarily better than another. Dialects exist simply because groups of people are, or were once, separated from one another.

dialogue

Conversation recorded in writing is called dialogue. In a short story or novel, dialogue is enclosed in quotation marks, and the speakers are indicated by phrases like *he said* or *she asked*. A new paragraph begins each time the speaker changes. Occasionally, phrases like *he said* or *she asked* are left out when it is clear who the speaker is. To be effective, dialogue should advance the action of the story. Also, it should tell something about the characters. Their words and the way they respond to each other should give the reader an insight into the kind of people they are.

"Want to go to the show tonight, Ann?" asked Cindy.

"I'd like to," Ann replied. "But I've got a problem. Want to hear about it?"

"No, not really. Think I'll call Sue. Bye, now."

In a play, quotation marks are not used. The name of the speaker appears before each line of dialogue.

(*See also* **indention; quotation marks;** WRITER'S GUIDE, pages 175, 177-179.)

diction

The choice of words in a composition is called diction. Good diction means choosing the right words. That is, the words you use are appropriate for your audience, your subject, and the occasion.

(*See also* WRITER'S GUIDE, pages 213-215.)

different from and different than

In formal writing and speaking, *different from* is preferred to *different than*.

Her opinions are usually different from mine.

Often, however, the use of *different from* may make a sentence somewhat wordy.

The restaurant was different from what we remembered.

In such cases *different than* is usually acceptable, especially in informal writing.

The restaurant was different than we remembered.

disinterested and uninterested

In formal usage a distinction is made between these two words. *Disinterested* means "impartial" or "free from selfish motive."

A judge who is not disinterested in the case should be disqualified.

Uninterested means "indifferent" or "not interested."

We explained our plans to Cal, but he seemed uninterested.

In informal usage the distinction between these words is often not made; both may be used to mean "not interested."

division

See **classification and division.**

doesn't and don't

In formal situations *doesn't* is used only with the pronouns *he, she,* and *it* and singular nouns. *Don't* is used with the remaining pronouns—*I, you, we, they*—and plural nouns.

Maria doesn't like to skate, and I don't either.

If he doesn't know how to swim, why don't you teach him?

For practice see page 243.

double negative

In modern English one negative word is enough to make an entire sentence negative. Double negatives, once widely used in English for emphasis, are now considered nonstandard—for example, *don't have no* and *won't never.*

Words like *never, none, hardly, scarcely, not,* and the contraction *n't* are all negative. They provide a variety of ways to make a statement negative.

We haven't ever seen a comet before.

We have never seen a comet before.

There wasn't anyplace to go.

There was no place to go.

I don't have any change.

I haven't any change.

I have no change.

I have none.

For practice see page 243.

(*See also* **can't hardly.**)

drama

See WRITER'S GUIDE, pages 174-181.

E

editorial

A short essay of opinion on some current event or problem is called an editorial. In newspapers the editorials usually appear

on a special page, separated from news stories, which are supposed to be factual and without opinion. Editorials are also
broadcast on radio and television. Whatever the medium, the
opinions expressed in editorials are those of the owner or man-
agement of the paper or station. Most editorials are serious in
tone, but some employ a humorous approach.

(*See also* **essay.**)

effect
See **affect and effect.**

ellipsis points
These marks ⌐ . . ¬ consist of three periods in a row. They
are used to show the omission of one or more words from a
direct quotation. If the omission, or ELLIPSIS, occurs at the end
of a sentence, a fourth period is added.

> Chesterton's ideas on work were clear and up-to-date.
> He once remarked, "It is perfectly obvious that in any
> decent occupation ⌐ . . ¬ there are only two ways of
> succeeding ⌐ . . . ¬One is by doing very good work,
> the other is by cheating."

(*See also* WRITER'S GUIDE, page 219.)

emotional appeals in persuasion
See WRITER'S GUIDE, pages 140, 142-143.

elliptical sentence
See **sentence fragment.**

emphasis
In any composition some ideas are more important than others
and, for this reason, deserve greater emphasis. To make sure that
each idea receives its proper emphasis, you may use a number
of different devices.

Perhaps the most obvious, and least effective, device is
underlining. Suppose the main idea in the following sentence

is contained in the word *that*. You could underline the word and give it greater emphasis.

I could never believe <u>that</u>.

But a better and less artificial way to achieve this emphasis would be to shift the order of the words in the sentence.

That I could never believe.

Now *that* receives the greatest emphasis because of its position. Position, then, often determines emphasis in a sentence. As further proof, examine the following pair of sentences. Notice that the emphasis in the first falls on *the campers;* in the second, on *a UFO.*

The campers sighted a UFO.

A UFO was sighted by the campers.

In paragraphs and compositions, the most emphatic positions are the beginning and the end. So, important sentences and important paragraphs should be reserved for either of these positions.

Another common device of emphasis is repetition. You may sometimes repeat a key word, phrase, or sentence.

There is no personal escape, no personal salvation, no personal solution. —BEVERLY JONES

Frequently, several devices of emphasis may be used in combination. In the following paragraph, for example, the device of repetition is combined with that of position to emphasize the main idea.

But you see the eyes. You see that the eyes are alive. They are pale blue or gray, set back under the deep brows and thorny eyebrows. They are not wide, but squinched up like eyes accustomed to wind or sun or to measuring the stroke of the ax or to fixing the object over the rifle sights. When you pass, you see that the eyes are alive and are warily and dispassionately estimating you from the ambush of the thorny brows. Then you pass on, and he stands there in that stillness which is his gift.

—ROBERT PENN WARREN

Finally, an obvious, but effective, device for achieving emphasis is space—that is, the more important an idea is, the more words, sentences, and paragraphs are given to it. By using space in this way, you develop the ideas that are most important.

(*See also* **coherence; sentence forms; sentence length; summarizing sentence; underlining; unity;** WRITER'S GUIDE, pages 192, 208-209.)

epic

A long narrative poem that celebrates the adventures of a hero of history or legend is called an epic. Epic heroes are portrayed larger-than-life, as superhuman in strength, skill, or cunning. The supernatural usually plays an important part in an epic. Many epics were written to glorify a nation or an empire. The *Luciadas,* for example, was written to glorify Portugal, and the *Aeneid,* Rome. Other epics include the Greek *Iliad* and *Odyssey,* the French *Song of Roland,* the Old English *Beowulf,* the *Ramayana* of India, the Spanish *Cid,* and the German *Nibelungenlied.*

(*See also* **narration.**)

essay

A brief prose discussion of a single topic, often from a personal viewpoint, is called an essay. The term *essay* covers compositions having an almost limitless variety of styles and subjects, making a satisfactory definition difficult. There are, for example, the solemn, moralizing essays of Francis Bacon and the light, funny ones of Phyllis McGinley. James Baldwin uses the essay to convey the grimness of his youth; Harry Golden, to sentimentalize his youth. Mary McCarthy and Gloria Steinem have written essays of social and literary analysis. Newspaper editorials and some magazine articles can be called essays.

(*See also* **article; editorial.**)

etc.

This is the abbreviation for the Latin words *et cetera,* which mean "and other things." *Etc.* should be used as little as possible. It should never be used with *and* or after the phrase *such as.*

> Sporting dogs—golden retrievers, pointers, weimaraners, and etc.—hunt by smelling the air.
> Some rather unusual sports, such as jai alai, lacrosse, curling, etc., are being offered as part of the gym program.

Sentences like those above should be revised as follows:

> Sporting dogs—golden retrievers, pointers, weimaraners, etc.—hunt by smelling the air.
> Some rather unusual sports, such as jai alai, lacrosse, and curling, are being offered as part of the gym program.

euphemism

A pleasant or indirect expression used in place of a harsher, more direct expression is called a euphemism.

Some familiar examples of euphemism are *passed away* for *died, intoxicated* for *drunk, dentures* for *false teeth, protective reaction strike* for *bombing raid,* and *senior citizens* for *old people.* For the most part, euphemisms are used to soften or sweeten reality and should, for this reason, be avoided.

(*See also* WRITER'S GUIDE, page 213.)

everyone, anything, and somebody

Certain words, called INDEFINITE PRONOUNS, do not represent specific persons or things. Many of these words are singular—like *anything, each, everyone, nothing,* and *somebody.*

In formal speaking and in writing, you use a singular pronoun to refer to a singular indefinite pronoun.

Somebody lost her hat.
Everybody expressed his opinion.
Nothing is the way it seems.

In informal speech, however, you may sometimes use a plural pronoun to refer to a singular indefinite pronoun.

Everybody forgot their umbrellas.

To avoid this mixing of singular and plural, you can change a singular word like *everybody* to a plural noun.

The students forgot their umbrellas.

For practice see page 244.

(*See also* agreement; his, her, and their.)

example and illustration

One common way to develop an idea for a paragraph or for a series of paragraphs is to illustrate a general statement with examples. In the following paragraph the writers illustrate with some carefully selected statistics their generalization that Americans are well-off.

On the average, Americans are in clover. According to the Federal Reserve Board, six out of ten own their own homes, seven in ten own automobiles, eight in ten can lay their hands on [savings].

—ROBERT and LEONA T. RIENOW

Each of these statistics is a separate example that illustrates the generalization. This is one way of illustrating a generalization. However, instead of listing several short examples, you might select one or two longer examples and describe them. This is what the writer of the following paragraph does. He makes the generalization that a baseball player waiting to catch a high fly may be distracted by the chatter of other people. Then he describes two examples.

> Now about the high fly. Your own thoughts are not the only distractions when you're looking for a ball somewhere up there in the blinding blue infinity of outer space. People are chattering all around you. Once I heard my sister call to me, "Hey, I'm going to play on the swings now, OK?" Another time, when we were playing State Street, Butch Mendoza hit a real rainmaker somewhere in my neighborhood. Running down the line to first, Butch had plenty of time on his hands, so he hollered, "Hey, kid, you're gonna miss it, you're gonna miss it!" Of course I was; nobody had to broadcast it.   —LAURENCE SHEEHAN

(*See also* **methods of development**; WRITER'S GUIDE, pages 118-119.)

exclamation point

This mark [!] is used after a word, phrase, or sentence expressing strong emotion.

Fire [!]
Not me [!]
Is he the one [!]
You're driving the wrong way [!]

Notice that an exclamation may take the form of a declarative sentence or even a question. In speech, the speaker's pitch indicates whether a sentence is a statement, a question, or an exclamation. In writing, punctuation signals the intention.

An exclamation point is a mark of emphasis. Used too often, it loses its impact. Two or three exclamation points after a single exclamation is a kind of false emphasis and should be avoided.

(*See also* **quotation marks; sentence functions**.)

exclamatory sentence

See **sentence functions**.

experimental poetry

   See WRITER'S GUIDE, pages 187-189.

exposition

   The term *exposition* has two related meanings. It means, first, that kind of writing which explains, which tells how to do something or how something works. News reports, owners' manuals, recipes, and textbooks are a few examples of exposition.

   Exposition also refers to that part of a story or play in which the writer "explains" essential facts to the reader. Here the writer may indicate the time and the place of the action, introduce the characters, and specify their **conflict.** Since these facts are necessary to understanding the actions which follow, the exposition usually occurs early. In a novel or a play, the exposition may occur in the first chapter or scene.

   (*See also* **article; essay; feature story; research paper;** WRITER'S GUIDE, pages 111-139.)

extended definition

   See **definition.**

F

feature story

   A newspaper story intended mainly to entertain is called a feature story. A feature story differs from a news story—which reports facts about significant events—and from an editorial—which expresses opinions. A feature story does not deal with important people or events. Instead, it deals with the unusual and the odd, with the amusing and the interesting. The feature story also has a literary quality—not only *what* is said but *how* it is said is important. Because a feature story contains opinions as well as facts, it is usually signed.

   (*See also* **article.**)

fewer

See **less and fewer.**

figure of speech

An expression in which words are used in an unusual, non-literal way is called a figure of speech. Figures of speech lend force or clarity to writing and speaking. The three most commonly used figures are **simile, metaphor,** and **personification.**

(*See also* **analogy; hyperbole; irony; pun; synecdoche.**)

final-draft preparation

See WRITER'S GUIDE, pages 221, 231-235.

first person

See **point of view.**

folktale

A traditional story of unknown authorship, preserved over the years by retelling, is called a folktale. Eventually, most folktales are either written down or lost.

Folktales are stories by and about common people. Their main characters are often laborers and farmers and soldiers rather than lords and princesses.

Several kinds of stories are classified as folktales. MYTHS are tales told to explain the natural world. LEGENDS are folktales based on real events or the lives of real people, such as Molly Pitcher and John Henry. Folktales in which the main characters are animals that speak and act like human beings are called FABLES. And folktales about the exaggerated adventures of imaginary characters like Paul Bunyan and Pecos Bill are TALL TALES.

footnote

A report making use of the writings of other people should give these people proper credit. Usually, this is done with footnotes, notes at the bottom of a page referring to something on the page. In addition to crediting sources, footnotes are also used to provide information that is not important enough to be included in the body of the report but may still be of interest to the reader. Footnotes are numbered consecutively throughout a report. And these numbers, placed above the line, key the footnote to its reference in the body of the report. When crediting sources, a footnote always lists the author, the title, and page number on which the quotation or idea may be found.

(*See also* **bibliography; plagiarism; research paper;** WRITER'S GUIDE, pages 232-234.)

formal English

See **standard English.**

free verse

Poetry that lacks, or is free from, a regular pattern of **rhyme** and **meter** is called free verse. Some modern poets known for free verse include H. D. (Hilda Doolittle), D. H. Lawrence, Amy Lowell, Marianne Moore, Ezra Pound, Carl Sandburg, Wallace Stevens, and William Carlos Williams. The following poem is written in free verse.

> THE REBEL
>
> When I
> die
> I'm sure
> I will have a
> Big Funeral . . .
> Curiosity
> seekers . . .
> coming to see
> if I
> am really
> Dead . . .
> or just
> trying to make
> Trouble. . . .
> —MARI EVANS

Free verse should not be confused with **blank verse,** which does have a regular meter.

(*See also* WRITER'S GUIDE, pages 183-184.)

friendly letter

Usually addressed to someone you know well, the friendly letter is informal in language and style. A friendly letter has five parts: the heading, greeting, body, closing, and signature.

Unlike a **business letter,** it does not have an inside address. Friendly letters include letters written to entertain, to give news, to express sympathy, to invite someone to a party, to reply to an invitation, or to thank someone for a gift.

G H

good and well

The adjective *good* is used to modify nouns. It is also used after the verb *be* and verbs like *feel, smell,* and *seem.*

They received a good response to their questionnaire.

That cocoa certainly smells good.

The sun feels good after two days of rain.

The adverb *well* is used to modify verbs.

She skated well.

Well is also used after *be, feel,* and *seem,* with the special meaning of "in good health."

He didn't look well last week.

He felt well after resting for a day.

He seemed well when he returned to work.

Both *good* and *well* have the same comparative and superlative forms—*better* and *best.*

For practice see page 245.

haiku

The haiku is a form of poetry that originated in Japan. It has seventeen syllables that are arranged in three lines. The first line has five syllables; the second line, seven syllables; and the third line, five syllables. The haiku is set in the present and contains a reference, either direct or indirect, to one of the seasons.

A rainy spring day—
umbrellas bloom like flowers
on city sidewalks.
—MARY KELLY

(*See also* **cinquain.**)

his, her, and their

Choosing a pronoun depends on the word the pronoun refers to—on its ANTECEDENT. If the antecedent is plural, choose a plural pronoun; if singular, a singular pronoun. Trouble may arise, however, when a singular antecedent is not clearly masculine or feminine. For example, words like *hiker, artist, member,* or *student* can represent either a male or a female.

If you know the antecedent is female, use a feminine pronoun like *she, her,* or *hers.* If you know the antecedent is male, use a masculine pronoun like *he, him,* or *his.*

Each hiker is responsible for her own equipment.
Each hiker is responsible for his own equipment.

In formal writing, if the antecedent could represent either a male or a female, a masculine pronoun is generally used. Some people, however, prefer to use a phrase like *his or her.*

Each hiker is responsible for his or her own equipment.

This is rather awkward. A good way to avoid the problem altogether is to recast the sentence in the plural.

Hikers are responsible for their own equipment.

In informal speech, people sometimes use a plural form of the pronoun even though its antecedent is singular.

Each hiker is responsible for their own equipment.

In formal speech and writing, however, **agreement** between a pronoun and its antecedent is maintained.

For practice see page 245.

(*See also* **everyone, anything, and somebody; pronouns and nouns before** *ing* **verb forms.**)

hisself, theirself, and theirselves

These words are nonstandard forms of *himself* and *themselves.* They are not used in writing or in formal speech.

hopefully

In both formal and informal usage, *hopefully* modifies a verb and means "in a hopeful manner."

The cat ran hopefully to the refrigerator door.

In informal usage, *hopefully* is also used to mean "it is hoped that."

Hopefully, someone remembered to feed the cat.

This second usage of *hopefully* is widespread in informal English, but it is generally avoided in formal writing and speaking.

hyperbole

An exaggeration used as a **figure of speech** is called hyperbole. Hyperbole is not intended to deceive, but to emphasize.

Waves as high as mountains broke against the shore.
This suitcase weighs a ton.

Hyperbole is an important part of many American folktales. Paul Bunyan's ox Babe was so strong that it could haul an entire forest of logs by itself.

hyphen

This punctuation mark ⊟ is used in a variety of ways within words and between words:

DISTINGUISHING SIMILAR WORDS   A hyphen is sometimes used to avoid confusion between similarly spelled words, such as *re-solve* and *resolve* or *re-mark* and *remark*.

DIVIDING WORDS   It is often necessary to divide a word at the end of a line of writing. Such divisions are marked with hyphens. Generally speaking, words are divided between syllables. Thus, a word of one syllable cannot be divided. If you are unsure where to divide a word, look it up in a dictionary and follow the division used there.

FORMING COMPOUND MODIFIERS   When two or more words are used as a modifying unit before a noun, they may be joined by a hyphen. No hyphen is used if the first modifying word in the unit ends in *-ly*.

The twins built a six ⊡ foot snowman.
Maria gave an up ⊡ to ⊡ date report.
The newly baked bread smelled delicious.

FORMING COMPOUND WORDS   Words formed by joining two or more words are called compound words. They are often written with a hyphen, like *tailor-made* and *great-grandmother*. Or, they are written as one word, like *sidewalk* and *drugstore*, or even separate words, like *high school* and *department store*.

There is no general rule covering the spelling of compounds. If you are unsure about a particular spelling, check a dictionary.

JOINING NUMBERS   A hyphen is used with numbers from *twenty-one* to *ninety-nine* and with fractions when they are spelled out.

As **two** ⊡ **thirds** of the building was without electricity, about **eighty** ⊡ **five** employees went home early.

JOINING PREFIXES   A hyphen is used when *self-* precedes a word, as in *self-conscious* and *self-disciplined*. A hyphen is also used with prefixes like *post-*, *anti-*, and *pre-* when they are joined to proper nouns and adjectives, such as *post-Renaissance*, *anti-American*, and *pre-Columbian*.

For practice see page 246.

I

imitative words

Words whose sounds echo their meaning are called imitative words. The technical name for this is ONOMATOPOEIA. Examples of imitative words are *boom, burp, buzz, fizz, sizzle,* and *sneeze*.

imperative sentence

See sentence functions.

imply and infer

Many people insist on a strict distinction between the meanings of these two words. *Imply* means "to express indirectly."

Miss Marks didn't accuse us of lying, but her questions **implied** that she did not believe our story.

Infer means "to conclude" or "to guess."

We **inferred** from Miss Marks' questions that she didn't believe our story.

However, *infer* is also frequently used, as is *imply,* with the meaning "to express indirectly."

indefinite pronouns
See **everyone, anything, and somebody.**

indention
Beginning a line in from the left margin is called indention. The first lines of paragraphs should be indented; so, also, should lines of **dialogue** each time there is a change of speaker. In handwriting, the amount of indention is one-half to one inch; in typewriting, four or five spaces. Although the amount of indention may vary with different writers, all paragraph indentions within a composition should be the same.

(*See also* **paragraphing.**)

indirect question
A sentence that reports someone's question but does not quote the person directly contains an indirect question. A period, not a question mark, is used to mark the end of the sentence.

Gerry asked if we could help her.

Louisa wanted to know where the map was.

indirect quotation
A sentence that reports what someone has said but does not quote that person's words exactly contains an indirect quotation. Quotation marks are not used with indirect quotations.

The president announced that she plans to retire at the end of the fiscal year. [indirect quotation]

The president announced, "I plan to retire at the end of the fiscal year." [direct quotation]

(*See also* WRITER'S GUIDE, page 218.)

infer
See **imply and infer.**

informal English
See standard English.

interrogative sentence
See sentence functions.

interview
See WRITER'S GUIDE, pages 165-166, 167.

inverted sentence
See sentence forms.

irony

A **figure of speech** in which the writer says one thing but intentionally means something else is called irony. In the following quotation, the writer says he likes work, but he means just the opposite.

> I like work: it fascinates me. I can sit and look at it for hours. I love to keep it by me: the idea of getting rid of it nearly breaks my heart.   —JEROME K. JEROME

irregardless

Irregardless, sometimes used in informal speech, is a nonstandard form of *regardless.* It should be avoided in writing and in formal speaking.

it

The pronouns *it* and *its* usually refer only to objects and places. But they may also be used to refer to babies and animals, especially when the sex is not known.

> There's a new baby next door; I heard it crying last night.
> A dog left its paw prints in the fresh cement.

When *it* appears without a specific reference, it is called INDEFINITE IT. While this usage should be avoided when possible, it does have legitimate uses.

> It is raining.
> It is 250 miles to Memphis.
> It is too late to help him.

(*See also* its and it's.)

italic type

This style of type has letters that slant to the right. *These words are in italics.* In handwritten and typed materials, italic type is indicated by a single underline.

(*See also* **underlining.**)

its and it's

Its is a pronoun like *his, their,* and *our.*

Bill followed his sister out to the car.

The dog followed its master along the trail.

It's is two words written as one and may mean *it is* or *it has.* The apostrophe shows that one or more letters have been left out.

It's faster if we take the bus.

It's been a long cold winter.

For practice see page 247.

(*See also* **it.**)

it's me

It's me is widely used in informal speaking and writing. Many people feel that *it's I* sounds too formal and prefer expressions like *it's me, this is me,* and *it's not only me. It's him, it's her, it's us,* and *it's them,* however, are still not generally accepted, but are rapidly becoming so, particularly in the western and midwestern regions of the country.

J K L

jargon

See **shoptalk.**

kind of and sort of

These two phrases are often used in informal speech with the meaning "rather" or "somewhat."

I felt kind of embarrassed.

We were all sort of tired anyway.

Kind of and *sort of* are not used with this meaning in writing or in formal speech.

I felt somewhat embarrassed.
We were all rather tired anyway.

lay and lie

Lay is a verb meaning "to place" or "to put." That is, *someone lays something* or *something is laid by someone.* Its forms are *lay, laying, laid, laid.*

Lay the parcels on the kitchen table, please.
The carpenter is laying a new floor in the hall.
They laid the cornerstone for the new school yesterday.
The cornerstone for the new school was laid yesterday.

Lie is a verb meaning "to recline," "to remain at rest," or "to be in a position or location." So, *something* or *someone lies.* Its forms are *lie, lying, lay, lain.*

Grandfather always lies down after dinner.
The mail is lying on the table in the hall.
The road lay along the riverbank.
The ship has lain at anchor for the past week.

In informal speech, *lay* often does double duty, being used to mean *lie* as well as *lay.* But in formal speech and in writing, the distinction between these two verbs is observed.

lead

The opening of a news story, usually the first paragraph, is called the lead. It summarizes the important facts of the story to follow. It does this by providing answers to any or all of six questions about the event being reported. The following lead answers the questions *who? what? where?* and *when?* in that order. Some leads also answer the questions *how?* and *why?*

An army of workers struggled to restore power to thousands of Connecticut homes without heat or light yesterday, but faced the prospect of more snow and freezing rain.   —Chicago Tribune

Leads are usually restricted to news stories. They are generally unsuitable for other types of compositions.

less and fewer

Nouns like *homework, furniture,* and *milk,* to which the question *how much?* may be applied, are MASS NOUNS. *Less* is used with mass nouns—*less homework, less furniture, less milk.*

Nouns like *friends, books,* and *problems,* to which the question *how many?* may be applied, are COUNT NOUNS. *Fewer* is used with count nouns—*fewer friends, fewer books, fewer problems.*

In informal English *less,* rather than *fewer,* is sometimes used with count nouns, as in *less accidents, less headaches.* This informal usage of *less* is not yet found in formal writing and speaking.

let and leave

In nonstandard English *leave,* rather than *let,* is often used in sentences like these:

Leave Bobby go with you.

Leave me use your bike.

Mindy left the assignment go until the last minute.

In standard English, however, a distinction is made between the meanings of the two words. *Leave* means "to go away from."

Please leave the room.

Mrs. Rogers left the office at 5:15.

Let means "to permit" or "to allow."

Let Bobby go with you.

Let me use your bike.

Mindy let the assignment go until the last minute.

Only when used with *alone* are *leave* and *let* interchangeable.

Leave us alone.

Let us alone.

let's

Let's is a contraction of *let us,* written with an apostrophe. The negative form is *let's not.*

Let's go to the movies.

Let's not study tonight.

In informal speech *let's us* and *let's don't* are often heard, but these forms are not used in writing or in formal speaking.

letters

See business letter; friendly letter.

library paper

See research paper.

lie

See lay and lie.

like and as

In formal speech and writing, *like* is used only as a preposition before phrase structures like *a baby* and *pieces of green glass; as* is used as a conjunction before such sentence structures as *he smiled yesterday* and *I do*.

The puppy cried like a baby.
Our cat has eyes like pieces of green glass.
Bob is smiling now as he smiled yesterday.
Hold the wheel as I do.

However, in informal speech and writing and increasingly in formal speech, *like* is used before sentence structures like *he smiled yesterday* and *I do*.

Bob is smiling now like he smiled yesterday.
Hold the wheel like I do.

Some people feel that *like* is too informal here and *as* is too formal. So instead of *like* or *as*, they use the words *the way* before such sentence structures.

Bob is smiling now the way he smiled yesterday.
Hold the wheel the way I do.

For practice see page 247.

(*See also* as; as if and as though.)

limerick

A form of humorous verse having a set **meter** and five lines that rhyme *aabba* is called a limerick. The following is by one of the most famous writers of limericks.

There was an Old Man with a beard,   a
Who said: "It is just as I feared!   a
   Two Owls and a Hen,   b
   Four Larks and a Wren   b
Have all built their nests in my Beard."   a
      —EDWARD LEAR

literary reference
See allusion.

loose sentence
See sentence forms.

M

metaphor
An implied comparison between dissimilar objects or ideas is called a metaphor. The first line of the following poem is a metaphor.

> Fame is a bee.
> It has a song—
> It has a sting—
>   Ah, too, it has a wing.
>   —EMILY DICKINSON

Although metaphors are based on comparisons, not all comparisons are metaphors. For instance, to write, "Grandma Moses' fame is greater than Mary Cassatt's" is to make a simple comparison, not a metaphor. This is because the items of the comparison are basically similar.

(*See also* analogy; figure of speech; mixed metaphor; simile; synecdoche; WRITER'S GUIDE, page 183.)

meter

One of the chief differences between prose and verse is rhythm. The rhythm of verse is more regular and patterned and therefore more obvious. The technical name for verse rhythm is meter. And meter is measured in feet. A FOOT is a unit of two, or sometimes three, syllables. The most commonly used foot in English verse is the IAMBIC foot. This is made up of one unstressed syllable followed by a stressed syllable. The most commonly used number of feet in a line of English verse is five. The name for a five-foot line is PENTAMETER. Thus, the meter of the following line of poetry is iambic pentameter.

Shall Ĭ | cŏmpáre | thĕe tó | ă súm | mĕr's dáy?
—WILLIAM SHAKESPEARE

Note that the division of syllables into feet may occur in the middle of a word. A foot may, therefore, have syllables from different words.

(*See also* rhyme; WRITER'S GUIDE, pages 182, 184-186.)

methods of development

After choosing a topic, you must decide upon an effective method for expanding your ideas into a piece of writing. That is, you must develop your ideas—adding details, explanations, and facts—and arrange them so that they are clear and understandable for your readers. The method of development you choose will depend on your topic, your purpose, and your audience. Suppose you want to explain how an automobile engine works. To develop this topic, you might divide the engine into its major systems and describe the function of each. You might compare an automobile engine with a steam engine. You might define *internal combustion* or *reciprocating engine*. Or you might explain what causes reciprocal power to change into rotary power. Often, however, you will need to combine several methods—describing, defining, comparing, showing causes—to fully develop your ideas into a finished piece of writing.

(*See also* analogy in persuasion; cause and effect; classification and division; comparison and contrast; definition; example and illustration.)

mixed metaphor

A metaphor is an implied comparison. A mixed metaphor occurs when two inconsistent comparisons are combined. Though often unintentionally funny, a mixed metaphor will usually weaken your intended meaning and confuse your reader.

> By midsemester Elaine was in deep water, stumbling over course requirements and grade averages.

Here, the first metaphor compares Elaine to a swimmer in deep water, and the second compares her to a hiker. Both comparisons are apt separately, but not together. To avoid the mental picture of Elaine trying to swim and walk at the same time, you might drop one metaphor.

> By midsemester Elaine was in trouble, stumbling over course requirements and grade averages.

Or, you might extend one metaphor by adding details that are consistent.

> By midsemester Elaine was on a rocky road, stumbling over course requirements and grade averages.

myself

The two standard uses of *myself* are illustrated in the following sentences.

> I hurt myself.
> I myself am to blame.

However, in informal speech and writing, *myself* is often used in place of *I* or *me*.

> My sister and myself were in charge.
> Ms. Steinberg asked Vince and myself to lead the discussion.

In formal usage, *myself* is not generally accepted in these situations.

> My sister and I were in charge.
> Ms. Steinberg asked Vince and me to lead the discussion.

N

narrating a process
See WRITER's GUIDE, pages 120-122.

narration

The kind of writing that tells a story is called narration. Its main purpose is to entertain and inform. Usually, events are told in the order of their happening, whether the narrative is factual, like a biography, or imagined, like a novel. News reports, short stories, folktales, epic poems, and most ballads are narratives.

(*See also* **allegory; article; autobiography; ballad; biography; epic; feature story; folktale; short story;** WRITER'S GUIDE, pages 115-122, 161-174.)

narrator

See **point of view.**

nonrestrictive and restrictive

See **comma.**

nonstandard English

Certain words, pronunciations, and grammatical forms that differ from those generally used by educated people are considered nonstandard.

NONSTANDARD	STANDARD
they was	they were
he done	he did
them books	those books
didn't have no	didn't have any

Nonstandard usages, while often natural in casual conversation with friends and family, are not considered appropriate for most writing and speaking situations. Nonstandard forms should be carefully avoided whenever their use might interfere with smooth and effective communication.

(*See also* **standard English.**)

note-taking

See WRITER'S GUIDE, pages 226-227.

number of

See **amount of and number of.**

O

o'clock

The phrase *o'clock* is often used to refer to an hour either before or after noon.

Debbie left at six o'clock.

It is used to refer to an exact hour. You would not say, for example, *six-fifteen o'clock*, but merely *six-fifteen*.

Notice that the hour is spelled out when written with *o'clock*. Many people prefer to use the more precise abbreviations *a.m.* and *p.m.*

(*See also* **a.m. and p.m.**)

one and you

In formal English *one* may be used to mean "people in general." Most often, the forms *one's* and *oneself* or *he, his*, and *himself* are then used to refer to *one*.

One should always try to complete one's own work.
One should always try to complete his own work.

However, if *one* means "a woman" or "a girl," then the forms *she, her,* and *herself* are used.

One should always try to complete her own work.

One is singular and third person, like *he* and *she.* So, forms like the plural *they* or the second person *you* should not be used in referring to *one,* as in "One often finds that you can't hear the speaker."

Many people find *one* too formal and prefer to avoid it. Instead, in informal English they use the word *you* to mean "people in general."

In Nebraska you can drive for hours through the farmland.

But it is important to be sure that this general sense of *you* is not misunderstood as personal.

You should answer the telephone courteously.

This sentence should be recast if there is a possibility of mis-understanding.

Everyone should answer the telephone courteously.

The telephone should be answered courteously.

(*See also* **agreement.**)

one of those who

In formal English a plural verb form generally follows expressions like *one of those who.*

Fran is one of those students who are always cheerful.

The pronouns *who, which,* and *that* can refer to either singular or plural nouns. In this sentence, the pronoun *who* refers to the plural noun *students,* and the verb form following *who* is plural.

In informal speech and writing, the verb form following *who* is often singular. This informal usage is long-standing and is gaining in acceptability.

Fran is one of those students who is always cheerful.

(*See also* **subject-verb agreement; who, which, and that.**)

onomatopoeia

See **imitative words.**

open punctuation

See WRITER's GUIDE, pages 219-220.

order of importance

The details in a paragraph may be arranged in the order of their importance. So also may the paragraphs in a composition. Often you will want to begin with the least important detail and build up detail by detail to the most important one. That is how the details in the following paragraph have been arranged.

To assess development of the [vegetable] known in the Orient for forty centuries as "the chicken without bones," scientists met in Munich last month for a world soy-protein conference, sponsored by the American Soybean Association. Some experts saw soy enhancing an affluent way of life but sadly questioned how far this planet's supply of soy can stretch to feed the world's poor. The bitter truth is that the hungry may be priced out of soy foods just

as they have been priced out of other high-quality pro-
teins.   —GERALDINE PLUENNEKE

Occasionally, you may reverse the usual order of importance,
leading off with the most important detail. News stories, written
for hurried readers, are arranged in this way. Compare the following paragraph with the previous one. It is actually the same
paragraph with the order of details reversed. Note how the paragraph seems to wind down or trail off. The original paragraph,
in contrast, builds toward the point of greatest interest.

> Scientists have recently learned the bitter truth that
> the hungry may be priced out of soy foods just as they
> have been priced out of other high-quality proteins. Meet-
> ing in Munich last month for a world soy-protein confer-
> ence sponsored by the American Soybean Association,
> experts sadly questioned how far this planet's supply of
> soy can stretch to feed the world's poor. The soybean,
> known in the Orient for forty centuries as "the chicken
> without bones," will, however, continue to enhance an
> affluent way of life.

(*See also* **chronological order; spatial order;** WRITER'S GUIDE,
pages 141-142, 159.)

outline

The plan of a composition is called an outline. It shows the
order of ideas in a composition, their relative importance, and
the relationships between them. Outlines are useful tools in summarizing reading you have done. They are even more useful
in arranging material you have collected for a report. There are
two kinds of outlines—the sentence outline and the topic outline. In a sentence outline, each heading is expressed as a complete sentence. In a topic outline, a word or a phrase is used to
express a heading. Either kind of outline may be prepared
formally. Formal outlines follow a set pattern using Roman
numerals, capital letters, Arabic numerals, and small letters,
in that order, to identify major headings and their subdivisions.

(*See also* **research paper; unity;** WRITER'S GUIDE, pages 192,
228-229.)

overused words

Words like *great, awful, fine,* and *nice,* called COUNTERWORDS,
are so widely and vaguely used that they have lost precise mean-

ing. For example, when people say *that's fine* or *it's nice*, they are expressing only a cloudy, generalized attitude of approval. Counterwords are common and accepted in conversation. But in writing they are an irritation, taking up space but adding little.

(*See also* **slang**; Writer's Guide, page 213.)

P

paragraph structures

See **chronological order; order of importance; spatial order;** Writer's Guide, pages 197-202.

paragraph types

Paragraphs may be classified according to their position and function in a composition. Within any composition there may be four types of paragraphs:

INTRODUCTORY PARAGRAPHS   These are intended to arouse the reader's attention and focus it on the main idea of the composition. An introductory paragraph may take the form of a generalization, a statement of purpose, a description of a process, or a definition of a problem. Short compositions rarely need an introductory paragraph.

DEVELOPMENTAL PARAGRAPHS   These paragraphs specify the details contained in the main idea. Usually, there will be at least one developmental paragraph for each major division of the main idea set forth in the introductory paragraph. Developmental paragraphs, which make up the bulk of any composition, are arranged so that an overall pattern is established.

TRANSITIONAL PARAGRAPHS   These are used to smooth the shift from one part of the composition to another. The function of transitional paragraphs is to link the main divisions of the composition. But a transitional paragraph is not needed before every developmental paragraph. Used infrequently, transitional paragraphs are usually short and function solely as signals to the reader.

CONCLUDING PARAGRAPHS   These paragraphs are used to end compositions. A concluding paragraph stresses the importance of the main idea. It may also present a brief summary or pose a **rhetorical question**. Like the introductory paragraph, a concluding paragraph is rarely needed in a short composition.

(*See also* **coherence; paragraphing;** WRITER's GUIDE, pages 193-197, 230.)

paragraphing
There is no rule for determining how many words a paragraph should have. Breaking up writing into paragraphs is basically a visual device. It is done to make writing easier to read. So far as structure is concerned, a composition could just as well be written in an unbroken mass of words.

Paragraphing, however, can be used to point up the relationship and order of ideas, especially in writing that explains. For instance, sentences that relate to the same idea can be grouped together in the same paragraph. This makes it easier for the reader to absorb the writer's thoughts and follow the order of their presentation. But in other kinds of writing, particularly narrative writing, the sentences do not cluster around ideas. Then, paragraphing becomes mostly a matter of appearance. In other words, the writer is concerned with how words look on the page. And too many long or too many short paragraphs in a row look bad. So the writer may merge a series of short paragraphs or break up a series of long ones. The variety that results makes for easier reading.

(*See also* **indention.**)

parallelism in sentences
When two or more elements serve the same function in a sentence, those elements should have the same form; that is, they should be parallel. If they are not, the sentence will be awkward. Note how parallelism is violated in these sentences:

Swimming, jogging, and even a walk are good forms of exercise.
Our new neighbors are noisy, inconsiderate, and snobs.
Roger thought happiness consisted of a large house and driving a flashy car.

Such sentences should be revised to give the same form to elements having the same function.

Swimming, jogging, and even walking are good forms of exercise.
Our new neighbors are noisy, inconsiderate, and snobbish.
Roger thought happiness consisted of a large house and a flashy car. *or* Roger thought happiness consisted of owning a large house and driving a flashy car.

Closely related to the problem of unparallel construction is the problem of needlessly shifted construction. Both betray a lack of consistent thinking. And both produce awkward and confusing sentences.

If one is really interested, you might ask the dean.
As soon as the game ended, all the fans run onto the field.
The members considered the problem for three months, and in January a recommendation was finally made by them.

Inconsistent sentences should be revised to avoid the needless shifts in construction.

If you are really interested, you might ask the dean. *or* If one is really interested, one might ask the dean.
As soon as the game ended, all the fans ran onto the field. *or* As soon as the game ends, all the fans run onto the field.
The members considered the problem for three months, and in January they finally made a recommendation. *or* The problem was considered by the members for three months, and in January a recommendation was finally made by them.

For practice see page 248.
(*See also* **one and you.**)

paraphrase

Restating someone else's writing or remarks in your own words is called paraphrasing. A paraphrase is not a summary. That is, it is not necessarily shorter than the original. Paraphrasing is helpful in note-taking and as an aid to understanding a difficult or technical text.

The following sentence, for example, is from a familiar speech:
Fourscore and seven years ago our fathers brought forth on this continent a new nation, . . .

—ABRAHAM LINCOLN

This sentence is a paraphrase of Lincoln's:
Eighty-seven years ago our ancestors founded a new government here.

(*See also* **précis.**)

parentheses

This pair of marks $\boxed{(\quad)}$ is used to enclose an explanation or reference that is not considered a part of the sentence in which it is used.

Contestants from Richmond $\boxed{(}$ California $\boxed{)}$ placed second and third.

The Bear Flag Revolt was led by a frontiersman named Ezekiel Merritt $\boxed{(}$ see pages 98-101 $\boxed{)}$.

Parentheses are used to enclose numbered or lettered divisions within a sentence.

Be sure to bring $\boxed{(}$ a $\boxed{)}$ your permission slip, $\boxed{(}$ b $\boxed{)}$ a bag lunch, and $\boxed{(}$ c $\boxed{)}$ a warm jacket or coat.

(*See also* WRITER'S GUIDE, pages 217-218.)

passed and past

Though these words sound the same, they are different. They are spelled differently and have different meanings. The word *passed* is a form of the verb *pass*.

The forward passed the ball rapidly to the center.

The word *past* functions in several ways, but never as a verb. In this sentence *past* functions as a modifier.

For the past two months, Joan hasn't missed a single band practice.

In this sentence *past* is a noun.

Cynthia enjoys recalling the past.

period

This mark ⟨.⟩ is used at the end of a declarative or an imperative sentence.

My mother is a surgeon⟨.⟩

Please leave the letters on the table⟨.⟩

Sometimes a sentence in the form of a question ends with a period. This is because the sentence is not really a question, but a request. The writer is not asking, but telling—in a polite way.

Would you have that delivered⟨.⟩

Will you please pass the gravy⟨.⟩

Periods are used after initials and after most abbreviations.

Dr⟨.⟩ Carla R⟨.⟩ Fracchia will speak at 8:15 p⟨.⟩m⟨.⟩

Periods are also used with numerals to mark the division between dollars and cents and between whole numbers and decimal fractions.

The seersucker costs $1⟨.⟩19 per yard.

The city has a population of 2⟨.⟩3 million.

(*See also* abbreviations; quotation marks; sentence functions.)

periodic sentence

See sentence forms.

personification

A figure of speech in which ideas or things are given human qualities is called personification. In the following poem, human qualities such as caution and fear are given to the sun.

WAR

Dawn came slowly,
almost not at all.
The sun crept over the hill
cautiously
fearful of being hit
by mortar fire.

—DAN ROTH

(*See also* WRITER'S GUIDE, page 183.)

persuasion

The kind of writing that attempts to convince a person to do something or to change an attitude is called persuasion. Political speeches, editorials, ads, sermons, debates, and sales talks are some of the many forms of persuasion. Persuasion, like the other kinds of writing, seldom appears in pure form. Usually, it is mingled with and supported by **exposition** or **description.** Similarly, it is rare for persuasion to be based solely on an emotional appeal or solely on a logical appeal. The most effective examples of persuasion are a blend of both.

(*See also* **editorial**; WRITER'S GUIDE, pages 139-161.)

plagiarism

Offering someone else's writing or ideas as one's own is called plagiarism. It is a form of theft. However, using someone's words or thoughts and giving that person credit is not plagiarism. In fact, it is the normal way to prepare a report or research paper. In some kinds of reports, the credit is given in a **footnote.** But whatever form it takes, credit should be given to sources, even of short phrases or ideas. This does not apply to undisputed, well-known facts, like the population of a city or the distance between two planets.

planning writing

See WRITER'S GUIDE, pages 106-110.

plot

The arrangement a writer gives to events in a story is called a plot. A plot has three parts—a beginning, a middle, and an end. This implies that a plot will be made up of at least three events. The difference between a narrative with a plot and a narrative without a plot is the difference between a parade and traffic. Both have an order, or sequence, but the order of the parade is arranged and selected. A news report is a narrative without a plot. A string of events are recorded in the order of their happening. A short story is a narrative with a plot. One event grows out of another. That is, the second event occurs because of the first one and the third because of the second.

In formal literary analysis, the beginning corresponds to the exposition, the middle concludes with the **climax**, and the end corresponds to the **denouement**.

(*See also* **narration**; WRITER'S GUIDE, pages 172-174, 175-176.)

point of view

The position, or "angle of vision," from which a story is told is called the point of view. Basically, a writer has two choices— a story can be told from the first-person point of view (*I*) or from the third-person point of view (*he, she, they*). Whichever point of view is chosen, the writer should stick to it—or risk losing the illusion of reality. Here is part of a story told in the first person:

> One summer morning when I was a child I lay on the sand after swimming in the small lake in the park. The sun beat down—it was almost noon. The water shone like steel, motionless except for the feathery curl behind a distant swimmer. From my position I was looking at a rectangle brightly lit, actually glaring at me, with sun, water, a little pavilion, a few solitary people in fixed attitudes, and around it all a border of dark rounded oak trees.   —EUDORA WELTY

In telling a story from this point of view, the writer creates a NARRATOR—the teller of the story—who must be a character within the story. This means that the writer cannot describe what is going on in the mind of any other character in the story. The writer is restricted to the mind of the narrator, and events must always take place in the presence of the narrator or be reported to him. The first-person narrator gives a story the impact of an eye-witness account. But it also limits the range of the writer. The alternative is a third-person narrator. Here is part of a story told from the third-person point of view:

> The children assembled first, of course. School was recently over for the summer, and the feeling of liberty sat uneasily on most of them; they tended to gather together quietly for a while before they broke into boisterous play, and their talk was still of the classroom and the teacher, of books and reprimands. Bobby Martin had already stuffed his pockets full of stones.   —SHIRLEY JACKSON

The third-person narrator is someone outside the story, not a character in it. This point of view allows the writer to move freely from event to event and enter the minds of the characters at will. Usually, however, a writer will report the thoughts of only one or two characters—the main characters. Some writers, especially modern ones, will restrict themselves from reporting any of the characters' thoughts, giving only descriptions and dialogue. In doing this, they are approaching drama. They are constructing scenes in which description is limited and dialogue makes up most of the story.

(*See also* **narration**; WRITER'S GUIDE, pages 116-118, 122, 163-165, 167.)

précis

A summary of written text that preserves the writer's point of view but uses other words is called a précis. Neither quotations nor phrases like *the writer says* appear in a précis. Instead, a précis is written as a condensed version of the original. The following is a précis of "Humpty Dumpty":

The massive attempts to reassemble Humpty Dumpty, who fell from a very high wall, failed.

(*See also* **paraphrase**.)

principle and principal

The word *principle* is a noun meaning "a basic law" or "a rule of conduct."

Sports are based on the principle of fair play.

Principal is an entirely different word. It has two functions. As a modifier it means "most important" or "chief." As a noun it refers to a person or thing of primary importance.

The principal players were from our local theater group.

Ms. Cardeira is the new principal of our school.

pronouns and nouns before *ing* verb forms

The *ing* form of a verb often functions as a noun. In formal English, especially in writing, pronouns like *my, his,* and *their* and noun forms like *Mary's, truck's,* and *cat's* are used before these verbal nouns.

My repairing the broken screen really impressed Dad.

We just heard of their canceling the concert.

I can't believe Mary's lying like that.

However, in other situations, when a verbal noun is not in the subject position, forms like *me, him, them, Mary, truck,* and *cat* are used very frequently. This usage is informal but occurs often in formal speech. It shifts the emphasis from the action to the performer of the action.

We just heard of them canceling the concert.

I can't believe Mary lying like that.

For practice see page 249.

(*See also* **his, her, and their.**)

proof in persuasion

See WRITER'S GUIDE, pages 140-142, 146, 155-159.

proofreading

See WRITER'S GUIDE, pages 215-221.

pun

A **figure of speech** which involves a play on words is called a pun. In some puns a word is used in two senses at the same time. In others a word is substituted for another word of similar sound but different meaning.

Hazel is one **nut** that never grew on a tree.

The water fountain is known as **Old Faceful.**

Most puns are intended to be humorous, but unintended puns are merely embarrassing. When you revise your writing, be on the alert for unintended puns and weed them out.

Q

question

See **sentence functions.**

question mark

This mark ⟨?⟩ is used at the end of an interrogative sentence.

What was the judge's decision ⟨?⟩

When the last part of a sentence is a question, the final punctuation is a question mark.

Ms. Dunn is teaching Film Study, isn't she [?]

A sentence which is in the form of a statement but is intended as a question ends with a question mark.

The plane has left already [?]

Notice that a sentence containing an **indirect question** does not end with a question mark, but with a period.

Ruth asked when the meeting would be over [.]

(*See also* **quotation marks; sentence functions.**)

quotation marks

This pair of marks [" "] is used to enclose a person's exact words.

["] When will this end? ["] she wondered.

Quotation marks are used to indicate **dialogue** in a narrative. A new paragraph begins each time the speaker changes.

["] Who are you? ["] I asked in a faint voice.

["] I'm the hotel nurse. ["]

["] What's the matter with me? ["]

["] Poisoned, ["] she said briefly. ["] Poisoned, the whole lot of you. I never seen anythin' like it. Sick here, sick there, whatever have you young ladies been stuffin' yourselves with? ["]   —SYLVIA PLATH

When more than one paragraph by the same person is quoted, each new paragraph begins with an opening quotation mark, but a closing quotation mark is used only at the end of the quoted passage.

William Woodward wrote of George Washington: ["] There were hard, harsh streaks in his personality, though on the whole he was magnanimous and kindly. Anyone who knows the long resentments of human nature cannot help being impressed by his generosity toward his personal enemies.

["] He was not a man of first-rate ability, but in many ways he was a great man—not only great, but very great. ["]

Quotation marks are used to enclose the titles of short stories, poems, chapters, essays, and songs.

> Yesterday the class discussed Ann Petry's short story "In Darkness and Confusion."

Single quotation marks are used to enclose a direct quotation or a title within a quotation.

> "Then Mr. Williams asked, 'Who's in charge here?'" explained Michelle.
>
> "Tomorrow we will read 'The Lottery' by Shirley Jackson," announced Mrs. Chan.

Quotation marks frequently occur with other marks of punctuation. Periods and commas always appear before the closing quotation mark; colons and semicolons, after it. A question mark or an exclamation point occurs before the closing quotation mark if the quoted material is a question or an exclamation; otherwise, it occurs after the closing quotation mark.

> He yelled, "I have found it!"
>
> Was it James Marshall or John Sutter who said "Eureka"?

For practice see page 250.

(*See also* **indention; indirect quotation;** WRITER'S GUIDE, pages 218-219.)

R

raise and rise

Raise is a verb meaning "to cause to move upward."

> Sally raised the flag at dawn.

Raise is also used to mean "to rear or bring to maturity" and "to gather or collect." Thus, *someone raises something* or *something is raised by someone.*

> They raised the puppies on a special diet.
>
> The puppies were raised on a special diet.
>
> The class will raise the money for the trip.

Rise is a verb meaning "to move upward." Unlike *raise*, its forms are irregular—*rise, rising, rose, risen.*

The pollution level rose dangerously last week.

Concern for the environment has risen sharply.

reference materials

See WRITER'S GUIDE, pages 223-224, 225-226.

research paper

A report telling what you found out about a specific subject is called a research paper. It may also be called a LIBRARY PAPER or a TERM PAPER. Usually three to six typewritten pages long, a research paper is based on information gathered through wide reading. A research paper should usually have (1) a title page, which includes the title, the writer's name, the name of the course, and the date; (2) a table of contents; (3) a final outline; (4) the paper itself; and (5) a bibliography. When you write a research paper as a class assignment, you may also be asked to hand in your note cards and bibliography cards.

(*See also* **bibliography; footnote; outline;** WRITER'S GUIDE, pages 222-235.)

restrictive and nonrestrictive

See **comma.**

revising

See WRITER'S GUIDE, pages 190-221.

rhetoric

The term *rhetoric* has several meanings. Originally, it meant "the art of persuasion." A current, unfavorable meaning is "inflated, insincere, elaborate speech or writing." But today's scholars and teachers use *rhetoric* to mean "the study of the effective use of language." To them rhetoric deals with the selection of words and forms that most fully express a writer's or a speaker's meaning and purpose to a particular audience.

(*See also* **diction; style; tone.**)

rhetorical question

Writers sometimes ask questions for which they expect no answer or questions which they answer themselves. These questions—called rhetorical questions—are used to emphasize an idea or introduce a topic.

> What is the use of saying that we need federal world control of the air? The whole question is how we are to get it. What is the use of pointing out that a World State is desirable? What matters is that not one of the five great military powers would think of submitting to such a thing.
> —GEORGE ORWELL

rhyme

Words having the same last sound are said to rhyme. To be exact, there are four common kinds of rhyme used in poetry. The first and most common is FULL RHYME. To rhyme fully, two words must have the following characteristics: The sounds coming before the stressed vowels must be different, and the stressed vowels and any sounds following them must be identical.

> "Is there anybody there?" said the Traveller,
>   Knocking on the moonlit **door**;
> And his horse in the silence champed the grasses
>   Of the forest's ferny **floor.**
> —WALTER DE LA MARE

Full rhyme may be either MASCULINE or FEMININE. In the previous lines, *door* and *floor* are masculine rhymes because both the stress and the rhyme fall on the final syllables. If the final syllables are unstressed, as in the following lines, the rhyme is feminine.

> Then to come in spite of **sorrow**
> And at my window bid good-**morrow**
> —JOHN MILTON

A second type of rhyme is called SIGHT RHYME. Here the words look as though they rhyme, but when pronounced, do not.

> Things fall apart; the center cannot **hold**;
> Mere anarchy is loosed upon the **world**
> —W. B. YEATS

A third type of rhyme is ASSONANCE. In assonance only the vowel sounds are identical—all other sounds are dissimilar. For example, *hat* and *cat* are full rhymes, but *hat* and *man* are assonant. Assonance is actually a partial rhyme, but it provides a pleasing and subtle variation from full rhyme.

> How do I love thee? Let me count the ways.
> I love thee to the depth and breadth and height
> My soul can reach, when feeling out of sight
> For the ends of Being and ideal Grace.
> —ELIZABETH BARRETT BROWNING

A fourth type of rhyme is CONSONANCE. In consonance the final consonant sounds are the same, but the vowel sounds are different.

> I shortcut home between Wade's tipsy shocks,
> And lookout crows alert in the bare elm
> Ask each other about this form that walks
> Stubbled mud they considered their own farm.
> —LEAH BODINE DRAKE

(*See also* **ballad; couplet; limerick; meter; sonnet; stanza;** WRITER'S GUIDE, pages 185-186.)

rhythm
See **meter.**

rise
See **raise and rise.**

run-on sentence
Two or more sentences joined without a connecting word or a semicolon form a run-on sentence. Because a comma is often incorrectly used in such sentences as a connecting device, this is also sometimes called COMMA FAULT.

> Mr. Davis did not receive his party's support, as a result, he lost the election.
> Jorie wanted to go to the concert, her parents wouldn't let her.
> This is a good magazine, I'm glad you recommended it.
> Max introduced us to the new exchange student, he is from Japan.

Run-on sentences can be corrected in four ways. They can be split up into separate sentences; their parts can be joined by a connecting word like *and, but, for,* or *or;* their parts can be joined by a semicolon; or their parts can be joined by a word like *who, which,* or *that.*

> Mr. Davis did not receive his party's support. As a result, he lost the election.
>
> Jorie wanted to go to the concert, but her parents wouldn't let her.
>
> This is a good magazine; I'm glad you recommended it. Max introduced us to the new exchange student, who is from Japan.

For practice see page 250.

S

semicolon

This mark [;] is used to join two sentence structures not connected by a word like *and, but, for,* or *or.*

> We'll have to hurry[;] it's almost three o'clock.
>
> Jon laughed aloud[;] Derek smiled mysteriously[;] Marvin just shook his head.

Semicolons are used to join two sentence structures that are connected by words like *however, moreover, therefore, for example, in other words.*

> Mr. Houston said the decision is up to us[;] in other words, he doesn't want any responsibility for the outcome of our project.

Semicolons are used between the items in a series if any of the items contain a comma.

> The members of the panel included Sue Poinsett, a senior at Acalanes High School[;] Mr. Stanley Perelman, the principal of Miramonte High School[;] and Dr. Louise

Thomas, a professor of education at the University of California.

We also plan to visit several smaller cities: Svendborg, Denmark⌐; Uppsala, Sweden⌐; Bergen, Norway⌐; and Turku, Finland.

(*See also* **quotation marks**; WRITER'S GUIDE, page 216.)

sentence classification

It is common practice to classify English sentences in two ways: They may be classed according to their function and according to their form. Function is determined by the purpose for which a sentence is used. Form is determined by the way basic elements are arranged within a sentence.

(*See also* **sentence forms; sentence functions**.)

sentence faults

See **dangling modifier; run-on sentence; sentence fragment; squinting modifier**; WRITER'S GUIDE, pages 210-211.

sentence forms

Grouped according to their form, sentences may be divided into four categories:

BALANCED SENTENCE   This kind of sentence contains two or more matching word groups. These word groups are not only matching grammatically, but are also similar in length. Often, words from one word group are repeated in another. Balanced sentences are most effective in expressing comparisons and contrasts.

If they are to fight, they are too few; if they are to die, they are too many.   —CHIEF HENDRICK

INVERTED SENTENCE   In this kind of sentence the usual word order is reversed, or inverted. By inverting word order, a writer gives special emphasis to the idea at the beginning of a sentence. When emphasis like this is desired, an inverted sentence is an effective way to achieve it. But used too often, inverted sentences make writing sound artificial.

His children he ignored completely. [inverted sentence]
He ignored his children completely. [usual word order]
On the desk, in plain view, lay the secret documents. [inverted sentence]

> The secret documents lay in plain view on the desk.
> [usual word order]
> The Ritz it's not. [inverted sentence]
> It's not the Ritz. [usual word order]

LOOSE SENTENCE   In this kind of sentence, also called a CUMU-
LATIVE SENTENCE, the essential meaning is made clear in the beginning. Later parts of the sentence, usually modifying elements
strung together, add detail and explanation: Much contemporary writing contains a high proportion of loose sentences.

> **She ironed again,** faster now, as if the more she engaged
> her body in the work the less she would think.
> —RICHARD WRIGHT

PERIODIC SENTENCE   In this kind of sentence the essential meaning is held up until the end. Periodic sentences may be used
occasionally to offer some variety from loose sentences. But
they are most effective when used to express suspense.

> If I read a book and it makes my whole body so cold no
> fire can ever warm me, **I know that is poetry.**
> —EMILY DICKINSON

(*See also* **emphasis; sentence functions; sentence length.**)

sentence fragment

A part of a sentence carelessly punctuated as a complete
sentence is called a sentence fragment.

> The child looked up at me. **And suddenly started to cry.**
> **While we were waiting for the bus.** Mrs. Ratzch drove by
> and offered us a ride.
> The box contained a set of woodworking tools. **Which was**
> **exactly what Theresa wanted.**

Sentence fragments can be corrected in two ways: they can be
joined with other sentences, or they can be rewritten as complete
sentences.

> The child looked up at me and suddenly started to cry.
> *or* The child looked up at me. Suddenly he started to cry.
> While we were waiting for the bus, Mrs. Ratzch drove by
> and offered us a ride.
> The box contained a set of woodworking tools, which was
> exactly what Theresa wanted. *or* The box contained a set
> of woodworking tools. It was exactly what Theresa
> wanted.

In some cases an incomplete sentence may make good sense and be easily understood. Such sentences, in which the missing elements are clearly implied, are called ELLIPTICAL. Elliptical sentences occur most often in conversation and are therefore very common in dialogue. However, they also appear in both formal and informal writing.

> "I'm not so sure about that. I've made arrangements with Mr. Nash for you to take the test again."
> "What?"
> "I've made arrangements for you to take the test again."
> "The test again?"
> "Just part of it. Half of it, I think."
>
> —JOYCE CAROL OATES

> They surveyed the terrace. A problem! Only one of the tables remained in the sunlight.   —DORIS LESSING

For practice see page 251.
(*See also* WRITER'S GUIDE, pages 210-211.)

sentence functions

Grouped according to the function, or purpose, they are meant to serve, sentences may be divided into four categories:

DECLARATIVE SENTENCE   This kind of sentence makes a statement.
> Oberlin College was the first college in the country to award degrees to women.

EXCLAMATORY SENTENCE   This kind of sentence expresses strong feeling.
> That's terrific!

IMPERATIVE SENTENCE   This kind of sentence makes a request or gives a command. Imperative sentences, especially when they are polite requests, often take the form of questions. These, however, are usually punctuated with a period.
> Fasten your seat belts, and extinguish all cigarettes.
> Will you please leave my door open.

INTERROGATIVE SENTENCE   This kind of sentence asks a question.
> Which airlines fly to Mexico City?

(*See also* **exclamation point; period; question mark; sentence forms.**)

sentence length

Variety in sentence length is basic to interesting writing. Without this kind of variety, writing will be choppy or dull. For example, a writer may want to emphasize an important idea by putting it in a short sentence. But if this sentence is surrounded by other short sentences, the emphasis is defeated. Similarly, a writer may find that a long, complicated sentence is the best means of expressing a subtle relationship of ideas. But if all the sentences are long and complicated, they will weigh the reader down and make for very dull reading. There is no special virtue in long sentences. Nor is there any in short sentences. But there is a virtue in having both kinds in a single piece of writing.

(*See also* **emphasis; sentence forms;** WRITER's GUIDE, pages 203-208.)

sentence punctuation

The marks used to punctuate sentences may be considered in two groups: those used at the end of sentences, and those used within sentences. End punctuation includes periods, question marks, and exclamation points. Punctuation within sentences includes commas, semicolons, colons, quotation marks, underlining, dashes, parentheses, brackets, and ellipsis points.

(*See also* **brackets; colon; comma; dash; ellipsis points exclamation point; italic type; parentheses; period; question mark; quotation marks; semicolon; underlining;** WRITER's GUIDE, pages 215-221.)

set and sit

The verb *set* means "to place" or "to put." Thus, *someone sets something* or *something is set by someone*. The forms of the verb are *set, setting, set, set*.

They **set** the plants in the shade.
The plants **were set** in the shade.

In contrast, *sit* means "to occupy a place." The forms of the verb are *sit, sitting, sat, sat*.

Please **sit** down.
Their house **sits** on a hill.

Two special uses of *set* are found in these sentences:
The sun **sets** in the west.
The cackling hen **is setting** on an egg.

several, each, and some

It is not always clear whether words like *several, each,* and *some* are singular or plural. Such words fall into three categories.

Words like *several, few, both,* and *many* are always plural.

Many of the paintings have been damaged.
Several are ruined.

Words like *each, either, neither, anyone,* and *everybody* are always singular.

Each of the teams has arrived.
Everybody is waiting.

A third group of words, like *some, any, rest, part, all,* and *most,* may be either singular or plural, depending on the meaning of the sentence. If the sentence answers the question *how much?* the word is singular.

Some of the house was still unpainted. [how much?]
Most of the milk is sour. [how much?]

If the sentence answers the question *how many?* the word is plural.

Some of the houses were still unpainted. [how many?]
Most of the sandwiches are gone. [how many?]

For practice see page 252.

(*See also* subject-verb agreement.)

shall and will

In American English *shall* is used primarily to ask questions with *I* and *we.*

Shall we ride or walk?
Shall I open the window?

Most Americans use *will,* both formally and informally, to express the ideas of determination and future time.

I'll (I will) finish this report if it takes all night! [determination]
I'll (I will) probably take the six o'clock train. [future]

shoptalk

The language of a particular occupation is called shoptalk, or JARGON. The following sentence, for example, consists mainly of printers' jargon.

Copy should be set flush left and ragged right.

Jargon is usually difficult or impossible for those outside the occupation to understand. For this reason, it should be avoided in speech or writing directed at a general audience.

(*See also* **slang**.)

short story

A brief, fictional narrative in prose is called a short story. Usually, a short story has only a few characters—sometimes only one—and a minimum of description and plot complication. Modern short stories, especially those of Chekhov, James Joyce, and Katherine Mansfield, often focus on the revelation of character. That is, the main point of the story is to reveal some insight into the personality of one of the characters.

(*See also* **narration**; WRITER'S GUIDE, pages 168-174.)

should of

See **could of and should of**.

simile

A stated comparison between dissimilar objects or ideas is called a simile. Usually the items compared are linked by the words *like* or *as*.

Writing free verse is like playing tennis without a net.
—ROBERT FROST

Had Robert Frost said, "Writing free verse is playing tennis without a net," he would have produced a **metaphor**, an implied comparison. The difference between simile and metaphor is often a difference in form rather than substance. Which way a writer expresses the comparison depends more upon "feel" than on any general rule. Of course, many comparisons cannot be expressed both ways. It would be difficult, for example, to express the following simile as a metaphor.

Life goes on forever like the gnawing of a mouse.
—EDNA ST. VINCENT MILLAY

(*See also* **analogy**; **figure of speech**; WRITER'S GUIDE, page 183.)

sit

See **set and sit**.

slang

Certain expressions in informal and nonstandard speech are labeled slang. Actually, slang is much like poetry; both spring from a desire to create new, vivid, forceful language. Slang, in a way, is failed poetry. It passes out of fashion very quickly, sometimes in a few weeks. Older slang, for instance, not only sounds dated, but is often hard to understand. What does *twenty-three skiddoo* mean? What does one do when one *takes a powder?* What is a *dream boat?*

In talking with friends, you probably use slang frequently. In informal writing, particularly **dialogue**, it is sometimes appropriate. But in formal speech and writing, slang should be avoided.

To use slang appropriately, you must first be able to recognize it. You must be aware that there is another way of saying *uptight* or *rip-off.* In many cases, dictionaries that label certain words or meanings as *slang* are of little help. *Webster's New Collegiate Dictionary* admits, "There is no satisfactory objective test for [determining what is] slang." In the end, you must rely on your own ear and your own experience to determine what slang is and when it may be used without offense.

(*See also* **overused words; shoptalk.**)

so

The word *so* is overworked as a connector. Also, it is often used very loosely.

Our car ran out of gas, so we had to hike home.

If a more exact word can be used, it should be, even though this means rewriting the sentence.

Our car ran out of gas, and we had to hike home.
Because our car ran out of gas, we had to hike home.
Since our car ran out of gas, we had to hike home.

sonnet

A poem that has fourteen lines and follows a conventional rhyme scheme is called a sonnet. Usually, each line of a sonnet has ten syllables, with stress on every other syllable beginning with the second. The following is an example of a sonnet:

Where are we to go when this is done?
Will we slip into old, accustomed ways,
finding remembered notches, one by one?
Thrashing a hapless way through quickening haze?

Who is to know us when the end has come?
Old friends and families, but could we be
strange to the sight and stricken dumb
at visions of some pulsing memory?

Who will love us for what we used to be
who now are what we are, bitter or cold?
Who is to nurse us with swift subtlety
back to the warm and feeling human fold?

Where are we to go when this is through?
We are the war-born. What are we to do?
　　　　　　　　　　　　　　　—ALFRED A. DUCKETT

(*See also* **meter; rhyme.**)

sort of
See **kind of and sort of.**

spatial order

In describing a person, an object, or a place, you must arrange the details in a pattern that the reader can follow. This could mean imposing a spatial order on the description. You might, for example, describe something according to the space it occupies—from top to bottom, from left to right, from far to near. But the point is that the description should be orderly, not haphazard. To be orderly, a description does not have to include every detail that an observer could see. In the following description, for example, the writer sorts out and selects details. She does not describe every brick in the school wall nor every window. She focuses only on a few suggestive details. And she arranges these details in a pattern that produces a clear picture in the reader's mind.

A wide concrete walk led from the street to the front doors of the school, dividing the yard exactly in two. Trees had grown in the yard at one time, but now only three stumps remained. . . . To the left of the building was a narrow side street and on its right was an asphalt playground that ran the length of the school building, back to a rear street that was also narrow. A six-foot fence protected the playground from the street, an ordinary chain-link fence that had begun to rust and come loose in places. In fact, in eleven places. Scraps of newspaper and children's lunchbags and wax paper and other harmless debris had been caught in the fence, soaked with rain and then baked dry, shredded. The asphalt of the playground was cracked everywhere and weeds grew up through the cracks, highest along the fence. Some of the weeds had begun to flower in small yellow buds.

—Joyce Carol Oates

(*See also* chronological order; description; order of importance; Writer's Guide, pages 114-115, 198-199.)

squinting modifier

Words which qualify the meanings of other words are called MODIFIERS. A squinting modifier is one that, because of its placement, can qualify more than one word or group of words at the same time. In the following sentence *yesterday* is a squinting modifier.

José said yesterday the trophy was missing.

It is not clear whether José spoke yesterday or the trophy was missing yesterday. A sentence containing a squinting modifier should be revised so that its meaning is clear.

Yesterday José said the trophy was missing.

José said the trophy was missing yesterday.

standard English

The **dialect,** or variety of English, spoken and written by educated people is called standard English. It includes the words, pronunciations, and grammatical forms most often used in schools, on radio and television, in newspapers, magazines, and books.

This standard dialect can be further divided into INFORMAL and FORMAL ENGLISH. Informal standard is the variety of English used in casual, everyday situations: that used in talking with friends and relatives; that used at school, at parties, and in the office. The following are some examples of informal standard English:

He didn't used to be afraid to fly.

She'll try and find you a ticket.

The two who you saw are here now.

Formal standard is the variety of English used on special occasions—term papers, lectures, letters of application, and academic discussions. The following are some examples of formal standard English:

He used not to be afraid to fly.
She'll try to find you a ticket.
The two whom you saw are here now.

(*See also* **nonstandard English.**)

stanza

A grouping of lines within a poem is called a stanza. Stanzas are often determined by their rhyme schemes. Some stanzas have a set number of lines. The ballad stanza, for example, has four lines and is called a QUATRAIN. A stanza of two lines is called a **couplet.** Other stanzas, such as those in **free verse,** vary in the number of their lines.

(*See also* **ballad; rhyme;** WRITER'S GUIDE, pages 184-186.)

statement

See **sentence functions.**

statement of intent

See **thesis statement.**

style

The selection and arrangement of words in a piece of writing is referred to as style. The term is also used in describing a writer's characteristic use of language—for example, "the terse, bare-bones style of Ernest Hemingway."

subject-verb agreement

A singular subject in English requires a singular verb form, and a plural subject requires a plural verb form. This relationship between a subject and a verb is called **agreement.**

COMPLETERS   A noun phrase coming after the verb *be* or a linking verb like *seem* or *remain* may look like a subject. Actually, it is a completer. The verb still agrees with the subject noun phrase, not with the completer.

Our favorite present was the homemade cookies.
The homemade cookies were our favorite present.
The chief hazard remains the icy roads.
The icy roads remain the chief hazard.

MODIFYING PHRASES   A modifying phrase following a subject does not affect the form of the verb.

The apples from the farm were delicious.

The action of the players was surprising.

Phrases joined to a subject by *as well as, in addition to, with,* and *together with* are usually set off by commas and also do not affect the form of the verb.

Theresa, as well as her sister, speaks fluent Spanish.

PLURAL SUBJECT WITH SINGULAR VERB   A plural subject expressing time or measure, if considered as a unit, often takes a singular form of the verb.

Two weeks was a long time to be sick.

Five dollars seems a lot to pay for that book.

RELATIVE PRONOUNS   A relative pronoun—*who, which,* or *that* —functioning as a subject takes a singular verb form when it refers to a singular noun.

The apartment which is being remodeled will be ready in two weeks.

A relative pronoun functioning as a subject takes a plural verb form when it refers to a plural noun.

The apartments which are being remodeled will be ready in two weeks.

SUBJECT AFTER VERB   The verb agrees with the subject, even when the subject follows it.

There's a woodchuck at the side of the road.

Here are the tickets I picked up for you.

In the corner were two frightened kittens.

Among the winners was a ten-year-old boy.

Has Jo found her books yet?

SUBJECT WITH PLURAL FORM   A subject that is plural in form but singular in meaning takes a singular verb form.

Politics is her overriding interest.

Competitive athletics for girls is an important part of our school's curriculum.

For practice see page 253.

(*See also* **collective nouns; compound subject; one of those who.**)

subjects for writing
See WRITER's GUIDE, pages 101-106, 224-225.

summarizing sentence
The final sentence of a long or complicated paragraph is often used to restate the topic sentence or to generalize about a series of details. Such a sentence is called a summarizing sentence. It may be used for clarity or for emphasis or for both. Used too often in a composition, however, the summarizing sentence becomes irritating. The last sentence in the following paragraph is a summarizing sentence. It repeats the idea of the topic sentence, which here is the first sentence.

> . . . The smalltimer . . . thought and talked only about his act and about show business. Nothing else interested him. If you said to him, "Do you remember the Johnstown flood?" he would probably reply, "Remember the Johnstown flood? Are you kidding? I and the wife were playing Pittsburgh that week. . . ." Everybody in Johnstown could have been swept out of town: the smalltimer wouldn't know or care. He had nothing in common with anybody who was not in his profession.   —FRED ALLEN

(*See also* emphasis; topic sentence.)

summary
See précis.

synecdoche
A form of **metaphor** in which a part of something is used to stand for the whole or the whole is used to stand for a part is called synecdoche.

> If Diane can't get wheels on Saturday, we'll have to take the bus to the ball game.

Here a part, the wheels, is used to stand for the whole, an automobile.

> Yesterday's game tied the record for the most runs Houston had ever scored.

And here, the city of Houston is used to stand for an important part—its baseball team, the Astros.

Although this form of expression occurs in everyday speaking and writing, the technical term *synecdoche* is usually reserved for formal literary analysis.

(*See also* **figure of speech.**)

synonyms

Words that are very similar in meaning are called synonyms. For example, *rescue, save,* and *redeem* are all synonyms, as are *feminine, womanly,* and *ladylike.*

Although the meanings of synonyms are very close, they are rarely identical. You must choose carefully which of several synonyms best fits the meaning and style of a sentence. In the following sentence, for example, *rescue* is the most appropriate of the three synonyms; *save* might also be used, but *redeem* would be inappropriate.

Liz is trying to rescue the stranded kitten.

(*See also* **antonyms; thesaurus.**)

T

take

See **bring and take.**

than I and than me

Usually a pronoun like *I, he,* or *she* is used after *than* and *as* in comparisons.

Carl can run faster than I.
Maria is almost as tall as he.

You can see why these pronouns are used if you complete the comparisons.

Carl can run faster than I can run.
Maria is almost as tall as he is tall.

In informal speech, pronouns like *me, him,* and *her* are often used instead, as in *Carl can run faster than me*. But this usage is not found in formal speech or in writing.

Sometimes the choice of a pronoun affects the meaning of a sentence. It may even make the sentence ambiguous.

Joe knows Sally better than me.
Joe knows Sally better than I.

To make the comparisons clear, you might recast the sentences.

Joe knows Sally better than he knows me.
Joe knows Sally better than I do.

their, there, and they're

These three words sound alike. But each one has its own meaning and its own spelling.

Their means "belonging to them."

Angela and Terri gave their reports this morning.

There means "in that place." It is also sometimes used to introduce a sentence.

Manny left his notebook there.
There are still a few difficulties.

They're is a contraction of *they are*.

They're too busy to help us.

them and those

Them is used only alone and as a substitute for a noun in an object position. Using *them* as a noun modifier, as in *them apples*, is nonstandard.

Jan picked the apples.
Jan picked them.
I ate three of the apples.
I ate three of them.

Those can be used as a substitute for a noun—in either a subject or object position—or as a noun modifier.

Those are Jan's apples.
Those apples are Jan's.
Jan picked those.
Jan picked those apples.
I ate three of those.
I ate three of those apples.

For practice see page 253.

thesaurus
A reference book which lists words and their **synonyms** is called a thesaurus. Usually the words in a thesaurus are arranged according to related topics, with an alphabetic index at the back of the book.

thesis statement
The subject of a composition is called the THESIS. What you assert about this subject is called the thesis statement. You might, for example, have the following for a thesis: the term of office for members of Congress. For a thesis statement, you might have this: The term of office for members of Congress should be extended from two to four years. A thesis statement is prepared before the composition is written. It is intended to be a guide for selecting and arranging details and seldom appears in the finished composition. A thesis statement is especially helpful in writing **exposition** and **persuasion.**

(*See also* **coherence; unity;** WRITER's GUIDE, pages 107-108, 110, 140-141, 144-146, 228.)

third person
See **point of view.**

titles
See **abbreviations; capitalization; quotation marks; underlining.**

tone
The general effect produced by a writer's treatment of material is called tone. Tone is a reflection of the writer's attitude. The tone of a piece of writing may be described as funny or serious, comic or tragic, sarcastic or sad—or whichever word seems appropriate.

topic sentence
The sentence which states or implies the **central idea** of a paragraph is called the topic sentence. It is often the opening sentence, as in the following paragraph:

> **He was a monster of conceit.** Never for one minute did he look at the world or at people, except in relation to

himself. He was not only the most important person in the world, to himself; in his own eyes he was the only person who existed. He believed himself to be one of the greatest dramatists in the world, one of the greatest thinkers, and one of the greatest composers. To hear him talk, he was Shakespeare, and Beethoven, and Plato, rolled into one. And you would have no difficulty in hearing him talk. He was one of the most exhausting conversationalists that ever lived. An evening with him was an evening spent in listening to a monologue. Sometimes he was brilliant; sometimes he was maddeningly tiresome. But whether he was being brilliant or dull, he had one sole topic of conversation: himself. What *he* thought and what *he* did.

—DEEMS TAYLOR

For variety or for emphasis, a writer may place the topic sentence in the middle or at the end of a paragraph. The function of the topic sentence in the paragraph is similar to that of the **thesis statement** in the composition. Both help to limit the writer's subject and act as a guide to the selection of details.

(*See also* **coherence; unity;** WRITER's GUIDE, pages 194, 200.)

transitions

See **coherence.**

types of writing

See **description; exposition; narration; persuasion;** WRITER's GUIDE, pages 111-139, 139-161, 161-174, 179-181.

U

underlining

In handwritten and typed materials, words that are to be printed in **italic type** are indicated by a single underline.

The names of books, magazines, newspapers, journals, ships, aircraft, motion pictures, and works of art are underlined.

> Miss Conforti asked us to read "Feeding on Dreams in a Bubble Gum Culture" in The Atlantic Monthly.
>
> Our favorite painting was The Potato Eaters by Vincent van Gogh.

Foreign words or phrases which are not yet a part of American English are underlined.

> Nureyev and Fonteyn danced the final pas de deux.

Words used as words, letters used as letters, and figures used as figures are underlined.

> Is this numeral a 9 or a 4?
>
> I can never remember how many l's there are in parallel.

Words are sometimes underlined for emphasis. This device, however, should not be used too frequently.

> He knows prices, not values.

For practice see page 254.

(*See also* **emphasis.**)

uninterested

> *See* **disinterested and uninterested.**

unity

When each paragraph in a composition relates directly to a main idea, the composition has unity. To help achieve unity, you may want to form a **thesis statement** before beginning to write. This is usually a sentence telling what general point you intend to make about the main idea. Such a statement is used to determine which details relate to the main idea and which do not. As a check of how unified a composition is, an outline is very useful. You might find that outlining your first draft helps you bring all the parts of a composition into focus. Then, for example, you may see that a step is missing or that a paragraph should be dropped.

A paragraph has unity when all the sentences in it relate to a **central idea** or to a **topic sentence.** In the following paragraph, the sentence in color does not relate to the topic sentence. The writer should remove this sentence to gain unity.

Michigan is an outdoor paradise. Hunters find the dense woods of the upper peninsula quick with wild game. Michigan's extensive shoreline provides opportunities for swimming, boating, camping, and fishing. In addition, countless inland lakes abound with fish. For skiing enthusiasts, northern lower Michigan offers steep hills and ridges. **The development of the automobile industry has made Detroit one of America's largest cities.** During both summer and winter months, Michigan is a popular vacation spot.

(*See also* **coherence; emphasis; outline;** WRITER'S GUIDE, pages 191-192, 228-229.)

usage

The way in which words and phrases are actually used is called usage. Usage sets the standards for what is appropriate in speech and writing. Often, these standards are summarized as "rules" in books about usage. Since usage changes, so do these standards, and so should the rules. Some words and expressions gain acceptance; others become obsolete. Modern usage books thus distinguish between "appropriate" and "inappropriate" contemporary English rather than between "good" and "bad" English. Changes in usage occur constantly, but gradually.

(*See also* **nonstandard English; standard English.**)

W

who and whom

In formal English *who* functions as a subject, like *I, she,* and *they*. *Whom* functions as an object, like *me, her,* and *them*.

Who said that?
Whom did you see? [object of *see*]
I don't know who is going.
I don't know whom you mean. [object of *mean*]
To whom was the package sent? [object of *to*]

In informal English *who* may also function as object at the beginning of a sentence structure.

Who did you see? [object of *see*]

I don't know who you mean. [object of *mean*]

Who was the package sent to? [object of *to*]

who, which, and that

Who is used to refer to people or animals. *Which* is used to refer to things or animals. *That* may be used to refer to people, animals, or things.

The geologist who (that) talked about Iceland has lived there for six years.

The puppy who (that) followed us home belongs to my cousin.

A wild animal which (that) comes close to camp may be looking for food.

The bicycle which (that) is for sale has ten gears..

-wise

The suffix *-wise* may be added to a word to indicate manner, direction, or position.

He cut the cloth lengthwise into two even pieces.

Sometimes people form words with *-wise* meaning "with reference to."

Salarywise, Jan has the best job.

In this sense, however, *-wise* is usually associated with commercial writing and generally not accepted in formal usage.

wordiness

Unnecessary words dilute the emphasis of a sentence and sometimes make the meaning unclear.

It may for these reasons be asserted that the view which he held in regard to the war is of some importance.

Such sentences should be revised to eliminate unnecessary words and express the meaning more clearly and directly.

His view of the war therefore counts.

—QUENTIN ANDERSON

(*See also* **emphasis**; WRITER'S GUIDE, pages 211-212.)

Writer's
Guide

THE WRITING PROCESS   Writing begins in thin air and ends on paper. And between the beginning and the end lies a complicated process. The process includes thinking, planning, and organizing. It includes putting words down on paper, scratching some of them out, and adding others. It includes assembling what's left into a polished, readable form. Says author Patrick Dennis, "Writing isn't hard; no harder than ditchdigging."

There are three general stages in the writing process. The first involves discovering a subject, thinking about it, and organizing your ideas. The second stage involves recording your ideas on paper. And the third stage involves revising and reworking what you have written. These three stages can be called prewriting, writing, and rewriting.

When you are actually involved in the writing process, you will find that there are no clear divisions between stages. You usually won't say, "Now I'll stop prewriting and start writing." In fact, you will often work back and forth between two or even three stages. And as you do more writing, you might change their order slightly. Or you might spend much time with one stage and little with another. But that will come later. Now, to learn how you write best, you need to know what the stages are and what's involved in each stage.

Some people believe that the only stage that really counts is the second—writing. This isn't so. You need thoughtful prewriting to develop something worth writing about. And you need careful rewriting to develop something worth reading. Each stage is an essential part of the writing process.

Before You Write

Good writing doesn't just happen—at least not very often. Good writing is planned. It's a process that moves through stages, taking shape as it goes along, like a statue being hammered out of a block of stone.

What is unusual about the first stage in the writing process is that it may involve no writing at all. You may simply sit around, turning things over in your mind. But this stage—called prewriting—is very important. It involves discovering a subject, finding out what you think and feel about your subject, and deciding what you want to say about it. Time spent in prewriting is not wasted. It makes the work of each of the following stages in the writing process easier.

GETTING STARTED

Finding something to write about is usually the first step in prewriting. Sometimes it can be very easy. You may have no choice of subject, or you may have a subject already in mind. At other times choosing a subject can be one of the most difficult parts of the writing process.

There are generally three kinds of writing assignments. Your teacher may make a very specific assignment: Write an essay telling why the other boys in *Lord of the Flies* killed Piggy. You probably don't know immediately just what you're going to write, but you do know what you're going to write *about*. And you know where to look for information—in *Lord of the Flies*—and where to focus your thoughts—on the question of why they killed Piggy.

Or your teacher may make a more general assignment: Write an essay about sports. That puts some limits on your topic, but there are a lot of different sports—and a lot of different things to say about them. You may be interested in weight lifting, or volleyball, or swimming, or soccer. You may want to explore the importance of keeping fit. Or you may think that sports are overemphasized in America. Turn the assignment over in your mind. Look at it from several different angles. Try to find an aspect of the assignment that will really interest you—one you will want to work with, involve yourself in, and write honestly about. Faking interest in a subject only makes your work harder and practically guarantees that your writing will be flat and uninteresting.

Finally, your teacher may make a completely open assignment: Write an essay on any subject you like. Now you have no limits. But you may also have no sense of direction. Having everything to write about, you may suddenly feel you have nothing to write about. This isn't true. You just need to spend some time considering the possibilities and choosing one for this assignment.

You will always write best about something you know and care about. So think about your personal experiences. Think about the people or events that have been most important in your life—your uncle who was killed in the war, your older sister who has always been the one person you could talk to, your first day as "the new kid" at school, your first job. Think, too, about less important experiences that have somehow impressed you—that funny couple you saw on the bus, the bit of conversation you overheard and couldn't forget, the mornings you delivered newspapers and watched the sun come up. Think about public issues that particularly affect you—your state's legal driving age, sports programs for girls, weekend curfew hours for teenagers. And think about the media messages you get—your favorite songs on the radio, the latest dog-food commercial on TV, a boring movie you saw, the magazine article about "today's youth," a science-fiction novel you couldn't put down.

Run through some of the possibilities in your mind. Don't take time to examine them all. Do that and you'll never get around to writing. But take enough time to find a subject that interests you, one you care enough to write about.

Your subject doesn't have to be unique. Lots of people have watched the sun come up, and almost everyone has seen that dog-food commercial. But maybe being out alone when the sun comes up gives you a special feeling of independence. Or maybe seeing how that commercial plays unfairly on viewers' emotions makes you angry enough to tell someone about it. If so, then you'll be able to take one of those common subjects and make it your own. You'll be able to involve yourself in the subject; you'll have feelings and ideas to write about.

TRY IT   Suppose you have a completely open writing assignment. Jot down several ideas for subjects. Try to include at least one person, one event, one public issue, and one movie or TV program. Now think about your ideas. Which one interests you most?

It's not yet necessary to know what the main point of your writing is going to be. All you need is a subject to explore. When you have one, you're ready to go on—to develop your ideas on the subject, to discover other people's ideas, then to focus your ideas, and finally to start organizing them.

As you brainstorm your subject, you might want to make some notes. You might want to jot down ideas so that you can consider them more carefully. You might want to write out a few key sentences or make some tentative outlines. On the other hand, you may prefer not to write anything yet. It might be easier for you just to sit quietly in a corner and think. Or you might mull over your ideas while you're busy doing other things. There is no one way to go about prewriting. Try more than one approach; find out what works for you.

DISCOVERING YOUR IDEAS

Choosing a subject is only the first step in prewriting. Exploring that subject is usually the next. This is the time to discover your own thoughts and feelings. This is the time to make up your own mind, to form your own opinions, and perhaps even to reject the subject you have chosen.

Your writing will be interesting only if you are honestly interested in your subject. That is what makes this step in prewriting so important. Discovering your own ideas involves you in the subject. It helps make the subject—whether it was assigned or chosen—uniquely yours.

To make a subject your own, you have to find out what you think and feel about it. It's not, for example, picnics in general or shoplifting in general that you are going to write about. It's your reaction to one of these subjects. And simply deciding that you favor picnics and oppose shoplifting is not enough. No one is going to be very interested in a general opinion like that.

To come up with something to say—something that might be interesting—you have to discover your personal reaction to the subject. Remember, for instance, the last picnic you went on. Didn't you get a bad burn from the grill? Wasn't the beach wall-to-wall people? And weren't there even more bugs than people? Actually, hasn't it been a while since you really enjoyed a picnic? Maybe you don't favor picnics after all. Now you're starting to make *a* subject *your* subject. And in discovering your own ideas on the subject, you're starting to pile up details that you can use in your writing.

Different people use different methods for discovering their ideas. Maybe you think best with a pen in your hand. If this is the case, then write down important words and phrases, even sentences, about your ideas. Reconsider them. Revise them. Rewrite them.

Or maybe you think best by yourself—no writing, no talking. Then find a place to be alone, and concentrate. Mull over your ideas. Accept them. Reject them. Improve them.

Or maybe you think best out loud. Then discuss your subject with a friend—or with yourself. Defend your ideas. Rework them. Expand them. One word of warning, though: if you do talk with someone else, be sure you end up with your own ideas, not with your friend's.

Whichever method you use—perhaps a combination of all three works best for you—examine your subject and your thoughts about it carefully. Ask questions: What are my reactions? Why do I feel that way? Don't just accept what you've always heard; decide what *you* think. And don't be afraid to disagree—with friends, with teachers, or with books. But if you disagree with someone or something, know why you do. Have details to back up your feelings. Consider the facts; consider your reactions to them. Find out why you think and feel as you do.

TRY IT   Think of a discussion you have heard recently in which two or more different opinions were expressed. Perhaps your parents and your younger brother disagreed about his bedtime. Or maybe you heard opposing TV editorials about the local curfew law. Consider the discussion carefully. Examine the arguments that were made, and think of others that could be made. Decide what stand you would have taken in the discussion. Don't automatically side with a person you like or with a popular opinion. Think about the issues and your reactions. Make up your own mind.

DISCOVERING OTHER'S IDEAS

As important as your own reactions are, they are often not the only thing you need to consider in prewriting. You may also need to find out what other people think and know about your subject. You can't know everything. And making up your own "facts" can get you into trouble with a knowledgeable reader.

You might, for example, have decided to write about a city ordinance that you consider unfair. Look up the law and find out exactly what it says. You may discover that it is not the law, but the way in which the law has been enforced, that seems unfair.

Or perhaps you want to respond to an editorial you read in the newspaper. Don't rely on your memory. Get a copy of the paper. Reread the editorial carefully; refer to it as you work through your ideas.

You may be planning to write about a personal experience. Talking it over with a friend or family member who shared the experience with you might be helpful. Maybe you can even find a photograph or a letter that will help focus your memories.

You might find that you need to check on facts even when you're planning a short story. Your entire plot may hinge on a factual detail—that red ants and black ants are mortal enemies or that wolves have often attacked and killed people. Find out if your factual detail really is a fact. Look it up.

You may even be preparing to write a paper that will be based almost entirely on research. You might be interested in the life of Lucy Stone, for example. In that case you will have to spend a major portion of your prewriting time gathering facts and ideas from various sources.

There are many sources available to you. Which ones you use will depend on your subject and the kind of information you need. The important thing is to use these resources now, in the prewriting stage. This is the time to sort through the ideas and form the opinions on which your writing will be based. And your ideas and opinions will be considered valid only if they are based on facts.

FOCUSING YOUR IDEAS

You have already spent time thinking about your subject and, if necessary, gathering information about it. Now you are ready to focus your ideas. Now you need to choose an approach to your subject and decide what point you wish to make in your writing.

This is one of the most important steps in the prewriting stage. It involves deciding what you want to say about your subject and then condensing your main point into a single statement. That statement will be the basis on which you will organize all your ideas.

The easiest and most helpful way to focus your ideas is to compose a sentence explaining what you want to write. This sentence is not the title nor the first sentence of your paper. Those will come later. It is a sentence for you to use both now, in deciding on your main point, and later, in planning, organizing, and writing.

If the purpose of your writing is to take sides in an issue or prove something, your sentence will be a thesis statement. It will name your subject and then assert something about the subject. You may have decided, for example, that you want to write about the sport of skydiving. After thinking about the subject and perhaps checking on a few important facts, you may have decided to make the point that this sport is too dangerous to be fun. Then you would write a thesis statement like this:

THE SUBJECT	YOUR ASSERTION
The sport of skydiving	is too dangerous to be fun.

Or you may have decided to make the point that skydiving requires skill and training. In that case, you would write a thesis statement like this:

THE SUBJECT	YOUR ASSERTION
The sport of skydiving	requires much skill and training.

Writing a thesis statement, then, takes you a step beyond choosing your subject. It involves deciding what you want to say about your subject.

TRY IT   From the following list of subjects, choose one that interests you. Or choose a subject that isn't on the list. Take some time to think about the subject and to decide what point you want to make about it. Then prepare a thesis statement that you could use in writing about the subject.

grades	hall passes
marriage	the Olympic Games
football	ballet
movie ratings	police
college education	the President of the United States
parents	marijuana

A thesis statement works well when you are writing to persuade someone. But not all writing is persuasion. Sometimes you will simply want to tell a story or relate a personal experience. Then, instead of a thesis statement, prepare a statement of intent, a sentence that explains what you want to write about. Both kinds of statements will help you to focus your ideas. For example, suppose you have actually been skydiving; you may have decided to write about your first jump. You might write a statement of intent like this:

> I will describe what happened on my first skydiving jump.

Or you may have decided to write about a specific aspect of that first jump: the mixed emotions of excitement and fear you felt at the time. Then you would write a statement of intent like this:

> I will describe the combination of excitement and fear I felt on my first skydiving jump.

Like a thesis statement, a statement of intent goes beyond the subject; it tells what you want to say about the subject. You should make your statement of intent as specific as possible.

TRY IT   Think of a personal experience you would like to write about. Consider major events in your life, like winning something or going away from home alone for the first time. And consider less important experiences that you remember, like spending a day at the beach with your friends or riding a bicycle forty miles. Think about the experience. Then write a statement of intent that you could use in writing about the experience.

Whether you use a thesis statement or a statement of intent will depend upon what you plan to write. Either one will help you by focusing your ideas and giving you a basis on which to plan and organize.

PLANNING AHEAD

Once you have decided on a thesis statement or a statement of intent, you are ready to start planning the details of what you want to write. At this stage you will probably want to make some notes—jot down main ideas, write out a few sentences, make reminders of specific details you want to include. If you prefer, of course, you can do this in your head. But most people find it helpful here to write at least some things down. And seeing something on paper will give you the feeling that things are really under way.

This is the final step in prewriting. It's your chance to get your ideas firmly in mind before you start a rough draft. You may want to look up some more facts or an important statistic. You may want to reconsider and revise some of your ideas. And you'll definitely want to make sure you can actually support your thesis or develop your story. So take your time here. Remember, there's a lot more to writing than stringing words and sentences together on paper.

This is the time to make a list of your ideas. Then cross some of them out, underline others, write in new ideas, draw arrows and stars, question marks and exclamation points. Use whatever methods and symbols work for you. But take time to consider how you are going to develop and organize your ideas.

If, for example, you're going to write an essay about a story you read, list your ideas for the main points of the essay. Check your list. See if each main point relates to your thesis statement. Reread the story. See which sections you might quote or refer to for support of your ideas.

Or if you're writing a story of your own, list your ideas for the major developments in the story. Be sure that each one is needed to make the story work. And be sure that you haven't left an important development out. Decide on the best organization for your story. Consider your characters—how they think and act. You might even prepare mini-biographies of your characters to make them more real.

This is also the time to think about your audience. Who are you writing for? Who is really going to read what you write?

How much do those readers know about your subject, and how much will you have to explain? How should you write to best capture the interest of your audience—to involve them in your story or make them want to read your essay?

This may also be the time to change your mind. You may find that your thesis statement won't hold up. Maybe you can't support your original statement that children should be able to decide whether or not they go to school. You might want to revise it: Children should be allowed to make certain decisions about their schooling. Or you might want to completely reverse your position and develop a thesis statement like this: Children should have to go to school until they are at least fourteen years old.

Similarly, you may find that your statement of intent isn't going to work. Maybe there just isn't much to describe about the last time you babysat the McVickers' kids. But maybe you do remember three or four funny incidents from various babysitting jobs. If so, you will want to develop a new statement of intent: I will describe some funny things that happened to me as a babysitter.

Whatever problems you are having with your subject, try to deal with them now. You're not committed to a particular approach, or a particular statement, or a particular subject. If you want to make changes, this is a good chance to do so.

When you are satisfied with your decisions, you should write out your plans in some form. A series of short notes to yourself may be enough. Or a list of the main points you want to make, in the order in which you want to make them, might be right for you. Maybe you want to write an informal outline, noting your major points and some supporting details. Or perhaps you prefer—or your teacher requires—a formal outline, with numbered and lettered headings. Again, choose the method that is best for you.

You'll find that having something down on paper, even though it's not what you finally want to say, gives you a feeling of confidence. You won't have to face that first blank sheet without support.

While You Write

You've spent some time in prewriting—getting ready to write. You've chosen a subject, considered what you want to say about it, and pinpointed your probable audience. You may even have jotted down some notes or put together a preliminary outline as a guide. What next? It's time to write.

This does not mean the end of planning and decision making. In fact, while you write, you'll have to decide *how* to say *what* you want to say—how best to present and develop your chosen subject. Which method you choose to develop your ideas will depend on your purpose in writing.

Basically, your writing will fulfill one of three purposes. If you want to tell your readers about something, your purpose is to inform. If you want to influence your readers' thinking or move them to action, your purpose is to persuade. If you want to use language to create—a story, a play, or a poem—your purpose is to entertain.

There are several methods of organizing and presenting material to achieve each of these three purposes. After you've decided your basic purpose in writing, you'll have to choose the method of development that best suits your particular needs. Then, you'll need to be consistent in following that method while you write.

WRITING TO INFORM

If your purpose in writing is to tell someone about something, you're writing to inform. Writing to inform may involve giving directions or narrating a personal experience or explaining the relationship between two events. So, giving information takes many different forms and requires different methods of presentation.

Which method you choose for a particular piece of writing will depend principally on the kind of information you want to give—facts, impressions, incidents, explanations—and on who is to receive it.

111

Informing by describing

Suppose you are writing an explanation about how to cook hamburgers on an outdoor grill. As one of the steps, you might write, "When the coals are ready, put on the hamburgers." But have you really given your reader useful information? Have you explained how long it takes before the coals are ready? Or what they look like when they are ready? To be informative, you'll need to add some descriptive details like these: "Allow 30 to 45 minutes for the coals to burn down before putting on the hamburgers. The coals will look ash-gray in the daylight but will have a red glow after dark."

What you've just done is to inform by describing. That is, your general purpose was to explain how to do something. But to explain fully, you had to describe appearances. You had to make your information precise and specific, to *show* your reader what you meant.

Literal and subjective descriptions   All description is made up of details—the size, color, smell, feel, shape, or sound of something. Suppose you heard a car being braked hard. You might describe the sound with details like these: "I heard the high-pitched sound of tires skidding over the road." On the other hand, you might write, "Through the open window I heard the sickening squeal of rubber tortured by blacktop." Both are descriptions of the same event. But notice this. The first description is factual, objective, impersonal. It's what anyone else who was listening might have heard. You might call this a literal description.

The second description, however, includes your own feelings about the sound—a "sickening squeal." This description, colored with your own emotional reactions, might be called subjective description.

So you have two kinds of description. Each is made up of different details. Each gives its own kind of information. The first describes things as they are. The second, things as you feel about them. The first kind, literal description, is appropriate in writing in which your personal feelings are not included—for example, in a factual report about a dangerous intersection. The second kind, subjective description, is appropriate in writing in which your reactions are part of the information you are giving your reader—for example, in a personal essay about an automobile accident you witnessed.

Your purpose in writing will determine whether or not your descriptions are literal or subjective. Notice the kinds of details in the following excerpt, in which tennis star Billie Jean King explains how she stands when she serves.

> . . . [M]y left foot is set about two inches behind the base line. My right foot is placed comfortably about twelve inches behind my left foot and about four inches to the right of it. A line connecting my feet would form about a sixty-degree angle with the base line. I am mostly sideways to the net but slightly facing it. —BILLIE JEAN KING

The purpose of this description is to inform the reader how to stand when serving. And the details are literal and objective. If Ms. King's purpose had been to describe a personal experience, say, a crucial serve in an important game, her description might have included her feelings and impressions as well.

In your descriptive writing, you may sometimes want to combine literal and subjective details. You want your reader to see first what is there and then to experience your reaction to it. In the following excerpt the writer describes a catwalk over a buffalo pen and then adds the subjective reaction of the boys trying to crawl along it in the dark.

> The catwalk was made of two 2 x 6's nailed side by side and braced atop the inner wall which bisected the rectangle. In the dark the planking seemed about as wide as a snake's hips and as high as the Empire State Building.
> —GLENDON SWARTHOUT

Whether your description is literal or subjective or a combination of both, it is important to be selective in your choice of details. Keep your audience and your purpose in mind. Try to select those details that add to the reader's understanding. And try to exclude those details that are irrelevant or that clutter the picture you are trying to give. Notice that, in the excerpt by Billie Jean King, she doesn't mention how she is holding the racket or what kind of court she is playing on. What is important, for the moment, is the position of her feet. And the details she uses all relate to this main point.

Patterns of organization   Whether your description is a few phrases or a complete essay, you should arrange its details in such a way that the particular picture they create is sharply in focus. This takes conscious planning on your part. If the details are given in a random or helter-skelter manner, the picture will be blurred and confusing to your reader.

There are several ways you can arrange the details in a description. If your description depends mainly on visual details, you can arrange them according to space—moving from far to near, for example, or from outside to inside, or from top to bottom, or from right to left. You could, on the other hand, begin with the most strikng detail, then move to less obvious ones—or just the reverse, build up to the most striking detail.

If you are describing an action or a change, you can arrange the details chronologically, presenting them in the order of their happening, from first to last.

In writing a description, first think about the main impression you want to make on the reader. Then present the details in an order that helps support and strengthen this impression. Perhaps you want to describe what you observed on a camping trip at three different times—in the darkness, in the predawn, and at sunrise. Here a chronological order would be effective. Or perhaps you want to describe your guitar teacher, emphasizing his long, sensitive hands. In this case, either starting off with or leading up to this most important detail makes sense.

In the following excerpt, the writer describes a cabin in West Africa where she and her family lived while studying wild animals. Here she uses a spatial organization. She begins with the general location and then narrows the focus to the cabin and its interior. By moving from far to near, outside to inside, she has enabled the reader first to visualize the surroundings and then to "zoom in" on the cabin itself.

> Built under the shadow of a giant fig tree, it is always cool, surrounded by dim green lights, the twittering and chirping of birds, and the constant babbling of a small muddy stream. . . . The cabin itself is a simple one-roomed wooden building, with a few basic items of furniture—tables, shelves, a cupboard and a large bed. The floor is stone, covered by rush matting, the windows are small, the ceiling low. —JANE VAN LAWICK-GOODALL

TRY IT You have just lost a sweater and want to put up a notice on the *Lost and Found* bulletin board at school. Would literal or subjective details be most informative in describing the sweater so that it could be recognized and returned? Which of the following details would you select for your notice? Would you group the details you choose in any special way? For example, would it be helpful to the reader if you grouped together details of appearance and then details of possible location?

The sweater:
> was a present from my parents
> is navy blue
> is often borrowed by my young brother
> was probably left in the gym last Friday night
> has a patch on the left elbow
> feels great on a windy day
> was perhaps lost in the parking lot
> is a cardigan

Informing by narrating

Narration is the kind of writing that answers the question "What happened?" Narrating is telling a story. Usually, when you think of telling a story, you think of fiction—of novels and short stories. But fiction is only one kind of narrative. There are narratives that are true—accounts of real incidents and events.

Because narration can be based on fact as well as on imagination, it can be used to inform as well as to entertain. For example, you can use narration to tell your reader about personal experiences—your first day on a new job—or historical events —the Apollo 13 space flight. You can use it to explain a process—how the body digests food—or the way to do something—how to play chess.

If description is like a photograph, then narration is like a motion picture. Narration follows events through time.

Personal narratives   If you are going to write about something that happened to you, you'll probably write a first-person narrative. You'll say things like "I did this" and "We did that." This is *your* experience, so you'll include your reactions to events, your feelings about them. But there is an important limitation to this approach. To be consistent, you can relate only what you know and feel or what others report to you— your point of view is restricted to your own thoughts, feelings, and observations. And since what happened has already occurred, you'll probably do your telling in the past tense. This is what the actress Shirley MacLaine has done in her autobiography. Here's an excerpt from it describing how she commuted to dancing class while she was in high school.

> Rehearsals ended at midnight. I would rush for the bus, which, it seemed, was always either late or early, but never on schedule. I'd stumble groggily from the bus an hour and a half later, and make my way down the quiet street to a dark and silent house. My dinner usually was saltine crackers smothered in ketchup and Tabasco, and with them a quart of ginger ale. I always ate standing up, and then I'd stagger to bed, rarely before two o'clock. . . .
>
> It was a lonely life, for a teenager especially, but I had a purpose—a good reason for being. And I learned something about myself that still holds true: I cannot enjoy anything unless I work hard at it.   —SHIRLEY MACLAINE

Sometimes, in a personal narrative, you'll want to give the reader a special feeling of immediacy. You'll want your reader to have a feeling of being there and experiencing what's happening along with you. Often, you can convey this feeling by using the present tense. Here's a writer narrating an event that he experienced thirty years ago. But he uses the present tense. The event was the Allied invasion of German-occupied France. He was on one of the thousands of ships that crossed the Channel from England to Normandy.

> It is three am; it is four am. We are six miles off shore. . . . By now the enemy must know what's up. Bombers roar overhead. Flares drop inland. I am so wrought up I do knee bends. A thousand youngsters are on board almost as inexperienced as I. It is pathetic to hear them ask my opinion. Everything's fine, I say. Now we wait three miles off shore. All nine guns point at the beach. 5:30 am. There are yellow streaks in the cloud cover. Now! The guns go off and [our ship] the *Quincy* bounces. Dawn finds us on Germany's doormat like the morning milk bottle.   —TRB

TRY IT   See if you can rewrite the excerpt by Shirley Mac-Laine in the present tense. What problems do you encounter? What information will you have to leave out? Try rewriting the excerpt by TRB in the past tense. Is it better this way, or do you lose something? What advantage is there to past-tense narrative? What disadvantage? What advantage is there to present-tense narrative? What disadvantage?

Objective narratives   When someone else—not you—is the center of your narrative, you will probably write in the third person. That is, you'll write, "She did this" and "They did that." And since you are not the focus of the narrative, your feelings and reactions will be kept in the background or omitted entirely. This is what is meant by objective narrative.

Because objective narrative doesn't require a restricted, first-person viewpoint, you have an advantage. You can describe events going on in several different places, even when you are not a witness to them.

Here is part of an objective narrative. The writer is explaining how a pioneer couple located their homestead on the Nebraska prairie in 1873. Does the writer appear at all?

> George Cather hired a man with team and wagon, measured the circumference of one of the back wheels, tied a rag on the rim so they could more easily count the revolutions and started across the prairie. George had a compass to keep him going in the right direction. His wife sat in the back of the wagon, counted revolutions and computed mileage. . . . When they had, according to calculations, reached their homestead, they drove on a bit to what they judged to be the center of their property, just to make sure they were really on their own land—and pitched a tent for the night.   —MILDRED R. BENNETT

This narrative is told in the past tense. Would you ever want to use the present tense for an objective narrative? Read the following excerpt and think about the effect of using the present tense.

> On the hunt, the bear is patient and cunning. Lying motionless in the congested ice for hours, it may cover its telltale black nose with one white paw. Let a seal only peek out of its breathing hole and the white mass springs, one clawed arm snatching its prey in a blur of movement. In the summer, the bear must sneak up to a seal basking lazily on top of the ice. Hiding behind ice hummocks, avoiding cracks, it edges closer and closer, until it can catch up to its meal in one-two leaps. Or, it may approach from the water, submerging deeply to come up close by, or swimming slowly, pushing a piece of ice before it as camouflage.   —SAVVA M. USPENSKIJ

Notice that the use of the present tense emphasizes the generalized, habitual nature of the bear's actions. So, when you want to suggest a habitual action, an action that repeats itself, you may want to use the present tense in an objective narrative.

TRY IT   Rewrite the excerpt about the polar bear using the past tense. What happens? Are you writing now about the habits of polar bears in general or about the actions of a particular polar bear?

Anecdotes and illustrations   Sometimes you'll find that you need to support a general statement with a specific example to fully express what you mean.

One way you can do this is with a brief story—an anecdote. Thus, you may include a small-scale narrative, or perhaps several, in a larger composition.

Here's an anecdote told about Jackie Robinson after his retirement from major league baseball. Notice how the writer uses it as an example to support his general statement about the character and strength of Jackie Robinson even in ill health.

> He accepted the blindness and the limping with a courage born of beauty. At an old-timers' game last season in Los Angeles, someone threw a baseball at him from the grandstands, ordering, "Hey, Robinson. Sign this." The unseen baseball struck his forehead. He signed it.
>
> —ROGER KAHN

An anecdote is a vivid way to back up a general statement. But you can't count on always having one handy. And sometimes an anecdote just doesn't seem to fit in. Then, rather than have your reader hang in the air with only a general statement, you should specify. You should back up your statement with an illustration. For instance, it isn't enough to state, "We've become a nation of wanderers. Few people can truly call a place their own." You need to go on from such a statement to illustrate what you mean, as this writer has done.

> It happens all around us. . . . It happened to me personally. My mother was from Poughkeepsie, New York; my father from Marietta, Ohio; my stepmother from Washington, Pennsylvania. I was born in Wheeling, West Virginia; raised in Athens, Georgia; educated in Pottstown, Pennsylvania, Ithaca, New York, and Baltimore, Maryland; and I now work in Rabun Gap, Georgia. I've learned a lot from all of that, but still I have no more idea of where I fit in space and time and community than if I had just landed inside a meteor from Pluto. I make my home where I am.
>
> —ELIOT WIGGINTON

When you use an anecdote or an illustration, remember that it is there for a purpose—to support or emphasize a point you are making in your composition.

‖ TRY IT   Here are some unsupported general statements. In each case, the experience is not specified. Pick one of these statements, complete it from your own experience, and support it with an anecdote or illustrate it with narrative details.

> Getting to — becomes more of a hassle every day.
> It was the wildest — I've ever seen.
> I'll never forget —.

Narrating a process   Narratives which are directions and explanations not only answer the question "What happens?" but also "How does it happen?" These kinds of narratives follow the movement of a process from one stage to the next.

You may narrate a how-to-do-it process in the first person or in the second person. For example, you may write, "I begin with a few simple breathing exercises" or "You should begin with a few simple breathing exercises." Using the second person has the advantage of sounding as though you were talking directly to your reader, having a face-to-face conversation.

But whether you choose the first or second person, you should "walk through" the steps of your directions in your mind to make sure that they are in the right order and that nothing has been left out. You may even want to number the steps, as this writer has done in explaining how to replace a fuse.

> 1. When the fuse blows, grope your way over to the flashlight and unplug the offending appliance (usually the last one turned on before the blow).
> 2. Get your spare fuses and open the fuse box door.
> 3. When you shine the flash on the fuses you'll see one with its little glass window all black and burned looking. Replace this fuse. . . .   —KAY B. WARD

Numbering the steps this way works well with brief, fairly simple directions. For more complicated directions, however, you may want to use transitional words like *first, then, next,* and *finally* as you move from step to step in the process. Also, you can use words like *if, when* and *after* to introduce the conditions required for the next step, as in "After the paint has dried, apply the second coat."

You may feel it necessary to illustrate your directions with diagrams or pictures. In that case, a word of warning. Don't depend on an illustration to make the meaning of your words clear. Write so that your reader can understand you even if there are no pictures or diagrams. Make sure your directions can stand alone.

Not every explanation of a process is a how-to-do-it. Often, you will need to tell how something happens—for example, how plants make food from sunshine. Such explanations are usually told in the third person. Sometimes, especially in explaining a process that is habitual, you will want to use the present tense, as this writer has done.

> In warm weather the local thunderstorm takes its place as an important water producer. It comes chiefly as a result of temperature differences on the earth's surface. There may be many causes for these differences. For example, the dark earth of a plowed field will absorb more heat than the surrounding forest, and over this warm field the air will rise. As it goes higher the moisture in the air begins to condense into water droplets, producing the towering cumulus clouds whose contours outline the movements of the rising air. Given the proper combination of heat, moisture, and subsequent chilling, the cloud will at last build up to produce a thunderstorm.   —John H. Storer

Whether you are giving directions or providing an explanation, you may need to do some research to be sure of your facts—of the exact sequence of events, for example, and their cause-and-effect relationship, if any.

And don't forget your audience. If you are writing for someone completely unfamiliar with the process you are explaining, don't leave out a step assuming your reader can figure it out. Put it in, in the right place. You will also want to use the kind of detail and vocabulary appropriate for your audience. An account of a process for the general audience of your school magazine, for example, would probably be less technical than a report to your chemistry class on the same subject.

TRY IT   A friend is coming to visit for the first time, and you want to write out directions for finding your house. Since your friend will pass the school you both attend, you should begin your directions at that point. Include whatever information your friend will need to get from your school to your house. You may need to mention the amount of time to allow, the direction to travel in, the names of streets, the number of blocks, the names of buses or trains and the fare, and the location and number of your house on the block.

Patterns of organization   Narrative writing characteristically describes a series of events in the order of their happening. If you change the normal order by shifting back to an earlier time or to an earlier event, be sure to alert your reader by using words like *earlier, when she was ten,* and *before we moved.*

Beyond this general pattern of chronological order, your choices in informing by narrating are many.

Your choice of first, second, or third person will affect the tone and the kind of information you give your reader.

Your choice of present or past tense will affect the sense of immediacy, habitual action, or distance that you want your reader to receive.

And your purpose—whether you want to relate a series of events, to give directions, or to explain a process—will affect the kind of narrative detail you use in moving from event to event. Once you have made these choices, you should try to be consistent so that the reader can follow without confusion as the series of events unfolds in your narrative.

Informing by dividing and classifying

Two common ways of arranging facts in informative writing are division and classification. When you divide, you separate something into its parts. When you classify, you group something with other things that are like it. These two ways of arranging facts are closely related and are often used together.

Analysis—separating into parts   Dividing, or analyzing, means breaking something down into its parts. This is fairly easy to do when you are explaining something like an automobile or an electric can opener. It is less easy to do when you are explaining something more general—parliamentary government, for example, or Manifest Destiny. But whether your subject is specific or general, you should divide consistently and fully. You should apply only one principle of division at a time. And your division should account for all the parts of your subject. Here is a paragraph that meets these standards.

> The typical jazz band of the time was a six-man group divided into two sections. The lead section carried the melody and was made up of a trumpet, a trombone, and a clarinet. The rhythm section was made up of a piano, a string bass, and drums. The job of the rhythm section was to lay down the beat. Or, to put that a little more fancily, they were expected to maintain the tempo. Of course, members of both sections often briefly switched roles during the playing of a number. The piano player, for instance, might perform a melodic solo while the trumpet player tooted a few rhythmic chords in the background.   —ALICE KIRSCH

This writer has divided a jazz band into two sections, according to their function—either playing the melody or maintaining the beat. This is her principle of division. You can test how well this division holds up by substituting other divisions. Suppose, for example, you divide the jazz band into a brass section and a rhythm section. Are you then applying one principle of division or two? Aren't the instruments and their functions separate things? In other words, dividing the band into a brass section (type of instrument) and a rhythm section (function of instrument) would be applying two principles of division at once. Further, this division does not account for one of the parts—the clarinet. This is neither a brass instrument nor is it used to maintain the beat.

If you like, try another division. Try dividing the jazz band into a brass section and a string section. Though you are now dividing by a single principle—the type of instrument—you still haven't accounted for all the parts. The clarinet, for example, and the drums fit in neither division.

Some subjects, like the jazz band, have fairly obvious divisions and are easy to analyze. But other subjects present a problem. For example, how do you divide a tennis swing? Isn't it one movement? How do you analyze something that has no parts?

> The forehand drive is best explained by breaking it down into its four main components: the early backswing, the maximum backswing, the moment of contact, and the follow-through. . . . But as you learn the shot step by step, remember that in fact it is one continuous, unbroken motion. You should remain aware of the whole swing even as you consider each of its four phases.   —BILLIE JEAN KING

What the writer has done is to invent parts for the sake of her explanation. The forehand drive, she admits, is "one continuous, unbroken motion." But she has imposed a division that her subject doesn't really have in order to analyze her subject clearly and precisely. Even so, her division is consistent and complete. She has used one principle—a time/position division—whose parts add up to a consistent whole.

TRY IT   Write a brief analysis—perhaps a paragraph—of some subject you know well. The subject could have obvious divisions—the sections of your school band—or divisions that you would need to invent—the parts of a golf swing. Test your analysis to make sure that the divisions are consistent and complete.

Classification—grouping together   When you classify, you put a thing or an idea into a group of other things or ideas that are in some way similar. How you classify will depend upon your purpose. For example, if you were cleaning out your bookcase, you might classify your books into three groups—those you want to keep, those you want to sell, and those you want to give away. On the other hand, if you were merely tidying things up, you might classify your books into fiction, poetry, and reference works. It all depends on your purpose.

Whatever you are sorting out—books in the bookcase or facts for a term paper—your classifications must be consistent, complete, and logical. You would not, for example, classify your books as fiction, poetry, reference works, and those with green covers. Nor would you classify your books as fiction and poetry if you also had some reference works.

In the following excerpt, the writer has taken the general subject of bikeways and grouped them into three distinct classes.

> Chicago has three different kinds of bikeways. A *bike path* is a small roadway of asphalt, concrete, cinder, or compacted earth, isolated from automobile traffic and reserved for bicycles only. The bikeways along the lakefront and through the forest preserves are bike paths. A *bike lane* is a separate lane marked off in a street and is reserved for bicycle traffic only. The city has only two bike lanes: They run along Clark and Dearborn from Elm Street to Wacker. A *bike route* is merely a street that city traffic engineers have decided is one of the better routes for traveling by bicycle to the Loop, the lakefront, or to some other spot of interest. Bike routes are marked by green and white signs.
> —JOHN CONROY

Notice that there is consistency in his classification. There is no overlap—each class of bikeway is distinct from the other two. And the classification is complete. There are no left-over bikeways that are not identified or accounted for by these three classes.

TRY IT   How you classify something depends on your purpose. For example, the swimming coach might classify a group of students according to physical abilities. The math teacher might classify the same students according to their reasoning ability.

Try classifying the members of some group—either people or things—according to some principle of your choosing. Then choose a different principle and classify the same group a second way. Be sure that you make the principle for your classification clear and that each classification is consistent and complete.

Patterns of organization   Both dividing and classifying provide an excellent means of ordering your material. You can inform your reader by identifying the structure of your subject—dividing—or by showing its relationship to other similar items—classifying. For both processes, you should follow two basic rules—be consistent and be complete. That is, follow one principle of division or classification at a time until you have accounted for all parts or items.

Often a good way to organize a composition using classification or division is to begin with a general statement about your subject. Then expand on this statement with the system of division or classification you have chosen. Notice that this is the pattern used in each of the excerpts in this section.

At times you may need to combine both classification and division in one piece of informative writing. When this happens, you could begin by classifying the items of your subject and then continue by dividing a typical item into its parts. For example, you might classify certain dogs as spaniels and then list the specific characteristics of a spaniel such as short legs, long wavy hair, and drooping ears.

Informing by defining

When you are trying to explain something, especially something technical, you may need to define key terms for your audience. Usually, such definitions are fairly short. Their purpose is simply to clarify. Longer definitions, sometimes extending over a whole essay, serve a different purpose. They provide you with a framework for your ideas, a structure for your composition.

Brief definitions   There are three basic reasons for offering your readers a definition. The most obvious is to explain a term you think they may be unfamiliar with. Also, you may wish to explain an unfamiliar meaning of a familiar term. Finally, you may want to pin down the precise meaning you are going to use for a term that has several meanings.

Whatever your reason, there is a common way to go about defining a term. First, classify the term. That is, place it in the next larger class of similar objects or ideas. Then, add the special characteristics which mark off this term from other members of the larger class. Here's how it works.

TERM		GENERAL CLASS	CHARACTERISTICS
Penuche	is	fudge	made with brown sugar and without chocolate.

In putting together a definition, be sure that your classification is not too large. For example, if you write "penuche is food" or even "penuche is candy," you would be placing the term *penuche* in too large a class. However, if you write "penuche is fudge," you are identifying it more exactly, as a certain kind of candy.

Also, you must be careful not to use your term to define your term. Don't, for example, define *penuche* as "a fudge that tastes like penuche." This is a circular definition and leads nowhere. Finally, avoid defining terms with constructions like "is when" and "is where," as in "Penuche is when you make fudge with brown sugar." Such constructions are unnecessary, and they cloud the meaning of your definitions.

What has been described here are the steps you take in putting together a formal definition, the kind you usually find in a dictionary. Often, in informative writing, this is the kind of definition you will need. But there are many times when a less formal definition will work as well—maybe even better.

Penuche, a brown-sugar fudge, is easy to make.

Whether you write a formal definition or an informal one will depend upon two things. It will depend on how much information you think your reader needs and how important a particular term is to a general understanding of your explanation. These are things you must estimate for yourself. Other than to know your audience, there is no hard-and-fast rule you can follow.

TRY IT   Rewrite the following as formal definitions, making them as clear and effective as possible. Then try rewriting the definitions informally as part of another sentence.

1. A confrontation is a meeting in which people confront one another.
2. Frostbite is when there is a partial freezing of some part of the body.
3. A schooner is a means of transportation.

Extended definitions   A brief definition is a good way to clarify the meaning of a particular term for your reader. If you were explaining classical music, you might, for example, drop in a brief definition of a symphony. On the other hand, if you were writing an essay on the symphony as a musical form, you would need more than a brief definition. You might instead describe the standard pattern of four movements and contrast the early forms of the symphony with the modern forms. You might also mention famous composers of symphonies and compare their work. If you choose this approach, what you are doing is informing through an extended definition, a full explanation of a particular subject.

An extended definition may run for several paragraphs or take up an entire essay. Usually the subject of an extended definition is abstract, like love and liberty, or it is general, like pop music and ecology. Here is part of an extended definition. The writer begins with a brief definition of chemistry, then goes on to more fully develop his opening statement.

> Chemistry is that branch of science which has the task of investigating the materials out of which the universe is made. It is not concerned with the forms into which they may be fashioned. Such objects as chairs, tables, vases, bottles, or wires are of no significance in chemistry; but such substances as glass, wool, iron, sulfur, and clay, as the materials out of which they are made, are what it studies. Chemistry is concerned not only with the composition of such substances, but also with their inner structure. Further, these materials are constantly undergoing change in nature: iron rusts, wood decays, sugar ferments, coal burns, limestone rock is eaten away by water, and living organisms digest their foods and build up their structures. Chemistry investigates such changes—the conditions under which they occur, the mechanism by which they take place, the

new substances that are formed as their result, and the energy that is liberated or absorbed by them.

—JOHN ARREND TIMM

Approaches to defining   There is more than one way to write a brief definition. And there is more than one way to build an extended definition. Here are some of the different approaches to defining you may find useful in your writing.

You can define an unfamiliar term with a familiar synonym.

> The woodchuck, or groundhog, is found in the northeastern United States and Canada.

You can compare a term to something similar or contrast it with something different.

> Both the porpoise and the dolphin are sea mammals, but the porpoise, unlike the dolphin, has no beak.

You can use examples to define, citing instances which illustrate the term.

> The weather was capricious—that is, one moment it was sunny and fair, the next it was rainy and cold.

If you are discussing a term that may have different meanings, you can explain the exact sense in which you are using it.

> By pride, I mean an unrealistic or undeserved self-esteem.

Sometimes you can use negation—that is, explain what something is *not*—as a way to help define what something *is*.

> An acoustical guitar does not have an electrical amplifier.

You can define something by dividing it into its parts.

> A submarine sandwich usually consists of a long roll sliced lengthwise and filled with cold cuts, onion, cheese, tomato, and lettuce.

You can define something by explaining what it does.

> A trip odometer, which can be reset to zero at the beginning of a trip, measures the total distance traveled by a vehicle.

TRY IT   Using one of the approaches to definition explained in this section, write a brief definition for three of the following words. Use a different approach for each definition. Define the word as it is used in the field indicated in parentheses. If you need additional help, you may consult a dictionary.

to spike (volleyball)	to crawl (swimming)
to beat (cooking)	a distributor (auto mechanics)
a fault (geology)	a stand (forestry)
a square (carpentry)	to tack (sailing)

Patterns of organization   When you write an extended definition, you may want to begin with a formal definition in your opening paragraph, briefly identifying the class and the special characteristics of what you intend to discuss. You could then explain any special sense or limited meaning that you want to use.

Your next several paragraphs might contain any of the various approaches to defining, such as classifying and dividing, comparing and contrasting, or the use of examples, synonyms, or negation. Finally, a concluding paragraph might sum up your interpretation of the term and any major points you want to make about it.

Informing by comparing and contrasting

When you use a comparison to explain, you show the similarities between two or more things. When you use a contrast, you show the differences. Comparison and contrast are so natural and so widely used it is hard to imagine explaining something without them. Often, they are used together in the same explanation.

An effective comparison or contrast is more than a mere list of similarities or differences between two randomly selected items. It wouldn't make much sense, for example, to contrast an eagle and an ocean. The two have so little in common that it would hardly be worth the effort to list all their differences. On the other hand, if you were interested in birds of prey, you might contrast an eagle and a vulture. Or, if you were interested in the laws of flight, you might compare an eagle and an airplane. In both cases, the items contrasted or compared have something in common which makes the contrast or comparison reasonable and informative. An eagle and a vulture are birds of prey, but with very different hunting habits. An eagle and an airplane are different kinds of things, but their similar shapes keep both in the air.

Comparisons   When you are making a comparison, what kind of similarities should you list? Do you have to list everything the items have in common? There is one answer to both of these questions. You should list only those similarities that relate to your purpose.

Suppose your purpose is to explain the disadvantages of buying a five-speed bike. To illustrate the disadvantages, you compare the five-speed bike with three-speed and ten-speed bikes. Here's how one writer has done it.

> Although some may appreciate a five-speed's trappings, most will discover this animal combines the worst of a three- and a ten-speed. The typical five-speed is built on the same heavy frame as the three-speed, often has the same wide saddle and upright handlebars, but has the five-speed gear cluster and changer bolted on in back. For two extra gears of dubious value, you pay almost as much as you would for a low-priced ten-speed, but pedal around as much weight as you would on a three-speed.
> —Stephen Marshall

All of these bikes have more in common than the similarities the writer has listed. They all have wheels and tires and handlebars and pedals. But these similarities do not relate to the writer's purpose. To mention these similarities would cloud the purpose of the comparison.

Contrasts   When you use contrasts, you don't list every difference between the items you are contrasting. As in a comparison, you list only those points that relate to your purpose.

Here, for example, Pat Jordan contrasts two styles of playing shortstop. Notice that he states the purpose of his contrast clearly in his opening sentence. And he sticks to this purpose by showing only those differences in the two styles of fielding. Other possible differences, such as batting stance, are not mentioned.

> There are two styles in which shortstops field their position in the major leagues: aggressive and fluid. The aggressive shortstops, such as Tim Foli of Montreal, attack a grounder as if the ball were their mortal enemy. They snatch it up so forcefully that one can hear it slap against the glove, and then they seem to grind the ball in their glove, choking it for a second before finally firing it to first base. The fluid ones, such as Mark Belanger of the Orioles, glide effortlessly after a grounder and welcome it into loving arms. They scoop the ball up with a single easy motion, bringing it to their chest for a moment's caress before making their throw.   —PAT JORDAN

Analogies   Most comparisons involve items that are basically similar—San Francisco and Tokyo, Lee Trevino and Arnold Palmer, Cadillacs and Lincolns, spaghetti and macaroni. But once in a while, you can explain something by comparing items that are basically different. This special kind of comparison is called an analogy.

> The glass used in the windshield of your car is a kind of sandwich. Instead of two slices of rye bread, you have two sheets of plate glass. Instead of corned beef or pastrami, you have a thin sheet of plastic vinyl. This glass sandwich is put in a press, heated, and squeezed. The plastic melts a little and binds the sheets of glass together.
> 　　　　　　　　　　　　　　　　　　—LILIAN ROSEN

The analogy drawn here is between safety glass and a sandwich. Except for a single characteristic—how they are put together—the two are basically different. But by pointing out this similarity, the writer helps explain what safety glass is. When you use an analogy, you can help your reader understand something unfamiliar by comparing it to something more familiar.

Patterns of organization   There are two general ways of organizing a comparison or a contrast. For the sake of illustration, assume that you are writing about a pair of items—item A and item B.

1. You can list first all the characteristics of item A that relate to your purpose. Then, list all the characteristics of item B. Your first section might begin like this: "My father likes to jog before breakfast and work in the garden after supper." Your second section might begin: "My mother likes jogging and gardening, too."

2. You can list a characteristic about item A, then a characteristic of item B, then A again, then B. You alternate characteristics between A and B until you have accounted for all that are related to your purpose. For example, you might begin: "My father likes to jog before breakfast and so does my mother. Both enjoy gardening, too."

The first method works best when you are dealing with a small number of characteristics. If there are many characteristics to mention, you should probably choose the second method. In this way, your reader can keep track of the points of contrast or comparison more easily.

When you want to combine comparison and contrast, you can follow either of the methods just described or use a third one. With this third method, you list all the *similarities* between item A and item B in one section. Then, you list all the *differences* between them in the next section.

By following one of these methods consistently throughout a composition, you will have a well-organized essay that will greatly help in informing your reader in a clear and effective way.

TRY IT   Suppose you are going to compare and contrast two candidates for the office of treasurer of the debating club. Your purpose is to inform other club members of the suitability of these two candidates.

First, pick from among the following characteristics the ones that are desirable in a treasurer:

likes bookkeeping
is a good swimmer
has ability in basic mathematical skills
is a girl
is popular with classmates
is able to work well with others
is willing to spend personal time maintaining club records

Now, decide how you will organize your report. Will you list all the appropriate characteristics about one candidate and then all those about the second? Will you take one characteristic at a time and apply it to both candidates? Or, will you list all the similarities between the two candidates and then all the differences? You may want to write an outline showing the organization of your paper.

Informing by identifying causes and effects

"What caused this to happen?" "What will be the effect if this is done?" The answers to questions like these may be only guesses. Often, no one knows for sure why something happened. And no one knows for sure what will happen. But there are good guesses and there are bad guesses. When you are trying to discover and explain causes and effects, there are some guidelines you can follow that will help you avoid a lot of bad guessing.

Telling why   In trying to find the cause of something, don't always assume that because one event occurred before another, the first event caused the second one. "It's starting to rain just because we're having a picnic," a person will say. Even though the statement isn't serious, it contains a serious mistake in thinking. It links two unrelated events simply because one comes before the other.

The strictest way to test a possible cause-and-effect relationship is to say that every time something—for example, a picnic—occurs, then something else—for example, rain—always results. And since there are plenty of picnics that are not followed by rain, the cause-and-effect relationship of these two events does not hold.

When you try to discover why something happened, look for a cause that is sufficient to explain the effects. If you are hammering a nail and accidentally hit your finger, you can be pretty sure of the cause of your pain. But in trying to explain why the Oakland A's won the World Series so many times or why the accident rate on highways has decreased, you'll find it hard to come up with one cause that is sufficient. In the case of complicated events like these, a sufficient cause usually means more than one cause. You should probably look for several causes.

Suppose, for example, you want to explain why a popular record has become a hit. It is not enough to say that it's a hit because everyone like it. What about the popularity of the performing group, the publicity surrounding the record's release, or the influence of the disc jockey promoting it? Quite apart from the music itself, there may be several causes at work here, not just one.

So, you need to be careful not to oversimplify your explanation. Don't suggest a single cause for a complex situation that probably is the result of many different causes.

Even when you think you've discovered the true cause or causes of an event, you must offer your reader some proof. You must give your reader some reasons for believing that you have really found out why something happened. Otherwise, you are dealing in unsupported opinions. You need facts, and to get these you will probably need to do some research.

TRY IT   In the following excerpt the writer describes the Eskimo custom of sharing food and suggests a reason for the custom. Read the excerpt and consider the questions following it.

> So, on a group hunting expedition there were strict rules and fixed customs for the division of all spoils. . . .
> Even after the hunter had brought his meat home, his

lucky household was expected to share generously with the families of those that were not so lucky. It is undoubtedly this custom of sharing food that has kept the small race of Eskimos surviving for these thousands of years. If every hunter had to depend entirely on his own luck and skill, instead of sharing in and contributing to the luck and skill of the whole village, a hostile nature would very shortly have picked them off one by one, for in the Arctic no hunter's fortune can be consistently good for several years running.   —Gene Lisitzky

According to this writer, why do Eskimos share their food? What facts does she give to support her explanation of the cause? Can you think of any other causes for this custom? Is this cause sufficient to explain the custom?

Designating effects   In suggesting an effect of a particular cause, you need to be sure there is a logical relationship between the two. Suppose, for example, you want to explain the results of a crop failure. You know that the crop failure was followed by a food shortage. But was the food shortage the result of the crop failure? Remember that two events may be closely connected in time but totally unconnected in terms of cause and effect. So, you cannot assume this relationship. You will need to investigate the facts and weigh the evidence carefully.

Second, don't oversimplify your explanation by suggesting just one effect in a complicated situation. You might find, for example, that the food shortage was not the only effect of the crop failure. Another effect was the increase in the cost of the available food.

Finally, you must offer your reader some reasons for believing that the effect you have designated is the real result of the cause you have mentioned. You must share the facts with your reader and present more than your unsupported opinion.

TRY IT   The following excerpt is from an article in which the writer presents facts suggesting a connection between the

typical American diet and some typical American health problems. Here she summarizes some of the possible effects of our
heavy consumption of sugar. Read the excerpt and consider the
questions following it.

> What price do we pay for living in a sugar-sweet society?
> For one thing, 98 percent of our population is afflicted with
> dental decay. Our yearly toll in dental bills is close to five
> billion dollars. About twenty million adults have lost more
> than half their teeth. . . . Obesity and general overweight
> have been major national health problems for years. Thirty
> percent of the population is too fat. The connection be-
> tween overweight and heart disease, and the strain obesity
> imposes on other body organs, is well known.
>
> —CLARA PIERRE

According to this writer, what are some of the effects of too
much sugar in our diet? Are there other causes for these conditions that could be involved here as well? Is the final sentence
well supported, or are more facts needed to back it up? In this
excerpt, is the emphasis on cause or effect? How do you know?

Cause-effect relationships   In a laboratory you can ignite
hydrogen in the presence of oxygen and obtain water. No matter how many times you perform the experiment, if you do it
properly, you will get water. And you can predict this result
with certainty.

But when you move out of the laboratory into the world of
people and events, you are moving away from certainty. In the
laboratory a controlled experiment can be repeated over and
over in exactly the same way. Outside the laboratory you cannot repeat an election or a quarrel, a battle or a traffic accident.
It is harder to be certain of the cause-and-effect relationship of
human events.

Often, the best you can do is predict a *probable* effect—what
you can reasonably expect to happen if some cause occurs or
continues to occur. Statements that begin, "If this person is
elected, then . . ." or "Unless we clean up the water pollution,
the river . . ." are really dealing with probable, not certain, ef-

fects. But dealing in probable effects is important. Manufacturers, for example, deal in probable effects when they estimate how many of their goods to produce. Doctors, too, deal in probabilities when they order treatment for a patient. Everyone with a plan, in fact, is dealing in probabilities. Still, when you write, you have a duty to your reader. You have a duty to make clear that you are dealing in probabilities, not certainties.

As with any cause-and-effect statement, when you predict a result, you need facts to support your opinion. You need to take the time to make your guess an educated one. So, you need to look for similar situations that may give you a clue to the effects. You need to discover what happened in a similar instance before or what usually happens in such an instance. Sometimes, however, there is no similar situation that you can examine in this way. You may be dealing with events that are unique—events that are unlike any that have ever happened before.

In this case you have to gather facts about the causes and try to see how they *might* interact to produce certain effects. This kind of prediction of a probable result is illustrated in the study described in the following excerpt. The writer is reporting on a group of business leaders and environmentalists who met to consider the probable effect of using more recycled paper. Notice the emphasis given to how the group gathered its facts. Showing their careful examination of all the causes helps make their prediction seem valid and reasonable.

> Participants . . . studied not only the paper industry and the wastepaper market but also corporate practices in the purchase, consumption, and disposal of paper. They consulted manufacturers of recycled paper, printers and designers using recycled stock, distributors, brokers, purchasing agents, and many more.
>
> Now they are seeking to impress on other corporations their principal conclusions: that more extensive use of recycled paper and the reclamation of wastepaper would effect substantial savings, conserve resources, and reduce solid waste . . .   —Philip W. Quigg

TRY IT   Pick one of the following topics—or create one yourself—and then briefly outline how you would develop a paper on it:

The probable result of abolishing the dress code at school.

The probable result of having shop and cooking classes available as electives for all students.

The probable result of eliminating grades for courses.

Patterns of organization   You may want to begin your explanation of cause and effect with a general statement and follow this with supporting facts and examples. Or, you may want to begin with facts and examples and build toward a general, concluding statement. In both cases, you should emphasize what you are trying to show your reader—a cause or an effect. If, for example, you are trying to show your reader the cause for something, then that cause, rather than its effects, should be given the most space in your analysis.

In explaining causes and effects, you may want to link the two with such phrases as *because, as a result, since,* and *therefore*. But this is not always necessary. Sometimes you can leave the relationship unstated.

> Frank skipped practice all this week. Last night, during the game, he missed three free throws.

Although the writer doesn't come out and say that *because* Frank skipped practice he missed the free throws, this is the clear intention of the statement. Similarly, if you feel the cause-and-effect relationship you are explaining is clear to your audience, you may want to omit such linking words.

WRITING TO PERSUADE

Your world is full of persuaders, people trying to get you to do things. They are trying to persuade you to buy this product, support that cause, join this group. Sermons, TV ads, editorials, campaign speeches, record reviews—these are only a few of the forms persuasion takes. But whatever the form, the purpose is the same: to get you to adopt a particular opinion or take a specific action or both.

Approaches to persuasion

All persuasion has two basic elements—a *what* and a *why*. The *what* is called the thesis. It is simply what the persuader is trying to get you to do—"Invest in a Marantz music system." The *why* is the reasons a persuader gives for the *what*—because "you'll be proud" and because "it delivers over 60 watts of continuous RMS power." Notice that there are two kinds of *why*'s. The first is aimed squarely at the emotions—at a sense of pride in ownership. This is called an emotional appeal. The second kind makes a statement about the product that can be proved or disproved. This is called a proof. Both emotional appeals and proofs can be used to support a thesis. But in using the first you choose *why*'s that focus on the audience's reactions. In using the second you choose *why*'s that focus on the subject.

Emotional appeals cannot be proved or disproved. It would be hard to determine, for example, whether a particular toothpaste can really make you more attractive. On the other hand, it could be determined whether this toothpaste can really help to prevent tooth decay. This kind of claim is a logical proof.

Emotional appeals are not necessarily bad. Nor are logical proofs necessarily good. Which kind you use in persuasion will depend upon your purpose, your audience, and your knowledge of your subject. And often both can be used in the same piece of persuasion. But you should know the difference between the two. And you should be able to judge which kind will be the most effective in supporting a particular thesis.

TRY IT   Here are some persuasive statements. See if you can identify the thesis. Then try to label the reasons given as either proofs or emotional appeals.
   1. The air smells fresher and food tastes better when you're physically fit. Get in shape and stay there.

2. Have you ever tired of paying taxes? Here's a way to save on your tax bill—and it's legal. Quit smoking. Every time you buy a pack of cigarettes you're paying taxes to the government.
3. Keep America beautiful—don't litter.
4. A bicycle uses no gas, it's inexpensive to keep up, and it's easy to park. For these reasons alone you should have a bike.
5. Support your President and preserve the dignity of the White House.

Logical persuasion   When you use proofs to support a thesis, you are persuading logically. To see how this is done, read the following excerpt. Note that the writer states a thesis and offers six proofs to support the thesis.

> Although dentists predict new techniques which will, in the next ten years or so, eliminate tooth decay as a general health problem, few of us can afford to neglect our teeth in anticipation of these advances. We should, rather, be conscientious about brushing our teeth regularly after eating. Food residue clings to the surfaces of the teeth and, if not removed by thorough brushing, will form acids. These acids destroy the tooth enamel, and then decay sets in. Bad breath will be one result. More seriously, teeth may be lost, abscesses may form, infection may spread to other parts of the body. And the ultimate result will be lengthy, perhaps painful, and certainly expensive trips to the dentist.   —AMERICAN DENTAL SOCIETY

This excerpt could be analyzed in this manner:

Thesis: You should brush your teeth regularly after eating.

Proofs: 1. Acids will form from food residue.
2. You will have bad breath.
3. You may lose some teeth.
4. You may get abscesses.
5. Infection may spread.
6. You'll have to go to the dentist.

What kind of proofs are offered? These are the consequences of *not* brushing your teeth. Are these proofs directly related to the writer's thesis? Can they be tested or measured in any way? Note the order these proofs are arranged in—from least to most serious. Is this logical arrangement effective? Suppose the writer had reversed the order. Would that be as effective? The writer's arrangement emphasizes the seriousness of the subject. And it demonstrates how the consequences of not brushing your teeth can get progressively worse.

Emotional persuasion   Emotional appeals are effective in persuasion, and they are used often. You've seen them in ads like this:

> Don't settle on any new luxury car
>   until you settle into this one. . .
>   until you let yourself sink into the comfort of the
> Olds 98 Regency. . .
>   until you've taken its magnificent ride . . .

Can you identify the emotional appeals in this ad? Can claims of luxury, comfort, and magnificence be tested or measured? Even though these are emotional appeals, they are effective. They are suited to the subject of the appeal—an expensive car—and to the audience—people with a taste for luxury. Suppose you were writing an ad intended to sell tractors to farmers. What kind of emotional appeals would you use? Would you claim durability and dependability? The point is that the emotional appeal depends on the subject and on the audience it is intended for.

You will find that sometimes emotional appeals can be blended with proofs to make particularly powerful persuasion. Here is an example of such a blend from a famous book— *Silent Spring,* by Rachel Carson. Miss Carson's thesis is that certain insecticides should not be used. She offers two proofs. Then she reinforces her proofs with a string of emotional appeals.

> These insecticides are not selective poisons; they do not single out the one species of which we desire to be rid. Each of them is used for the simple reason that it is a deadly poison. It therefore poisons all life with which it

comes in contact: the cat beloved of some family, the farmer's cattle, the rabbit in the field, and the horned lark out of the sky. These creatures are innocent of any harm to man. Indeed, by their very existence they and their fellows make his life more pleasant. Yet he rewards them with a death that is not only sudden but horrible.

—RACHEL CARSON

Think about the examples Miss Carson used to reinforce her proofs—the family cat, the farmer's cattle, the rabbit, the lark. Would she have been as persuasive if she had used a weasel, a coyote, a crow? Remember, Miss Carson was writing for a general audience. If she had been writing for a group of conservationists, she might have used those other animals as examples. Who you write for does make a difference. And when you use emotional appeals, you need to shape them to your audience. Emotional appeals can add a tone of genuine concern to a logical argument. But they should be reasonable and not overdone; genuine, not phony.

Persuading by classifying

The best of arguments is wasted on an audience already in agreement with you. For persuasion to take place, it must be directed at an audience either hostile or undecided about your thesis. Such an audience may not be eager to give your argument a fair hearing. And so your first problem is to establish a positive relationship with your audience, to gain their attention so they will allow you to state your case. One way to do this is to find a common ground with your audience, an area of mutual agreement, and link your thesis to it.

Here's how it works. Suppose you want to convince your audience that women doing the same work as men should receive the same pay. And suppose your audience consists of men who feel threatened by equality for women. These men may not agree that unequal pay for women is bad. Your task is to persuade them that it is. Therefore, you must link unequal pay with a larger issue, one that your audience will agree is bad.

In other words, you must show them that unequal pay for women is part of a larger class of undesirable things. Because you know your audience will feel that discrimination is bad, you might classify unequal pay for women as a discriminatory practice. Discrimination becomes your common ground.

Here, then, is your thesis: Unequal pay for women is a form of discrimination. If you can offer logical proofs that unequal pay is discriminatory, then your audience will probably accept your argument that women should receive the same pay as men for the same work. You've persuaded by classifying.

Here are some more examples of how persuasion by classifying works. Suppose you want to persuade an audience of parents and teachers that the dress code for students in your school should be abolished. Using classification you link students in your school with a larger class—mature people. Your thesis is this: A dress code is unnecessary for mature students. Since the members of your audience are mature people, people who feel that a dress code is unnecessary for them, it seems likely that they will agree with your thesis. Then by proving that most students in your school are mature, you can persuade your audience that the dress code should be abolished.

Or suppose you want to argue that students should have sole control over what goes into the school paper. If your audience might likely disagree, you can find a common ground by wording your thesis in this fashion: Taking editorial control of the school paper away from the students is press censorship. Because you know your audience will agree that censorship is bad, you classify withholding editorial control as censorship. Your persuasiveness will depend on the evidence you give your audience that control of the school paper and press censorship are logically connected.

Your persuasion will fail, however, if there is really no logical connection between the specific topic of your thesis and the class you put it in. If the connection is strained or far-fetched, your audience won't accept it. Suppose this is your thesis: Vision tests for drivers should be discontinued. The specific topic of this thesis is vision tests. You might try to classify vision tests for drivers as a form of prejudice. But this classification probably wouldn't hold up. Your audience would be more apt to classify vision tests as a reasonable safety requirement. And this classification would be more logical than yours.

Here is an example of classification used in a piece of persuasive writing. See if you can determine the writer's thesis and the larger classification he links it to. Ask yourself if his classification is logical or strained.

> The notion that any American, merely because he is one, has the privilege of proceeding to the highest university degree must be abandoned. . . .
>
> With . . . only carefully selected graduates . . . permitted to proceed to the university, we might have a truly democratic system of education, democratic in the purest . . . sense. . . .
>
> There is nothing undemocratic about saying that those who are to receive education at public expense should show they are qualified for it. On the contrary, it is most undemocratic to say that anybody can go as far as he likes in education, when what it actually means is he can actually have all the education he can pay for.
>
> —ROBERT M. HUTCHINS

Hutchins has a thesis—higher education should be restricted to a few carefully selected students. Since many people would object to his thesis, he classifies this restriction as a democratic practice. He is assuming that the audience will favor any practice that can be shown to be democratic. How effective is this classification? In the last paragraph Hutchins supports it. That is, he tells why his idea is democratic. Does he persuade you? Or do you think more evidence is necessary? Does the amount of evidence depend on the nature of the audience? Will a hostile audience require more evidence in support of a classification than an undecided audience will?

What are the steps you take in persuading by classifying? You start with a thesis, of course. And a knowledge of your audience. Then you find a general idea, or class, you can link your thesis to, one your audience will agree with. This means you may have to alter your thesis slightly. Finally, you give your audience evidence to support the classification you've made.

TRY IT   Match each thesis on the left with a general class listed on the right. Then, rewrite each thesis to link the specific topic to the general class.

_____1. Wiretapping should not be allowed.

_____2. Tax money should not be given to church-operated schools.

_____3. Military training (ROTC) should not be required of students.

_____4. The voting age should be lowered to 18 in all states.

a. Injustice
b. Academic freedom
c. Invasion of privacy
d. Separation of church, state

Patterns of organization   In persuading by classifying you begin by linking the subject of your thesis to a general class, one you know will serve as a common ground between you and your audience. For instance, if you were trying to persuade an audience of Democrats to vote for an independent candidate, you might classify your candidate as one who favors certain Democratic policies. If your audience were Republicans, you might classify your candidate as one who favors Republican policies.

Establishing the classification will take at least one paragraph —and perhaps several. Your next step involves arranging proofs. In the case of the candidate, you would have to list specific Democratic or Republican policies that the candidate favors. Listing these proofs would take up the bulk of your persuasive writing. In a final paragraph, then, you might sum up these proofs and urge the audience to support your candidate.

Persuading by defining

One of the most effective tools of persuasion is definition. If you are arguing for or against open housing, for instance, it's important that your audience agree with you about what "open housing" is. If their interpretation of that key term differs from yours, your argument is doomed to failure. So, in persuasion, definition is used not simply to explain or inform, as a dictionary explains the meaning of a term. Instead, it is used to give key words special meanings. By limiting the meaning of a key word or by using it in a special way, you can establish a common ground with your audience and head off objections to what you're trying to prove.

Here's how definition works in persuasion. This writer is trying to convince students to direct their enthusiasm toward other things in school besides the football team. Notice how the writer tailors his definition of school spirit, how he excludes the meaning "cheering ourselves hoarse."

> Of course we need more school spirit around this place. Doesn't everyone say so?
>
> But what do we mean by school spirit? Do we only mean going out on Saturday afternoons and cheering ourselves hoarse. . .? Does school spirit mean nothing but pride in a football team that numbers less than one percent of the student body?
>
> Don't we have some other things to cheer for? Maybe school spirit should get into the classroom and the library and the Union as well as the stadium. Maybe we should start cheering not with noise but with quiet appreciation for some of the things we have here. . . .
>
> So let's stop thinking of school spirit as nothing more than cheering for the team.   —DAVID ROYCE

What does Royce mean by *school spirit*? Does he mean "cheering ourselves hoarse"? Or does he mean "quiet appreciation"? If he used the first definition, would he run into trouble trying to apply school spirit to the "classroom, the library, and the Union"? How heavily does his persuasion depend upon a special definition?

In using definition to persuade, you must be careful not to make your definition so special that no reasonable person could accept it. For instance, to define *school spirit* as getting good grades or always agreeing with your teachers would be straining the limits of the term. Few students and even fewer teachers would accept either of these definitions.

The kinds of terms defined in persuasion are most often general terms like *school spirit, democracy,* and *freedom.* Such abstract words have many meanings. So, within reasonable limits, you can tailor your definition to fit your persuasive purpose.

TRY IT   Suppose many taxpayers oppose building a swimming pool for your high school because they consider the pool a luxury rather than a necessity. What sort of argument could you present based on a definition of the words *luxury* and *necessity?* Would you simply define necessity and then show how the pool qualifies as one? Or would you define both words and show by contrasting the two definitions that the pool is more of a necessity than a luxury? Look up both words in a dictionary. Would you give any special meanings to them? Then jot down a few ideas for mounting your argument.

Patterns of organization   In persuading by defining you find a common ground with your audience by limiting the meaning of a key term. Then you fit that meaning to your persuasive purpose. The key term is stated in your thesis. Usually, it is a word with several meanings, a word like *freedom, duty,* or *patriotism.* You can begin in your opening paragraph by giving your full definition of the key term. Then in the following paragraphs you show how your definition supports or disproves the specific points you're arguing for or against. If, for example, your key term is *freedom of speech,* you might begin like this: "Freedom of speech is the right to say or write what you believe as long as you don't interfere with or endanger others." You can then go on to illustrate specifically what this definition means.

On the other hand, you could spread the definition over several paragraphs, building up to a full, concluding definition. For instance, you might begin by writing, "By freedom of speech I don't mean allowing someone to shout 'Fire!' in a crowded theater." In a second paragraph you might continue, "When there is no danger of injury to others, there can be no restrictions on freedom of speech." And in following paragraphs, you could add to and qualify the meanings freedom of speech has for you. You might contrast what it does mean with what it doesn't mean. Or you might cite several definitions and explain why you don't think they are suitable. But the argument is not over the "correct" meaning of the term. Defining a term is merely a way of "choosing your own weapon."

Persuading by cause and effect

You're talking with a friend. You say, "The river's been polluted ever since that cement plant opened up. I think the city council ought to pass a law. Either make the plant clean up the waste or shut down operation. If they don't, the pollution will only grow worse." What you are doing is using cause and effect to try to persuade your friend. You started off with an effect—the polluted river. Then you isolated a cause for that effect—the new cement plant. Finally you proposed a remedy—the city council should pass a law.

This kind of persuasion is one of the commonest ways of getting people to change their minds or take a specific action. And the cause-and-effect relationship is usually stated directly, often in such terms as "if . . . then," "unless . . . then," "because . . . therefore." Here is another example. The writer's thesis is that mass transit—public buses, trains, and subways—should be subsidized, supported with money, by the Federal Government.

> For mass transit is the circulatory system of our cities, great and small. If some of our big cities have to cut service sharply or raise fares. . ., the whole country will suffer.
>
> Suburbanites who start their daily trips to jobs in the city by driving only as far as a commuter railroad or bus station and then taking urban transit to their offices will have to drive all the way. Even if enough gasoline were available, the ensuing pollution and traffic snarls would be intolerable. With breakdowns and gaps in the network of main

and feeder commuter lines, people who live farther from
the city would be similarly immobilized. Our tight-knit
economy would be dealt a serious economic blow.

The writer begins by linking a cause and an effect. He says
that if mass transit isn't supported, the country will suffer. He
goes on to specify how the country will suffer. If you were to
isolate his cause and its effects, you might produce a list
like this:

Cause: Lack of support for mass transit systems
General effect: The country will suffer.
Specific effects: 1. pollution
               2. traffic jams
               3. immobility
               4. economic setback

Notice the "if . . . then" arrangement of the cause and the effects. The writer wants the audience to see a need. His next
step is to show how these effects can be avoided or lessened.
He does this by proposing to eliminate the cause of these effects.

    The situation underscores the need for a federal oper-
ating subsidy for mass transit. By saving some of our most
hard-pressed systems, it will provide benefits that are by
no means restricted to the cities: 1) An immediate relax-
ation in the energy crisis. . . . 2) A dramatic decrease in
air pollution. . . . 3) A brake on inflation. . . . 4) More
mobility for those who cannot afford automobiles or sky-
rocketing transit fares. . . . 5) Better land use. . . .
    It is high time we face up to a basic fact: Mass transit,
like public health and social security, is a national respon-
sibility.   —William J. Ronan

Ronan's thesis—subsidizing mass transit—stands or falls on
his analysis of cause and effect. If he has linked the plausible
effects to a logical cause, an audience will accept his thesis.
And they will probably agree with him about the desirable
effects he says will flow from subsidizing mass transit. But if
his link between cause and effect is not logical, his argument
fails.

How do you test the logic of a cause-and-effect argument? To see how, go back to the discussion of the cement plant and the polluted river. Ask yourself these questions: Was there pollution in the river before the cement plant opened? If so, then you've got the wrong cause. Are there any other plants along the river that might be contributing to the pollution? If so, then there may be more than one cause. Asking questions like these will help you determine whether or not an argument is logical—your own or someone else's.

TRY IT Read the following statements. Which ones show a logical relationship between cause and effect? Which ones do not? What is wrong with those which are not logical?

1. Sylvia has a cold. She must have got her feet wet.
2. The soil here is very poor, and there is an awful lot of shade. A garden planted here will probably not do very well.
3. Bill and Eunice were playing ball in the driveway last night. This morning I found the basement window broken. They must have done it with their ball.
4. If the factory does not install antipollution devices on its furnaces and smokestacks, the air will become increasingly hazardous to breathe.

Patterns of organization   In persuading by cause and effect, you might begin, as this piece does, by stating the cause (locked playgrounds) that produces an undesirable effect (playing in the streets).

> In this country, there are thousands of places built for kids to play in.
> Ironically enough, most of the time most of them are kept locked up. And the kids kept locked out. (Not enough money for sports and recreation supervisors is the usual excuse.)
> So the street becomes the ballfield. And the kids have to play with one eye on the ball and one eye on the cars.

Whether this takes one paragraph or several will depend on how complicated your cause and effects are. Here they are fairly simple. In the essay by William J. Ronan, they were more complicated.

Next you will want to suggest changes that will remove the cause and thereby remove the undesirable effects.

> The situation makes so little sense, you'd think someone would do something about it.
>
> Which is just what we're asking you to do. Not to give any money, not even your time, but just to make a telephone call or two to the school officials in your area.
>
> Ask them to give the streets back to the cars. The recreation areas back to the kids.
>
> And if things work out that way, you might even want to stop by and show the kids a thing or two yourself.
>
> You'll not only do them some good; you just might do yourself some. . . .
>
> —THE PRESIDENT'S COUNCIL ON PHYSICAL FITNESS AND SPORTS

Often, especially in short persuasive essays, you won't have to go into detail about the new effects that might result. Usually, it is enough to argue that the undesirable effects will be eliminated.

However, if you're arguing not for change in a situation but for keeping things as they are, you would probably want to begin by listing all the desirable effects and linking them to a cause. Then you would point out that removing this cause would mean the loss of the desirable effects.

Persuading by analogy

An analogy is a comparison. When you use analogy to persuade, you suggest that because two things are similar in several ways, they will be alike in at least one other way important to your argument. For example, you might try to persuade someone to vote for Ralph Jones for President because he had been a good governor. The analogy here is between the qualities necessary for success as governor and those necessary for success as President. You are suggesting that since these qualities are similar in many ways, they will be alike in other important ways. A man who does well in one office should therefore do well in the other. A good analogy can be persuasive.

If an argument using analogy is to be effective, the two things compared must be undeniably similar in several important ways. You would not, for example, argue that Ralph Jones would make a good President because he had been a track star. The similarities between the qualities of a good President and those of a track star—if there are any—are far less significant than the differences.

Sometimes a special kind of analogy is used in persuasion. It is called a figurative analogy. It differs from the usual, or literal, analogy in that it compares things that are not commonly thought to be alike. A literal analogy would compare things in the same class—construction workers in America with construction workers in Australia. A figurative analogy might compare construction workers with ants. Here, for example, a writer compares fashions in clothes with fashions in political ideas.

> I have often noticed on my trips up to the city that people have recut their clothes to follow the fashion. On my last trip, however, it seemed to me that people had remodeled their ideas too—taken in their convictions a little at the waist, shortened the sleeves of their resolve, and fitted themselves out in a new intellectual ensemble copied from a smart design out of the very latest page of history.... —E. B. White

The writer here is not using this figurative analogy as his sole means of persuasion. Instead, he is using it to set a mood, to indicate the tone of the persuasive essay that follows.

If you try to use a figurative analogy as your only basis for an argument, you will run into trouble, especially if you push the analogy too far.

> Building a sound government is like building a sound house. Before the first nail is driven, someone must provide a blueprint, a design for success. Alfred Brown is a skilled architect. If he is elected governor, he will provide a blueprint for successful state government. If elected governor, he will direct the rebuilding of the political institutions of our state.

On first reading, this analogy may seem impressive. But on a closer reading, it doesn't really make sense. There is no actual similarity between a house and a government and between the skills of an architect and those of a governor. They are "built" and they "build" in different ways. Using a figurative analogy as the only support for a serious argument can become absurd.

TRY IT   Read the following analogies and analyze their effectiveness. Ask yourself these questions: What is being compared? Is the analogy literal or figurative? If it is literal, do the things being compared have more similarities or more differences?

1. Soldiers have to wear uniforms when they are on duty, and so, too, should students when they attend classes.

2. The body is a machine. Like any machine, it requires lubrication from time to time. Drink Mossback Mountain Dew.

3. Jill has been a success as president of the glee club, as captain of the tennis team, and as editor of the school paper. Each of these positions required aggressive leadership. She is therefore a qualified candidate for student council president.

4. A good book is like good food. Both provide nourishment. Your bookshelves should be as well stocked as your refrigerator.

Patterns of organization   A figurative analogy often functions as a beginning. It seldom extends for more than a paragraph or two in persuasive writing. The reason is simple. It is usually difficult to find a great many points of comparison for a figurative analogy without straining. Carried too far, a figurative analogy becomes artificial and unconvincing. Figurative analogies are used in persuasion to illustrate, to explain, or to set a mood, rarely as the entire argument itself.

Literal analogies often run longer than do figurative analogies. Sometimes they take up the major portion of a composition. They may be organized in one of two ways. Whichever way you use, you would begin by stating the comparison you're making: A is like B. Then you could list the important characteristics of A followed by a list of the similar characteristics of B. This pattern works best when you have only a few characteristics to list. The second way to organize a literal analogy is to list characteristics in pairs. That is, you list a characteristic of A, then a similar characteristic of B. You list another characteristic of A and a similar one of B. You do this point by point until your analogy is complete. This pattern is helpful when you have many characteristics to list.

Persuading by citing authority

Sound reasoning and solid proofs are needed for effective persuasion. In addition, you can lend extra force to your ideas by quoting the supporting opinions of experts. That is, you cite an authority to back up what you say. It's a technique widely used—and widely abused—in advertising.

> A. J. Foyt, champion race driver, car builder, and master mechanic, uses Valvoline Motor Oil—on the street as well as on the track.

In citing an authority, you should be sure the person you cite really is an expert on the subject in question. It would make little sense to cite A. J. Foyt's opinions on breakfast foods or antibiotics. And yet this sort of thing is done. People who are expert in one field—coaching football, for example, or acting— are cited as authorities on automobiles and snack foods. What the writer is trying to do is transfer authority. But in reality the famous quarterback may know no more about razor blades and soft drinks than the next person. He may even know less.

An authority should be up-to-date, too. This is especially important if your subject is a scientific or technical one, one to which new knowledge is constantly being added. An old-fashioned opinion, even though it may have been valid at one time, may be useless.

Where can you find an authority to cite in support of your

ideas? Standard reference books—encyclopedias, almanacs, dictionaries—may be one source. Magazines, biographies, histories, and newspapers are other sources. In any case you will probably have to make a trip to the library. And you will have to do some careful research.

Sometimes, however, you can go directly to an authority. For example, suppose you were trying to persuade people to allow the police of your community to form a union. It would make sense to interview some members of the department and get their opinions. Similarly, if you were writing about the need for new athletic equipment, it would be wise to talk to coaches and team members.

Finally, there is one more authority you should not over-look—yourself. You may be your own expert. You may have authoritative, firsthand experience that can support a thesis. Here, for example, is a writer who is arguing for admitting more girls to technical schools. This is her thesis:

> Public education should provide specialized training in technical and vocational fields . . . to those who desire it. When education reaches that stage, the word *coed* will become obsolete.

To back up this thesis, to show that girls can find places for themselves in technical schools, she cites her own experience.

> In the spring of 1971, 1,500 angry young men, waving fists and shouting, . . . walked out of school . . . to protest a Board of Education decision to admit girls into an all-male, technical high school.
> The school was Lane Tech, and I was among the first class of freshmen girls to enter that spring. It was a unique experience. . . .
> The female students [have] made themselves at home. . . . Girls are in machine shops, auto shops, and foundries. They take drafting, design houses, operate presses—in fact, I haven't heard of one request for a home economics class (from the girls that is).
>
> —Rochelle Harris

It's possible that you might find two authorities who disagree, one who supports your thesis and one who doesn't. What do you do then? Is it fair to cite the one who supports your thesis and ignore the other? If the authority who disagrees with you is plainly wrong, you have no obligation to deal with this opinion. It might, after all, be based on incomplete facts or outdated knowledge. But what if this opinion is not plainly wrong? Then, you have a duty to mention it and to explain why you sided with the other opinion. Bringing up responsible objections to your thesis and discussing them will not weaken your persuasion. Just the opposite, such an honest approach will make your arguments more believable.

TRY IT   Here are some statements supported by authorities. Which of the authorities cited for each would be more persuasive? Why?
1. Snake bites should be sterilized with alcohol.
   A medical book published in 1850
   The first-aid instructor at the YMCA
2. Changes in the school curriculum should be made at once.
   Students in the bottom third of the class
   The teachers' association
3. *Huckleberry Finn* is one of the best American novels.
   An ad on the cover of a paperback edition of the book
   Your English teacher
4. The country is headed for a recession.
   A talk-show host on TV
   The financial editor of *The New York Times*

Persuading by citing statistics

Statistics are impressive, maybe too impressive. Many people are afraid even to question them. For this reason, when you use statistics to support an idea, you should make sure they are accurate and fair. You'll need to do some research.

Suppose this is your thesis: Foreign languages should be dropped from the curriculum of our school. One of the reasons you offer in support of this thesis is a lack of interest in foreign languages. Of the, say, 500 students in your school, you have found that only 150 are enrolled in foreign language classes. This works out to 30 percent of the student body. So, you could write that 70 percent of the students in your school are not studying a foreign language. Your statement would be accurate, but would it be fair?

Suppose that in your school only students in the tenth and eleventh grades are allowed to take a foreign language. There are, say, 363 students in these grades. This means that of the students eligible to take a foreign language, more than 41 percent do. Or, to put it another way, less than 59 percent of the students eligible to take a foreign language are not doing so. This figure is less persuasive than the 70 percent figure. But it is fairer. And since it doesn't offer strong support for your thesis, you might want to omit the question of student interest from your argument.

Statistics can be distorted. They can be made to give the wrong impression, to lie. But in honest persuasion, they are used to give concise, forceful, and clear pictures of actual situations.

Patterns of organization   Statistics and opinions from authorities usually play supporting roles in persuasive writing. They are not the center of focus. Nor do they provide a pattern of organization, a structure, for the entire composition. Where they fit in depends on what you are saying at any given time. Sometimes you'll find it effective to lead off with an expert opinion.

> Could there be life on other planets? According to Robert M. Glasser, director of the National Space Observatory, there could be—in some distant solar system if not within our own.

At other times you may want to save an expert opinion for the end of your composition, using it as a kind of clincher to your arguments. Wherever you use it, though, you want to give the audience enough information about the authority so that they will accept the cited opinion as valid evidence. And be specific. Don't just say, for example, "A noted astronomer believes there might be life on other planets."

Individual statistics should be linked closely to the ideas they support. If you have a series of statistics, then you must decide how to arrange them. One common arrangement is to begin with the least significant figure and build to the one of greatest significance.

> Twenty percent of the population has no hospital-insurance coverage. Fifty percent of poor children are not immunized against common childhood diseases. The disability rate for families below the poverty line is at least 50 percent higher than for families with incomes above $10,000. The lifespan of nonwhites is seven years shorter than for whites in the United States.
>
> —DONALD C. DRAKE

You might, however, feel that it is better to begin with your most significant figure. Which order you choose is a matter of personal judgment. The point is that you can't just insert statistics and expert opinions anywhere. You have to put them where they will best support your ideas.

Refutation

Whenever you take a stand on an issue, you are doing two things at once. First, you are trying to persuade an audience that your thesis is correct. Second, you are trying to refute, or disprove, someone else's thesis. For example, if you come out in favor of a dress code or in support of a political candidate, you would obviously be opposing those who would abolish the dress code or vote for another candidate.

In many kinds of persuasion, you will need to spend little if any time and space in directly refuting a rival thesis. Instead, most of your efforts will be spent in presenting and supporting your own thesis. But when you do need to refute someone's thesis, how do you do it? On what basis do you say that an opinion or an idea is incorrect or inaccurate? One way is by using statistics which show that a thesis is wrong. Here is an example:

> Some say that there is not enough money to pay for a new expressway. Those who say this forget that there is now a surplus in the highway trust fund of 2.3 million dollars. According to estimates, the expressway will cost no more than 1.8 million dollars. Plainly the money is available.

Statistics like these are very helpful in refutation. If they are true, an opponent cannot contradict or deny them. Unfortunately, not all arguments can be refuted by statistics alone. You will need additional means.

Another way to refute a generalization is with an example.

> It is said that a new expressway will hamper industrial growth in the city. But this is not what happened in Detroit. There, land was set aside for an industrial park next to the proposed John Lodge Freeway. Even before the freeway was finished, new industries had moved in and begun building. This is just one instance of a new expressway aiding a city's industrial growth. There are others.

Or, you might refute the logic of a rival argument. You might point out that the thesis is based on a false analogy:

> Opponents have compared the new highway to a kind of "Berlin Wall." According to this analogy, people and businesses in the inner city will be cut off from the outside world. Commuters and shoppers will be shunted away from the downtown area. Actually, people will find it easier to get in and out of the inner city than ever before. New access roads, interchanges, and exit ramps will give people free movement into and out of the downtown area.

Finally, you might be able to turn an objection to your advantage, using an opponent's argument to support your own thesis:

> Opponents of the expressway have argued that it will displace thousands of people from their homes. Yes, it will do this. But what kinds of homes are they being displaced from? The expressway will cut through the heart of the worst slum area. in the city. New housing projects will be built. The city will benefit and the people will, too.

Note that refutation requires support. You can't simply write "This generalization is not true," or "This is a bad analogy." You have to give reasons. And this means knowing your opponent's thesis and analyzing it carefully.

The tone of your refutation is important, too. It should not be insulting or sarcastic. Personal attacks and name-calling usually backfire. They will turn the audience against you and your thesis.

WRITING TO ENTERTAIN

One major purpose of writing is to entertain—to bring insight, surprise, or delight to the reader. Language as art—literature—can inform or persuade, but its real purpose is to entertain, to bring enjoyment by stimulating the imagination. Literature, like informative and persuasive writing, stresses *what* is said. But literature also places great emphasis on *how* something is said. It demands that the writer find just the right words and express them in just the right order.

Much of literature—stories, plays, and poetry—is *fiction*. It includes facts about real people and actual experiences but really depends upon the writer's unique imagination. Fiction also uses special devices, such as figurative language and dialogue. Some literature—like the feature article—is *nonfiction*. Such literature demands that the writer present real-life situations in an interesting, entertaining way. Whether fiction or nonfiction, each literary form is unique. But all literary forms have the same basic goal—to entertain the reader through the artistic, creative use of language.

The article

Nearly everyone is interested in unusual or important people, like Melanie or Ralph Nader, or in unusual events, such as the Chicago River turning green on St. Patrick's Day. Articles deal with these and countless other topics. An article can be about almost anything, but its major purpose is to entertain. Articles include interviews with famous or unusual people, like John Lennon, Margaret Mead, or the man whose job is collecting earthworms. Articles describe interesting hobbies, such as model railroading, collecting books about Sherlock Holmes, or raising golden hamsters. Articles offer practical advice, such as how to restore an old farmhouse or prepare a homemade remedy for colds. They describe interesting events—a block party, a carnival in New Orleans, a ride in a steam locomotive. Articles also describe interesting places—a wine and cheese café, a pet shop that sells wild animals. The list of possible topics is endless.

Unlike the news story, the article is not directly about a significant event—a summit conference, an earthquake in California. The article may touch on such an event, but it does so from a human-interest angle. For example, an article might be a firsthand account by a man whose home was destroyed by an earthquake. An article about a noted scientist might describe her hobby of backpacking, but not her scientific theories. Usually, the topics of articles are not considered "news" at all. Instead they appeal to the reader's curiosity, sense of humor, and interest in people. Here is part of an article about exploring caves.

> Descending the cool throat of the cave into darkness, we came to a stream that fell away into a well-like chamber. Our flashlights showed water splashing on rocks 15 feet below.
>
> Posting Ken on the brink, I tied a rope around a rock slab beside the waterfall and started down, hand over hand. The wall curved away, out of reach of my groping feet.
>
> Like the weight of a pendulum, I began to swing, and a moment later I arced under the falls. Drenched and blinded, pounded and with my boots filled with water, I lost my grip on the rope and fell.
>
> The fall left me flat on the pitch-black floor of the pit. Soaking wet, choking, and bruised, I stood up and

> reached for the rope, ready to call it a day. But the
> wavering beam of my electric head lamp revealed the line
> dangling just out of reach.   —CHARLES E. MOHR

Most articles are based, at least in part, on personal experience. The writer interviews someone, goes somewhere, sees something. Mohr actually explored a cave. His article is not a simple transfer of facts about caves from an encyclopedia. Notice, also, that Mohr places himself in the article. This is a result of personally experiencing what he is writing about. It is a common trait of articles.

Perhaps you've never explored a cave, but you've done other things that are unusual or interesting. And you've seen things that are funny or unusual; you've known unusual people. Some of these would make good topics for an article.

Articles about people   There are three basic ways of writing articles about people. You can write your article from the first-person point of view, from the third-person point of view, or you can write a formal interview.

1. First-person articles   An article about an interesting person can take several forms. If you're writing mainly about yourself or someone you are close to, the article will probably be in the first person. That is, you write, "I saw this" and "She said this to me." Don't be bashful about using "I." Saying "we" or "this reporter" when you really mean "I" is stuffy, false modesty. Here, for example, is part of an article by a teenager who sailed around the world. He's talking about his experience, and he uses "I."

> The sea is glassy calm. If I lean over the rail I can
> see my sweat-streaked face in the water. The sails droop
> and flap in hazy, glary air that hurts my eyes. I'm barely
> moving, getting nowhere.
>
> But up ahead, over the curve of the world, is my journey's
> end. The next shore I stand on will be California's, which
> I left nearly five years ago, a schoolboy in a small boat,
> sailing westward alone. I've been going westward and
> westward ever since, leaving California farther and farther
> astern. Now it's on my bow, and getting nearer and nearer.

So I guess the world is really round. I mean, it's one thing
to know that, and another to experience it.

—ROBIN LEE GRAHAM

If you have a unique experience like this to write about,
you're lucky. But be careful. Even a good subject can be
flubbed. With a wealth of detail from which to choose, you
could overwhelm your reader unless you're very selective.

Notice how Robin Lee Graham makes his experience vivid
for you by such phrases as "I can see my sweat-streaked face in
the water" and "in hazy, glary air that hurts my eyes." Instead
of writing about the horizon, he calls it "the curve of the world."
This is how it appears to him. And putting it this way helps to
bring you closer to his experience. In fact it is the details, as
much as the subject itself, that make the writing interesting.
With just enough sharp, vivid details, even an ordinary subject can be made interesting. You might not think that your
job last summer or the camping trip to Yosemite is in the same
league as sailing around the world. But these subjects can be
made interesting if you supply your reader sharp, clear-eyed
details.

2. Third-person articles   Sometimes your subject will determine the form of your article. If your subject is about somebody else—what he or she did, who he or she is—then you'll
probably use the third-person form in writing your article. That
is, you'll write, "She did this" or "He did that." This does not
mean you'll never write "I." It only means that the focus of interest is on "he" or "she."

Who makes a good subject for an article? If you have a
movie star or an astronaut handy, that's fine. But suppose you
don't. Then perhaps one of your friends will do, someone who
has an interesting hobby or job, such as collecting political
campaign buttons or helping the zoo keepers feed the wild
animals. Perhaps your grandmother is ninety and has stories
to tell about the family exploring the countryside in one of the
first Fords. You could write about one of your teachers, the manager of the cafeteria, the school-bus driver.

Since you probably don't know all you need to about the person, you'll probably want to arrange an interview. Take notes during the interview. These notes don't have to be neat —their purpose is to remind you what was said. When you've finished the interview, look over your notes while your memory is still fresh. Decide which notes you'd like to use, choosing the most interesting ones.

In writing your article, remember that you're trying to give your reader a clear idea of what the person is like. So you'll not only use facts and quotes—you'll also want to describe the person. You'll want to describe what he or she looks like and mention any gestures or ways of speaking that will give your reader a vivid impression.

3. Interviews   Sometimes what a person has to say is so interesting or so important that you won't want to omit any of it. In that case your article will probably take the form of a formal interview. Unlike the third-person article, the formal interview follows a fairly set pattern of questions and answers— it's the exact written record of a spoken interview. And for this reason accuracy is vital. If a tape recorder is available, use it. Otherwise, work out a system of shorthand that you can read back later.

Before you begin a formal interview, you'll want to make a list of questions. Take some time to think out your questions so that you'll get the specific details you need. For example, if you interview the school-bus driver, you'll want to find out what route he travels, how long he's been driving the bus, what he's learned about students in that time, what his funniest experience was. During the interview, try to stay loose. If something interesting or amusing pops up, pursue it. Don't worry too much about asking all the questions on your list.

A formal interview follows a conventional pattern of question and response. Notice the pattern in this part of an interview with the playwright Edward Albee.

> INTERVIEWER: Why did you decide to become a playwright? You wrote poems without notable success, and then suddenly decided to write a play, *The Zoo Story.*

ALBEE: Well, when I was six years old I decided not that I was *going* to be, but with my usual modesty, that I *was* a writer. So I started writing poetry when I was six and stopped when I was twenty-six because it was getting a little better, but not terribly much. When I was fifteen I wrote seven hundred pages of an incredibly bad novel—it's a very funny book I still like a lot. . . . I was still determined to be a writer. And since I was a writer, and here I was twenty-nine years old and I wasn't a very good poet and I wasn't a very good novelist, I thought I would try writing a play, which seems to have worked out a little better.

—WILLIAM FLANAGAN

TRY IT   Make a list of people you have access to who would be interesting subjects for an interview. Choose one and set up an appointment to talk with him or her.

Articles about places and things   In writing about a place or an object, you'll want to show with details how this place or object is different from all others. You can do this by selecting the right kind of details, details that are unique to the place or thing you're describing. Here's part of an article about a special place—a club for magicians.

The foyer appears to be a well-appointed library complete with somber paneling and hunt-scene paintings. There is no visible doorway connecting the entranceway with the main rooms of the club. To enter those, you must whisper "Open Sesame" to a figure of a golden owl wedged into a row of leather-laden book shelves on one wall.

Presto! The bookcase slides away, and you are admitted into the Grand Salon . . .   —ANGELA ROCCO DECARLO

Here the author wants to emphasize that the club is a special place for magicians, not just an ordinary club. Notice her use of details—"you must whisper 'Open Sesame' to a figure of a golden owl" and "Presto! The bookcase slides away." These details emphasize magic and mystery—they give the reader a vivid picture of what the club is like.

In writing about an object, you should select details in the same careful way. Ask yourself what it is about this car or this store or this bicycle that sets it off from other cars and stores and bicycles. Sometimes, it's not the thing itself that is different, but your own special relationship or involvement with it.

> My older brother had a Volkswagen that was like no one else's. It gave fantastic mileage. He got forty miles to the gallon, then fifty, then sixty. Each night, when the yellow bug was resting in my father's garage, my sister and I would top up the tank. We never told Phil, of course. We let him go on bragging about his mileage to his friends with the large cars . . . .

TRY IT   For a day, make a special effort to observe everything around you. What interesting people, places, or things do you observe? Take notes. Pile up details that strike your imagination. Look for the unusual in the ordinary. Some of these notes could form the beginning of an article.

Patterns of organization   Different kinds of articles have different kinds of organization. You might arrange a first-person article about an event in chronological order, setting down happenings in the order they occurred. Or you might give the outcome of a personal experience and then describe the events that led up to it.

For a third-person article about a person, you might take the common approach of describing the person's hobby, job, or achievement that you're going to focus on. Then you might tell the events that led to the hobby, job, or achievement. Or you might want to start with a close-up of your subject: "Short, slight, and balding, Sol Schultz would be the last person you would pick to be a former Olympic shot-putter . . ."

For a formal interview, you will probably set the pattern of the interview by deciding upon a few key questions that you hope will bring out interesting responses. You might want to begin with a short introduction that sets the stage for the interview that follows. Where are we? Who are we with? Why?

In writing about a place, you will probably want to structure your article around a spatial description. For example, if you are writing about a famous old mansion that is going to be torn down, you might first describe what it looks like from afar. Then, move closer up. Then, describe the entrance. Then the rooms on the first floor. There are many spatial patterns you could use. But the point is that you arrange your details in a pattern that your reader can easily follow and that creates a strong impression. Then your reader can see clearly what you are trying to show and can get the specific "feel" of the place.

In writing about things, you should also have a pattern for your details. If you are writing about a new kind of bottle opener, for example, you might begin by telling what it is supposed to do, then what it looks like, then how it works. What you want to avoid is scattering your details, jumping back and forth from one thing to another.

The story

There were stories even before there was writing. And they were preserved orally and passed on from one generation to the next. Even though they were fiction, they sprang from the experiences of the people who told them and listened to them. They reflected the people's lives and values. Over the years many of the stories were lost. But some, like this one, were finally written down.

> Once there was a man who owned a fine hunting horse. It was black and fast and afraid of nothing. When it was turned upon an enemy it charged in a straight line and struck at full speed; the man need have no hand upon the rein. But, you know, that man knew fear. Once during a charge he turned that animal from its course. That was a bad thing. The hunting horse died of shame.
>
> —N. Scott Momaday

Though brief and simple, this story has all the basic elements you could find in the longest, most complicated novel. It has characters—a hunting horse and its rider. It has setting—the scene of a battle or hunt. Something happens—the rider turns the horse aside. There is a problem—the rider's fear. There is an outcome—the hunting horse dies of shame. These are the basic elements of a story.

The term *fiction* is applied to stories that tell about invented happenings and people, not real ones. The problem with this term is that for many people it implies that such stories deal in the false and the untrue, that they have no connection with real life. But fiction, good fiction, while not a factual record of real life, is grounded in real life. The story you just read, for example, reflects the life of the Kiowa Indians. They were hunters and warriors, and physical courage was looked upon as a virtue. Also, their horses were very important to them. Although this brief story is about an incident that never really happened, it does tell you something about the life and the values of the Kiowa Indians.

Similarly, the stories you invent should grow out of your life —your experiences, observations, the people and things you value. This is not to say that you can take an incident directly from life and record it without change. You have to let your imagination reshape your experiences. Change some details, add some details, and subtract others. Rework your ideas until your story says exactly what you want it to say.

The characters   Characters are an important part of any story—perhaps the most important part. In writing your story, you must let your reader know what your character is like. One way to do this is by physical description.

> Ralph's mother, wearing a faded cotton print dress, came out of the kitchen. She was a tall, gaunt woman in her early forties with dark circles under her eyes and an enormous pile of disheveled gray hair.
> —Alfredo Otero y Herrera

Notice that a good physical description tells its own kind of story. To see how, reread the description of Ralph's mother omitting the details in color. What happens? You still have a physical description, but it no longer tells a story. Details like "faded" and "cotton" tell of money problems. That the woman is "gaunt," has "dark circles under her eyes," and is prematurely gray tells the reader that her life has not been an easy one. Make your descriptions tell stories about your characters.

Closely related to physical description is the description of a character's mannerisms, how he or she moves, gestures, talks.

> David Turner, who did everything in small quick movements, hurried from the bus stop down the avenue toward his street.   —SHIRLEY JACKSON

Notice that the phrase "who did everything in small quick movements" helps suggest that David is nervous and precise. You can help make your characters real by giving them such traits as talking loudly when they are unsure of themselves, rubbing the side of their nose when they are lying, or standing first on one foot and then the other when they are hesitant.

Another way to show what a character is like is to show how he or she feels about things. But don't merely tell the reader. Instead, allow your characters to reveal themselves by *what* they say and *how* they say it. Here's a dialogue between a young man and his sister which reveals not only how the young man feels about the pigeons he's raising, but how he looks at life.

> "Well, why are we . . . ." Her voice had trailed off in a plaintive sound.
> "Why are we keepin' them [the pigeons]?" he sighed. "Spendin' money on their feed and time on their care? I ain't sure, but I think it's cause they're Beauty. Can't you feel it, Sis, inside you, when we open the cote and let them all out? They swirl up in the sky like a . . . a scarf, a white scarf, or maybe a white flag and then they sweep back and forth, wavin' through the air till we call them in."   —JEAN McCORD

In creating a character, you won't want to just copy someone you know. Instead, you might take one trait from one person you know, another trait from a second person, still another trait from a third person. Then you could combine these traits to create a unique character. Remember, however, once you've established your character's individual personality, that character must act consistently. If you create a character who is friendly and open, for example, you would not suddenly show this person being unfriendly and secretive, unless your story centers on the reasons for this change.

The setting   A story must happen somewhere—it must have a setting. Perhaps your idea for a story will start with an interesting place you know. What sorts of interesting incidents could occur in such a place? Perhaps, instead, your story idea concerns some exciting action. In that case, you'll have to supply a setting completely appropriate to and supportive of that action.

In describing your setting, you should do so as quickly and vividly as you can. Long-winded place descriptions tend to clog the flow of a story. and bore readers. Notice how the following writer describes the setting—with a few quick strokes of colorful detail.

> In August, down towards the Rio Grande, the rays of the sun beat vertically upon the sandy stretches of land, from which all tender vegetation has been scorched, and the white, naked land glares back at the sun; . . . In the thickets of brush the roadrunners, rusty lizards, mockingbirds, and all other living things pant. Whirlwinds dance across the stretches of prairie interspersed between the thickets of thorn. At six o'clock it is hotter than at midday . . . .   —JOVITA GONZÁLEZ

Here the author has carefully selected such details as "rays of the sun," "scorched," "glares," "rusty lizards," and "living things pant." All these add up to a single, clear impression of the setting—the story takes place in a scorched desert, not simply a hot, dry place.

How you select details will depend partly on your purpose. If you are trying to convey the feeling that a city apartment is a wonderful place to live, you might use such details as "a panoramic view of sleek gray skyscrapers," "the cheerful laughter of children playing below," "parsley and rosemary growing in small red pots in a sunny kitchen window." If the feeling you are trying to convey is that city apartments are unpleasant, you might use such negative details as "a view of dirty brick build-ings," "children wailing and screaming in the next apartment," "a small, cramped kitchen with a stained sink and a dripping faucet." Details of setting create a specific atmosphere in which the characters and their actions appear convincing and realistic.

The plot   Something must happen in a story—a story must have a plot. But plot is more than a string of events. For ex-ample, a news article about a hotel fire deals with a string of events, but it has no plot because there is no conflict. To have a plot, there must be conflict, problems that the characters must face and solve or fail to solve. Thus, the sequence of events making up the plot must be planned and arranged to present in-cidents that (1) introduce the conflict, (2) build toward a climax—the point where a solution to the conflict is unavoid-able, and (3) present the solution, or resolution, of the conflict. There are many types of conflict you could use as plot starters.

One type of conflict is the physical opposition of two char-acters—for example, the cowboy hero in a shoot-out with the villain. Does the hero win or lose? Why? On a more realistic level, you might have two students as finalists for a scholarship that only one could win. What happens?

Another type of conflict involves making an important de-cision. For example, a girl sees her best friend shoplifting—she must decide between loyalty and honesty. What does she do? Or a boy's friend has been rejected by the group they both be-long to, for a reason he considers unfair. He must decide if he should support his friend at the risk of also being rejected by the group.

Another kind of conflict involves solving a problem or over-coming a handicap. For example, a boy whose parents are very poor needs to buy new clothes for a job interview. Or a young athlete has been crippled in an accident and must learn how to live a meaningful life.

Real life is full of conflicts that can form the basis for story plots. It provides writers with a never-ending supply of ma-terial. You might also get ideas for conflict from magazine and newspaper stories. But remember to keep the conflict—and the plot—reasonably close to your own experience.

The story as a whole   It's helpful to look at story elements like characters, setting, and plot separately, in order to clearly define the special role each element plays. But in reality the elements of a story work together. Here's the opening of a story in which the character and setting are fused together in one paragraph.

> He was not interested in the snow. When he got off the freight, one early evening during the depression, Sargeant never even noticed the snow. But he must have felt it seeping down his neck, cold, wet, sopping in his shoes. But if you had asked him, he wouldn't have known it was snowing. Sargeant didn't see the snow, not even under the bright lights of the main street, falling white and flaky against the night. He was too hungry, too sleepy, too tired.
>
> —LANGSTON HUGHES

Note how much information this first paragraph gives the reader. It begins to establish the main character—the man's name is Sargeant, and because he has just got off a freight rather than a passenger train, he probably doesn't have any money. It also establishes the setting—a small town on a snowy night during the economic depression of the 1930's when millions of people were out of work and could not find jobs. Your first few paragraphs should establish the characters, setting, and conflict. Once established, these elements should continue to work together, each supporting the others throughout your story.

TRY IT   Suppose you want to write a story. How do you begin? Here's one way. You could start with a person. Maybe it will be someone you don't even know, but someone who's aroused your interest or curiosity. Perhaps the woman you saw on the bus the other day. Mink coat, expensive dress and jewelry, hair right out of the beauty shop. What made you notice her was the way she stood out from the other people on the bus—the lunch-pail and brown-bag bunch. She was in the wrong setting. Try to imagine what the right setting for her would be. Try to imagine why she was riding this bus in this neighborhood. Perhaps you have the beginnings of a conflict. So you have a character, a setting, part of a plot. You're on your way. Try writing a one-paragraph plot summary of one story suggested by the mink-clad woman.

Or try it from another angle. A friend of yours tells you that he wants to be a professional trumpet player, but his parents object. They want him to be an engineer. What does he do? How do they react? This conflict could give you the idea for a story. Try writing a one-paragraph plot summary for one story suggested by this conflict.

Patterns of organization   In writing your story, there are two common patterns you might use. You might begin with the first event and tell your story chronologically—first A happens, then B, then C. Also, you should take care that each event flows logically from the one that precedes it. For example, a hurricane causes a flood. Then the flood causes a family to evacuate their home and to fight for survival. A second pattern you might use is the flashback technique. In this technique, a story begins in the present but then goes backward in time to tell about a previous event or events. For example, a young athlete wins a medal at the Olympics. Then in a flashback the reader finds out how the athlete overcame an injury and disillusionment in order to go on to compete at the Olympics.

The play

Writing a play involves telling a story, but not in the usual sense. Plays are not meant for quiet reading. They are meant to be acted out by real people talking and moving about on a stage. You can't write a play the same way you would write a short story. A play is put together differently. Here's a brief scene from a play. In it are most of the basic elements of drama. See if you can tell what these elements are.

The scene is a school hallway. The bell has just rung. Mary and Brian are standing by a doorway as the scene opens.

BRIAN: Can you go with us this Saturday?

MARY: *(Starts to walk down hallway.)* I'd like to, but Dad always says no—no hitchhiking.

BRIAN: *(Following Mary.)* Tell him the team's playing out of town, at Westfield or something. He'll never know you've gone to New York.

MARY: *(Stops.)* I'd like to. *(Hesitating.)* But I don't know . . . .

Taking them in order, the first element is scene description. Then there are the characters—Mary and Brian—and what they say to each other—the dialogue. Enclosed in parentheses are stage directions that tell the actors how to move and how to speak their lines. And finally there is the conflict—should Mary obey her father or hitchhike to New York with Brian? The only element missing from this scene is the resolution—the action Mary takes to resolve the conflict.

The idea for writing a scene like this could have come from an overheard conversation or perhaps could have been drawn from a personal experience. The writer might have started with no more than this.

A girl would like to hitchhike to New York with some friends but knows her father would disapprove. What happens?

The problem of the writer is to get from this bare idea to a finished scene, to use the elements of drama to make the idea come alive, to make it happen.

Conflict and resolution   At the heart of any play is a conflict. This is the problem that the characters must face and work out in some way. The working out of the conflict keeps the audience interested, makes them wonder what's going to happen next. The resolution of the conflict, how the characters solve their problem, should leave the audience satisfied. They should feel, when the play is finished, that the events in the play make the resolution inevitable.

Probably the most basic of all dramatic conflicts is a physical one. You've seen this kind of conflict many times. Over and over again in westerns, you've seen the peace-loving sheriff goaded into a showdown with the outlaw gunslinger.

But there are other kinds of conflict in drama, as there are in life. Some conflicts involve making a difficult decision. For example, in Henrik Ibsen's play *An Enemy of the People,* a doctor discovers that the new health baths in his town are polluted. He must decide between depriving his town of its main source of income or allowing the visitors who use the baths to become seriously ill.

But whatever kind of conflict you build a play around, you must resolve it in a way that satisfies your audience, a way that fits their sense of how things happen. For instance, if the peace-loving sheriff were to find out at the last minute that the gunslinging outlaw wasn't that at all, but really his law-abiding, long-lost brother, the audience would feel cheated. Similarly, if the doctor in Ibsen's play discovered in the last scene that the baths really weren't polluted, the audience would again feel let down. In both cases, such an ending just wouldn't seem believable. The conflict would be ducked, not resolved.

TRY IT   Since conflict is at the heart of all drama, you might begin putting a play together by stating a conflict. It might be something like this:

> A girl is asked by her friends to hitchhike to New York on a Saturday afternoon. But she knows her parents would disapprove. She must decide between going with her friends and obeying her parents.

The next step is to think about this conflict. What would happen if the girl goes with her friends? What would happen if she doesn't go? You've got to think through the actions that would follow from her decision. As you do, ask yourself these questions: What happens next? Would this really happen, or would something else be more likely? What you will finally end up with is an outline of a plot, or scenario. This still has to be

translated into characters, scenes, and dialogue. Your scenario
is your map. It shows you a starting point, a route, and a desti-
nation.

Dialogue   When you see a play performed, you see people
on a stage talking to one another. This is a kind of a trick. The
actors only seem to be talking to one another. Actually, they are
talking to you in the audience. They are speaking lines of
dialogue, invented by the writer of the play, that tell you certain things about the story. What kind of things? What does
dialogue do?

The dialogue of a play must supply the audience with any
background information it needs to understand the actions of
the characters. It must make clear what the conflict is. It must
reveal what kind of person each character is. Here's some
dialogue, taken from Henrik Ibsen's play *A Doll's House,* that
does all three jobs.

> HELMER: Nora—what is this?—this cold, set face?
> NORA: Sit down. It will take some time; I have a lot to talk
> over with you.
> HELMER: *(Sits down at the opposite side of the table.)*
> You alarm me, Nora!—and I don't understand you.
> NORA: No, that is just it. You don't understand me, and I
> have never understood you either—before to-night. No,
> you mustn't interrupt me. You must simply listen to what
> I say. . . .[T]his is a settling of accounts.
> HELMER: What do you mean by that?
> NORA: *(After a short silence.)* Isn't there one thing that
> strikes you as strange in our sitting here like this?
> HELMER: What is that?
> NORA: We have been married now eight years. Does it not
> occur to you that this is the first time we two, you and I,
> husband and wife, have had a serious conversation?
> —HENRIK IBSEN

To make the actions of a character in a play believable, you
must first show your audience what kind of a person the character is. If you were writing a short story, you could simply say,
"Webster loved money more than anything else in the world.
His enemies were all those who were trying to take some of it

away from him—salesclerks in stores, waitresses in restaurants, bus drivers, and the electric-power company." In a play, revealing what a character is like is not as easily done. You would either have to have another character describe Webster's stinginess or have Webster reveal it in his own words and actions.

Here are two writers using dialogue to reveal character. The first writer reveals what his main character is like by having someone else describe him. This description is taken from the play *A Man for All Seasons*.

> MATTHEW: *(Referring to Rich who has given him a grudging small tip.)*—That one'll come to nothing. My master Thomas More would give anything to anyone. Some say that's good and some say that's bad, but I say he can't help it—and that's bad . . . because some day someone's going to ask him for something that he wants to keep; and he'll be out of practice . . . .
>
> —ROBERT BOLT

The second writer has the character talk about herself. This dialogue is taken from the play *A Raisin in the Sun*.

> BENEATHA: . . . When I was very small . . . we used to take our sleds out in the wintertime and the only hills we had were the ice-covered stone steps of some houses down the street. And we used to fill them in with snow and make them smooth and slide down them all day . . . and it was very dangerous you know . . . far too steep . . . and sure enough a kid named Rufus came down too fast and hit the sidewalk . . . and we saw his face just split open right there in front of us . . . And I remember standing there looking at his bloody open face thinking that was the end of Rufus. But the ambulance came and they took him to the hospital and they fixed the broken bones and they sewed it all up . . . and the next time I saw Rufus he just had a little line down the middle of his face . . . I never got over that . . .
>
> ASAGAI: What?
>
> BENEATHA: That that was what one person could do for another, fix him up—sew up the problem, make him all right again. That was the most marvelous thing in the world . . . I wanted to do that . . . .
>
> —LORRAINE HANSBERRY

In both cases character is revealed by a brief story. Matthew doesn't say simply, "Thomas More is a generous man." Beneatha doesn't say simply, "I like being able to help people." Instead of making flat statements like these, the characters tell stories that illustrate values and attitudes.

Stage directions   Another way a writer of plays has of indicating meaning to an audience is through stage directions. These are simply instructions to the actors. They tell the actors how to speak certain lines and which movements to make. Notice the stage directions—the lines in parentheses and italics —in the following speech. What do they tell you about the ways the character is feeling as she talks?

> MAMA: *(Looking up at the words "rat trap" and then looking around and leaning back and sighing—in a suddenly reflective mood—)* "Rat trap"—yes, that's all it is. *(Smiling.)* I remember just as well the day me and Big Walter moved in here. Hadn't been married but two weeks and wasn't planning on living here no more than a year. *(She shakes her head at the dissolved dream.)* We was going to set away, little by little, don't you know, and buy a little place out in Morgan Park. We had even picked out the house. *(Chuckling a little.)* Looks right dumpy today. But Lord, child, you should know all the dreams I had 'bout buying that house and fixing it up and making me a little garden in the back—*(She waits and stops smiling.)* And didn't none of it happen. *(Dropping her hands in a futile gesture.)*
>
> —LORRAINE HANSBERRY

Here the stage directions tell the actress to move through a series of gestures as she says her lines. The actress smiles, shakes her head, drops her hands. These gestures *show* the audience how the character is feeling as she talks. On stage, as in real life, talking isn't enough to show emotions. A character must gesture, smile, frown, talk softly or loudly so that the audience can tell exactly what the character is feeling.

Scene description   A play must take place somewhere—it must have a setting. The setting helps to establish the mood—

a gloomy, deserted room in an old house and a bright room filled with cheerful people provide very different moods. The setting also provides a place appropriate to the action and to the personalities in the play. Into the deserted room might come a detective trying to solve a crime—the bright, cheerful room might be the scene of a party.

In setting a scene, you must describe the setting clearly so that it can be accurately reproduced on a stage. The audience, when the curtain goes up, should be able to tell immediately the kind of place in which the actions of the play will occur. Here's part of a setting.

> . . . *The kitchen at center seems actual enough, for there is a kitchen table with three chairs, and a refrigerator. But no other fixtures are seen. At the back of the kitchen there is a draped entrance, which leads to the living-room. To the right of the kitchen, on a level raised two feet, is a bedroom furnished only with a brass bedstead and a straight chair. On a shelf over the bed a silver athletic trophy stands.*
> —ARTHUR MILLER

What does this setting tell you about the people that inhabit it? Why is there a trophy in the bedroom?

There are several approaches you might take to describing a scene. For example, your scene description could be very simple. You could use one or two objects which by their isolation *suggest* rather than minutely reproduce an environment. You could set a scene in a school hallway. All the scenery you might need would be the outline of a door or two—or perhaps the bare stage with a single locker could represent the hallway. Or you might, like Miller, use only a few props—Miller lets a table, three chairs, and a refrigerator represent a kitchen. Or you may wish to use a full set of props—a living room could have a sofa, several chairs, a lamp, several pictures on the wall, a window, perhaps a fireplace. In describing your scene, remember that what you describe must contribute to the total effect of the play. You should not just choose furnishings at random. For a short play, a simple setting with a few props would probably be best.

Of course, your play may have more than one setting. Each time you change the scene to a new setting, you must carefully describe that setting. In a relatively short play, you will probably not want to change the scene more than once or twice.

Patterns of organization   Unless you're writing a very short play, you will probably wish to divide the action into two or more scenes. Scenes are the building blocks of a play. Like the play itself, a scene has a beginning, a middle, and an end. To signal the beginning of a scene, you could indicate that the curtain should be raised or that the stage lights should slowly come on. To end a scene, you could indicate a reverse procedure. During a scene, both the characters and the conflict must be developed through action and dialogue. The scene should form a unit in itself.

One common reason for dividing a play into scenes is that the action occurs in different places. Another is that the actions occur at different times.

In a play, the scenes are usually arranged chronologically—A happens, then B, then C. For example, in one scene in *A Man for All Seasons*, Thomas More is made the king's chief minister. In a later scene, he opposes the king. In a still later scene, he's sent to prison. Each scene flows logically out of the previous scene. More's opposition is important *because* he's the king's chief minister; he's sent to prison *because* he opposes the king.

Poetry

It's likely that writing poetry would not appear on your Ten Favorite Activities list. Maybe this is because you think poems have to be about flowers and birds and streams and things like that. Or maybe you just don't know how to write a poem. Or maybe both.

First of all, a poem can be about anything. Second, a poem isn't *that* hard to write. Third, writing a poem can be fun, almost as much fun as having someone else read it and like it.

If you do want to write a poem, where do you start? What

do you write about? A good place to begin is with yourself. Write about you. Haven't there been special times and special feelings? Nothing big and solemn, but just moments like these?

DRIVING TO TOWN LATE TO MAIL A LETTER

It is a cold and snowy night. The main street is deserted.
The only things moving are swirls of snow.
As I lift the mailbox door, I feel its cold iron.
There is a privacy I love in this snowy night.
Driving around, I will waste more time.

—ROBERT BLY

Couldn't you write a poem like this? Couldn't you tell what it's like to be awake when everybody else is sleeping and everything is quiet?

If you read the poem again, you may think it doesn't sound like a poem. For one thing, there's no rhyme. For another, there's no regular rhythm—no pattern of stressed and unstressed syllables that repeats itself in each line. So what makes this poem a poem?

Take a look at the kind of words used—especially "swirls of snow" and "I feel its cold iron." These words appeal directly to the senses. Of course, words like these might be found in a straightforward prose description. But is this merely description, a portrait in words? If it is, there's a lot left out. You don't really know what the main street looked like. The writer hasn't shown you the bank and the hardware store and the police station and the supermarket. He's not really focusing on things, but on his feelings. Things like the mailbox, to guide the reader to thoughts and feelings.

If what you read is a poem, not prose, it has three characteristics that mark it off. It is packed with words that appeal to and prod the reader's senses. It focuses on an emotion. The third characteristic you may have already noticed—compression. It uses words very sparingly—just enough to do the job.

Are these three characteristics all there is to poetry? Not quite. There's another one in this poem. See if you can tell what it is.

ON WATCHING THE CONSTRUCTION
OF A SKYSCRAPER

Nothing sings from these orange trees,
Rindless steel as smooth as sapling skin,
Except a crane's brief wheeze
And all the muffled, clanking din
Of rivets nosing in like bees.
—BURTON RAFFEL

Another important characteristic of poetry is figurative language. That is, language in which things that are not alike are compared in a striking or original way. The poem itself, for example, is a metaphor comparing the steel framework of a skyscraper to bare trees. Within the poem there are other figures of speech—personification and simile. The construction crane, for example, makes a noise like a person—a "brief wheeze." The sound of the rivets is similar to the sound of bees.

These, then, are the major characteristics of poetry. But not every poem that you read will have them all. Nor will every poem that you write. But it won't be a poem—whether you read it or write it—if it has none of these characteristics.

Free verse   What should you write your poem about? Quite simply, you can write a poem about practically anything. You could even write a poem about writing poems, as this writer has done.

GONE FOREVER

Halfway through shaving, it came—
the word for a poem.
I should have scribbled it
on the mirror with a soapy finger,
or shouted it to my wife in the kitchen,
or muttered it to myself till it ran
in my head like a tune.

But now it's gone with the whiskers
down the drain. Gone forever,
like the girls I never kissed,
and the places I never visited—
the lost lives I never lived.
—BARRISS MILLS

This poem is written in free verse—that is, the verse is free from regular meter and rhyme. But poetry written in free verse is not entirely without a pattern. The difference is that when you write free verse, you have to invent a pattern appropriate for each poem—there are no ready-made patterns for you to follow.

Notice the patterns that hold this poem together. First, the poem is arranged around two ideas, so there are two stanzas. In the first stanza, the author talks about what he should have done; in the second, about what he has lost. The parallel verbs "scribbled," "shouted," and "muttered" help to give the first stanza its form. In the second stanza, the repeated phrase "I never" serves the same purpose.

How did the author create this pattern? He probably experimented, trying out different line divisions until he was finally satisfied. Maybe originally he thought the poem was all one idea and didn't divide it into stanzas. But on looking it over, he may have found two distinct ideas, so he divided it into stanzas. He probably didn't write the poem in its final form the first time around. Once in a while you can do that. But usually you'll need to experiment to find just the right words, just the right line divisions.

TRY IT   Free verse isn't really "free." But it does give you certain kinds of freedom. For example, you don't have to use complete sentences. Here's a poem in which the writer uses simple words or phrases to describe himself.

> Me
> Mean, hating
> Running, talking, falling
> Not liking anyone
> Sad
> —DANNY

Now write a poem like this. Start it with *me* and then use *-ing* words that describe you or that tell how you feel. You could use the pattern above or a different one. Experiment.

Traditional poetry   Instead of inventing a form for each poem you write, you could use a form that already exists. You could write a sonnet, or a ballad, or a couplet. These are traditional forms for poetry. That is, they've been around for a long time. But more important, each of these forms follows a specific pattern. Each form has a certain number of lines and a certain number of syllables in each line. Also, there is a pattern of rhyme that the last word of each line fits into. Here is a traditional poem. Read it and see how many patterns you can pick out. Does the poet sometimes break away from these patterns? Or does he apply them rigidly throughout?

STOPPING BY WOODS ON A SNOWY EVENING

Whose woods | these are | I think | I know.	a
His house | is in | the vil | lage, though;	a
He will | not see | me stop | ping here	b
To watch | his woods | fill up | with snow.	a
My little horse must think it queer	b
To stop without a farmhouse near	b
Between the woods and frozen lake	c
The darkest evening of the year.	b
He gives his harness bells a shake	c
To ask if there is some mistake.	c
The only other sound's the sweep	d
Of easy wind and downy flake.	c
The woods are lovely, dark, and deep,	d
But I have promises to keep,	d
And miles to go before I sleep,	d
And miles to go before I sleep.	d

—ROBERT FROST

In reading this poem, you probably noticed first the regular rhythm. Each line consists of four feet. These feet are marked in the poem by the vertical lines in color. Each foot in turn consists of unstressed syllable ( ) followed by a stressed syllable ( ). The poem also has a regular rhyme scheme, which is marked at the side of the poem in color. Notice how the rhyme scheme is repeated in each group of lines except the last. Each group of lines, called a stanza, contains a relatively complete idea, although each idea is related to the other ideas in the poem. Try reading Frost's poem again, perhaps out loud. Can you hear the regular pattern?

In following a regular pattern, you don't need to feel that you can't change anything. You can vary the rhythm a little, as long as you stick to your basic pattern. You can also vary the rhyme scheme. Notice that the last stanza of Frost's poem has a rhyme scheme different from the others. All four of the end-words rhyme. You could also, like Frost, use a refrain, the repetition of a line, to show that your poem is ending and to emphasize the idea in your last line.

All good traditional poets feel free to vary rhythm and rhyme a little. They do this because a completely regular poem might bore the reader—the poem might become singsong and monotonous. Also, they may really need an occasional word that doesn't fit completely into the regular rhythm. You should feel free to vary rhyme and rhythm in the same way, just as long as you stick to the basic pattern you've chosen.

TRY IT   Experiment with writing a short traditional poem. It need be no longer than two or four lines. Before you write, you might like to study this short, four-line poem.

> I do not love thee, Doctor Fell,
> The reason why I cannot tell;
> But this alone I know full well;
> I do not love thee, Doctor Fell.
> —THOMAS BROWN

Perhaps you could write a short poem like this, in which you make a comment about a person or about life. Or perhaps you could write a short poem about something you've observed— city streets reflecting the sky after a rain, a commuter train as it roars along its tunnel, the pattern of rain on a window, the smell of damp autumn leaves.

Experimental poetry   If you like to draw, and you like to play with words, then you might like to try an experimental poem. Here's such a poem.

—Sarah Gallagher

This may not look like a poem. In fact, it may not even make sense at first. But think about it a moment. Count the words in the poem. What this poem does is to make the meaning of its words visual. This is a feature of the experimental poetry called concrete poetry. It's a kind of "picture writing" in which the poem's physical shape and arrangement give visual support to its meaning.

Here's another concrete poem. How does its form or shape convey its meaning?

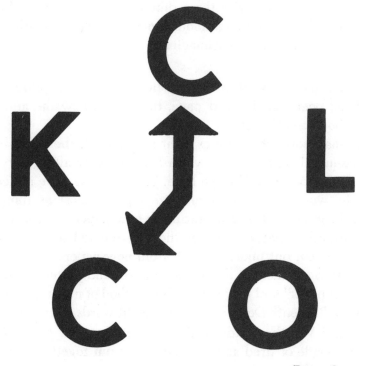

—Beth Oderkirk

Like most concrete poetry, this poem is really part poem and part drawing. The author has used the word *clock* to form the outer circle of the clock. Then she has added two clock hands to complete the poem/drawing.

TRY IT   Perhaps you could create a concrete poem about a clock or about time. Take, for example, the phrase *all the time in the world*. You know that refers to having a great amount of time. But think about the phrase from a new angle. Think, "What might this phrase mean if I didn't know what it meant?" Then you might draw a globe composed of the single word *time*. Or you could form the globe by repeating the word *time* many times within the drawing. Now try these two phrases.

clockwise

time flies

There is no one right way to create a poem from these words. Three people might write three different poems on *time flies*. That's one of the nice things about experimental poetry—there's plenty of room to use your imagination.

There's another kind of experimental poetry you could try. Read the poem on the next page, then guess how the author went about creating it.

You may notice two things right away. First, the poem has some unusual phrases—sunny gardens don't usually grow on the second floor of a Chicago barn. You may also have noticed that the words are in different size types, almost as though they'd been cut out of a magazine or newspaper. And in fact, that's exactly what the author did. He created a "paste-pot poem." He cut out unusual words from newspapers and magazines, arranged them in a pattern he liked, and pasted them to a sheet of paper. And why not? Is this method of making a poem really so different? Don't all poems use old words to create new meanings? Whether traditional or experimental, a poem that works is made of tired and familiar words put together in new ways, ways that startle and delight.

A sunny garden

now is   growing

on the second floor of

a Chicago barn

which once housed

the horses

for

fire wagons.

—NORBERT BLEI

TRY IT   You might like to create a "paste-pot poem." First of all, cut out any interesting words you find in magazines or newspapers—you might try to find words in several different type sizes, the way that Blei did. You could also cut out any small pictures that interest you. Then play with different combinations of words and pictures until you find some unique combination. Finally, paste everything to a sheet of paper to create a "paste-pot poem."

After You Write

Once you have finished a first draft, you may be tempted to cut the writing process short, to consider your work at an end. After all, you've thought and planned and organized. And you've recorded your ideas on paper. Even though this first try is really experimental and tentative, you may feel there is something special about the words and sentences you have written. Wouldn't it be best to leave them just as they are? Won't rewriting only spoil your first draft?

No. Believe it or not, rewriting is exactly what your first draft needs. In fact, it is exactly what anyone's first draft needs. Professional writers recognize rewriting as an essential stage in the writing process. Ernest Hemingway, for example, rewrote the ending of one novel thirty-nine times.

Writing is meant to be read by someone other than the writer. And your first draft isn't ready to be read by anyone else yet. It still needs rethinking, reworking, and polishing. In the prewriting and the writing stages, your work was essentially private. You were on your own—thinking, experimenting, changing your mind, trying a new approach. You even wrote your ideas down, to see how they looked and sounded. Now you have to prepare your work to be made public. It's time for those crucial finishing touches.

Basically, rewriting boils down to this: You must be able to switch roles. You must be able to put yourself in your readers' place. Is there something in what you've written that your readers might not understand? Is there a sentence or a paragraph that might be fuzzy or unclear? If there is, fix it now. Remember, you won't be there to explain to your readers what you meant to write. You have to write what you mean.

EDITING FOR CONTENT

It's not hard to start rewriting. The first thing to do is nothing. Just let your first draft cool for a while. If possible, put it

190

away for a day or two. Don't work on or even think about your writing. Then it will be easier for you to take a fresh, objective look at your first draft and to see what changes need to be made.

Your writing as a whole

When you first read through your rough draft, you will want to pay special attention to its organization and emphasis. Stand back a bit and look at your writing as a complete, well-rounded whole. Ask yourself questions like these: What are the different parts of the whole? Are any parts missing? Are any extra parts included? Are the parts in the best possible order? Will my readers know which parts I consider most important? Will they understand why I included these particular details? Could I defend my choices?

Organization   To find out whether or not the whole thing hangs together, think about the main point of your writing. Use the thesis statement or the statement of intent that you wrote—and perhaps revised—in the prewriting stage as your yardstick. Measure your first draft against the statement; see if your writing as a whole and all the parts of your writing clearly relate to your main point.

Consider the overall impression that your writing makes. Do you feel that the writing as a whole follows through on your main point? Have you really shown why private cars should not be allowed in the downtown area of your city? Have you really described how you felt when your parents decided to adopt another child?

Then consider each paragraph as a necessary part of the whole. Does each one help to make the main point clear? Does it directly support your thesis statement or statement of intent? Perhaps you have written about your first summer at camp. As you read your draft, you may find two paragraphs about the camping trip you made with your family last year. It was a fun trip, and the paragraphs are interesting—but do they relate directly to your subject? If not, take them out.

Finally, consider the order of the paragraphs. Does the order help build toward or support the main point? Are the paragraphs arranged so that they form a logical sequence? You may find, for example, that a paragraph explaining how to remove a worn fan belt comes before a paragraph explaining how to find the fan belt in a car. If you are trying to give your readers clear directions for replacing a fan belt, you should reverse the order of those two paragraphs.

Emphasis   In this rereading of your first draft, you will also want to check your writing for proper emphasis. That is, you will want to be sure you have given the most space to the most important ideas and less space to minor ideas. For example, you may have written an editorial recommending that soccer be included in your school's athletic program. And maybe you felt that the best reason for including soccer was the excellent physical conditioning it provides. But in rereading, you discover that after you developed two other reasons, you didn't have time—or space, or energy, or whatever—to fully develop your best reason. Your emphasis was misplaced. Remember, rewriting doesn't mean just changing or rearranging the words you have already written. In this case, rewriting means writing new sentences and even paragraphs to expand the most important part of your composition.

Outlining as a check   As a final check of the organization and emphasis of your writing, you may want to make an outline of your first draft. The headings of the outline will bring to the surface problems you may have overlooked before. They may help you see that you have included an idea that doesn't relate to your subject, or that you haven't developed one of your ideas completely, or even that you haven't presented your ideas in the clearest possible order.

Your paragraphs

After you have reread and rethought your first draft—and made sure that it hangs together as a whole—you are ready to focus on smaller, more particular segments of your writing. You are ready to examine your paragraphs.

As you examine the paragraphs you have written, consider each one from two points of view—function and structure.

Paragraph functions   Paragraphs can be divided according to their functions into four types: introductory, developmental, transitional, and concluding. As you reread a paragraph, decide which type it is. What function is it intended to serve? How well does it serve that function? How could it be changed to serve its function better?

Be alert, though. Not every piece of writing has all four types of paragraphs.

1. Introductory paragraphs   The purpose of an introductory paragraph is to capture the readers' interest and to give them a general idea of what is to come. But not all your writing will have—or need—an introductory paragraph. Usually, only a fairly long or complicated composition calls for one.

The following introductory paragraph is from an article about the sport of spinnaker flying. As you read it, notice how its direct approach arouses your interest.

> Take one 70-foot racing sloop, a costly, big-bellied sail called a spinnaker, an elk hide sling called a vang strap and a thrill seeker with more courage than sense, and you have all the essential ingredients of the newest water sport —spinnaker flying. Enthusiasts describe the sport as something akin to hang-gliding except that instead of floating free on gentle air currents, one is tethered to a masthead that may be as high as 90 feet off the water. A miscalculation or momentary panic in a strong gust can send the flier crashing into the mast or into the sea below.
>
> —FRANK ROHR

Frank Rohr has avoided the common problems of an introductory paragraph: a roundabout approach, unnecessary length, meaningless words, repetitious sentences. If, as you reread your introductory paragraph, you realize that it has one of those problems, rewrite the paragraph. Get to the point quickly. Take out the unnecessary phrases. Make each word count.

A paragraph, especially an introductory paragraph, does not need to be long. So aim for meaning and interest—not for length. Be direct. Be specific. Never begin like this: "I am going to write about spinnaker flying. . . ."

2. Developmental paragraphs   Most of the paragraphs in your writing will be developmental. These are the paragraphs that expand your main point, that introduce qualifications and explanations, that support the thesis of your writing. These paragraphs carry the weight of your thesis statement or statement of intent. They must be strong and well structured.

Each sentence in a developmental paragraph should be related to a central idea. That idea may be expressed in a topic sentence, or it may be only a thought you keep in mind as you write. In either case, every sentence in the paragraph should relate to this idea.

In the following paragraph, the first sentence expresses the central idea. And each sentence after that is related to this idea.

> Also, I had a change-of-pace, which Sal Maglie purports to be the most important pitch in any given repertoire. My version of the pitch, which big-leaguers throw pretty much off their regular motion, consisted of a big windmilling windup—grotesquely exaggerated to fake the batter into thinking the pitch was going to be smoked in—then at the last second letting up on the motion to take the speed off the pitch, like trying to make a fellow flinch without hitting him, and the pitch as I threw it, a soft, inaccurate lob, wouldn't have fooled your sister. I rarely threw it. But it was in the repertoire—like a useless but interesting instrument kept in a toolbox in case it should ever come in handy.   —GEORGE PLIMPTON

Why didn't the writer mention his fastball or his curve? Why didn't he include a sentence about Sal Maglie or big-league pitchers or his favorite catcher? Maybe he did, but they're not in this paragraph. This is a paragraph about his change-of-pace pitch; every sentence is about that pitch.

As you reread your own developmental paragraphs, watch

out for sentences that don't belong. Keep the central point of each paragraph in mind. Be sure every sentence relates to that point. And make certain the relationship will be obvious to your readers.

3. Transitional paragraphs   Like introductory and concluding paragraphs, transitional paragraphs are best suited to long or fairly complex compositions. If each of the main ideas in your writing is developed in a single paragraph, you probably won't need transitional paragraphs. This doesn't mean you won't use transitions. But in short compositions, transitional words and sentences are usually enough.

If you do use transitional paragraphs, be sure that each paragraph links a previous idea to one that follows. This doesn't take many words. A good transitional paragraph will often be only one or two sentences long.

The following transitional paragraph is from an article about girls taking part in amateur athletics. It comes after several paragraphs describing the efforts of three girls to be included in sports programs. It leads into several paragraphs about the legal action taken against Little League Baseball, Inc., for sex discrimination. Notice how it looks back and ahead at the same time.

> While these girls and young women are fighting their private battles, one battle has been fought in public and the whole country has watched its outcome.
>
> —LETTY COTTIN POGREBIN

This paragraph doesn't include much detail. It assumes that you have read the preceding paragraphs and that you will read the paragraphs that follow. Simply and directly, it serves its function: it leads from one subject to the next. If your writing includes transitional paragraphs, keep that function in mind as you read over your first draft.

4. Concluding paragraphs   The last paragraph of your composition isn't always a concluding paragraph. This is a special kind of paragraph used to wrap up a long or complicated piece of writing. A concluding paragraph should stress the importance of the main idea of your writing. But it should

be more than a rehash. It should somehow express the idea in a new and interesting way—with an anecdote, a rhetorical question, or perhaps a quotation. The following is the concluding paragraph of an article on communes:

> But many veterans of less-than-perfect communes are ready to try others. Alice, now in her fifth group, says, "Sure I know the problems. But I wouldn't consider any other way to live. . . . Even at its worst, the commune provides company. At its best, I have a family. And, anyway, it is *home.*" —ROSABETH MOSS KANTER

The writer might have concluded: "There are good and bad sides to living in a commune. But, at least for some people, it's the best way of life." This is a bare repetition of the point she had already made in her article. So, instead, she added something new and interesting by quoting a member of a commune who could sum up those ideas in a personal way.

You won't want to use the same device in every concluding paragraph you write. Choose one that fits your subject and your purpose. And remember, each paragraph—including the concluding paragraph—should add something new to your writing.

TRY IT   Do one or more of these rewriting exercises:

1. Rewrite the following introductory paragraph. Your rewritten paragraph doesn't need to be as long as the original one, but it should be direct and interesting.

> Everyone lives somewhere. And probably everyone thinks that that somewhere is the best place to live. I have a friend who lives in the city. And she likes it there. And some of my friends live in the suburbs. They think suburban living is the best. But I live in the country. And, even though you may have heard some bad things about country life, I can tell you that it's the best there is.

2. Rewrite the following developmental paragraph. Be sure your rewritten paragraph has one central idea.

> I really love to swim. Swimming always makes me feel better, both physically and psychologically. My muscles seem to wither during a day spent listening to lectures

and taking surprise quizzes. But a few quick laps in the pool bring those muscles back to life. And I can usually take out my frustrations on the water when I swim. Of course, there are a lot of things in life that can be frustrating. I find trying to say a whole sentence correctly in French and dealing with my little brother particularly frustrating. Last week, for instance, my brother picked up the other phone while I was talking.

3. Rewrite the following concluding paragraph. You may want to invent a quote or anecdote to make your rewritten paragraph new and interesting.

We have seen that public concern for campaign reform is high. And we have seen that our legislators are unwilling to enact the legislation that people want. We are faced with a serious problem indeed.

Paragraph structures   The structure of a well-organized paragraph will usually match one of six typical paragraph patterns. And in reading over your first draft, you should check each of your paragraphs to see how closely its structure conforms to one of these patterns.

The six paragraph patterns can be divided into two groups. There are those that follow natural order and those that follow logical order. Paragraphs organized in natural order are most often used in telling stories, explaining how something works, or describing what something looks like. Their organization follows the organization of what is being told, explained, or described. Paragraphs organized in logical order follow a pattern that you, as the writer, create. They are most often used in persuading.

Each of the two groups includes three specific patterns. Patterns of natural order include chronological structure, spatial structure, and associational structure. Patterns of logical order include deductive structure, inductive structure, and pro/con structure.

1. Chronological structure   *Chronological* means "in the order of happening." So a paragraph with a chronological structure lists events in the order in which they occurred.

The following paragraph has a chronological structure. In it the writer tells how to remove and replace the plug on an electric cord. Notice how the sentences are arranged.

> Assuming you want to replace the plug because the insulation on the cord has frayed, here's what you do. Cut the cord off beyond, but as close as possible to, the damaged part. Remove all the wire from the old plug (or use a new plug) and slide the plug back on the cord. Separate the two wires for a distance of about two inches and tie an Underwriters' knot . . . Now carefully, without cutting any of the small wires, scrape away a half inch of insulation from the end of each wire and give the exposed wire a clockwise twist. Pull the knot down firmly into the plug between the prongs. Pull each wire around a prong, wrap it clockwise around a screw, and tighten the screw. The insulation on the wire should come to the screw, but not under it. Put the insulation cover back on the plug. . . .   —BILL ELISBURG

One good way to test the structure of a paragraph like this is to switch some sentences around. For example, try reversing the order of the second and third sentences. Doesn't this disrupt the meaning of the paragraph? If the sentences can't be switched, then they are in the right order.

Another thing to check for in chronological paragraphs is gaps. Has an important step or event been left out? It's easy to skip over something, especially when you are writing about a subject you know well.

2. Spatial structure   If your writing includes a paragraph of description, the details will probably be arranged in a spatial pattern. That is, the details will follow one another in the same order that someone looking at what is described would see them. The order might be from left to right, from top to bottom, or from far to near. The point is that the details are arranged according to a pattern, not scattered around. And once the pattern is established, it is followed consistently throughout the paragraph. Here, for example, is a paragraph describing a small town in England called Leesden End. The details are arranged in a spatial order from far to near.

> At the end of the thirties Leesden End was an L-shaped town. Our house stood near the top of the L. At the other extreme was the market. Mr. Simmonds, the oculist, had his shop on the horizontal leg, and he lived there above the shop with his mother and sister. All the other shops in the row were attached to each other, but Mr. Simmonds' stood apart, like a real house, with a lane on either side. —MURIEL SPARK

This description is similar to the opening scene from a movie. First you get an aerial view of the town. Then the camera moves in closer until it focuses on a single house. The writer has arranged her details carefully, so that you, as the reader, can "see" what she is describing.

As you reread your own paragraph, check the arrangement of your details. Don't let your description jump randomly from one spot to another. That will only be confusing. Instead, help your readers "see" what you are describing by choosing a spatial pattern for your details and sticking to it.

3. Associational structure   A paragraph with associational structure does not follow an order of time or space. Instead, it follows an order of mental connections. For example, you may be writing about the smell of fresh roses at a florists' show. That makes you think of the rosebushes around your grandmother's house. One thing—a thought, a memory, a feeling, an idea—leads to another. That's association.

In the following paragraph, one man sees another carrying garbage cans. Seeing the other man at work makes the first man think of his son Sam.

> . . . He waved to the superintendent of the building on the corner. And watched him as he lugged garbage cans out of the areaway and rolled them to the curb. Now, that's the kind of work he didn't want [his son] Sam to have to do. He tried to decide why that was. It wasn't just because Sam was his boy and it was hard work. He searched his mind for the reason. It didn't pay enough for a man to live on decently. That was it. He wanted Sam to have a job where he could make enough to have good clothes and a nice home. —ANN PETRY

As you read the paragraph by Ann Petry, you can follow the development of the man's thoughts. But what if the paragraph had skipped from the second sentence directly to the last sentence? You would miss the connections that hold the paragraph together. It wouldn't make sense.

A paragraph with associational structure must have clear, controlled connections. Each idea should lead directly to the next. Look for the connections in your own paragraph. Be sure your readers will understand how each sentence develops from the one before it.

4. Deductive structure   A deductive paragraph begins with a statement—usually the topic sentence—and continues with facts or details that back up that statement.

> Selecting a jury is of the utmost importance. So far as possible, the lawyer should know both sides of the case. If the client is a landlord, a banker, or a manufacturer, or one of that type, then jurors sympathetic to that class will be wanted in the box; a man who looks neat and trim and smug. He will be sure to guard your interests as he would his own. His entire environment has taught him that all real values are measured in cash, and he knows no other worth. Every knowing lawyer seeks for a jury of the same sort of men as his client; men who will be able to imagine themselves in the same situation and realize what verdict the client wants.   —CLARENCE DARROW

Clarence Darrow's first sentence introduces the main idea of his paragraph. Each of the following sentences supports that main idea. As you reread your own deductive paragraph, see if it works the way Darrow's does. Does it begin with a clear, direct statement? Do each of the following sentences relate to the opening statement? Do the sentences offer enough support for your opening statement? When they finish reading the paragraph, will your readers understand why that opening statement is true—or at least why you think it's true?

5. Inductive structure   Inductive structure is deductive structure turned upside down. That is, an inductive paragraph begins with supporting facts and details and builds toward a general statement.

Librans hate to be rude, yet they'll straighten the crooked picture on your wall and snap off your blaring TV set. Librans love people, but they hate large crowds. Like gentle doves of peace, they go around mediating and patching up quarrels between others; still they enjoy a good argument themselves. They're goodnatured and pleasant, but they can also be sulky, and they balk at taking orders. Librans are extremely intelligent. At the same time, they're incredibly naive and gullible. They'll talk your ear off, yet they're wonderfully good listeners. Librans are restless people. But they seldom rush or hurry. Are you completely confused? You're not alone. There's a frustrating inconsistency to this Sun sign that puzzles the Librans themselves as much as it does others.

—LINDA GOODMAN

In checking an inductive paragraph, you follow essentially the same process you followed with a deductive paragraph. This time, though, your paragraph should lead up to, rather than support, a general statement. Does each sentence lead directly to the final statement? Have you left out any important ideas? Have you included any sentences that don't relate to the main point of the paragraph?

6. Pro/con structure   *Pro* means "for" and *con* means "against." So a paragraph with pro/con structure presents two conflicting opinions—arguments for and against. It moves back and forth, from one opinion to the other, as the following paragraph does:

Today many men enjoy wearing the hair long—below the ears, to the shoulders, or beyond. But other men consider long hair too much trouble. Those who favor long hair think it looks stylish. Those who oppose it think long hair looks messy. The pro-longhairs contend that women are attracted to men with long hair. But the anti-longhairs think that long hair is "feminine" and that "real men" are usually bald—or close to it. Both groups, however, ignore the history of fashion.   —BUFFY KAVANAUGH

If you have written a pro/con paragraph, don't let it be an excuse for a lack of organization. Check its structure carefully. Be sure your paragraph presents one opinion on a particular aspect of your subject and then an opposing opinion on the same aspect of your subject. And be sure each opinion is balanced by its opposite.

TRY IT   Choose one of the following rewriting exercises:

1. Rewrite the following paragraph. Be sure your rewritten paragraph has a clear chronological structure.

> Jamie was determined to find someone at home. When no one responded to the bell, he tried pounding on the door—still no response. Finally, Jamie walked around the house, peering in every window. Then he tried turning the knob, but the door was locked. He began by ringing the doorbell several times.

2. Rewrite the following deductive paragraph. Remember that the first sentence in a deductive paragraph states the central idea of the paragraph; each of the following sentences should relate to that central idea.

> More American lives were lost in the Civil War than in any other war in history. Deaths during that war totaled over 529,300. The war which caused the next largest number of American deaths was World War II, which took 405,400 American lives. There was a very severe inflation during the Civil War. In World War I, 116,500 Americans died; in the Vietnam War, 56,000. Estimates for the loss of American lives during the Revolutionary War range from 4,400 to 12,000. Of course, many Americans die from accidents, both at home and on our highways.

Paragraph groups   Sometimes you will need more than a single paragraph to say all you want to say about a particular idea. In a long composition you may have a group of two, three, or even more paragraphs about a single main idea.

You will want to check the organization of a paragraph group in much the same way that you check the organization of a single paragraph. Are the paragraphs within the group arranged in the best possible order? Do they build up to or firmly support the main point? Have any important ideas been left out? Have any confusing or unnecessary ideas been left in?

Your sentences

As you consider the sentences in your rough draft, you will be most concerned with their effect. Does each sentence convey exactly the meaning and the emphasis that you want? Does each sentence fit in with the other sentences around it? Does each group of sentences work together?

You may find that some of your sentences don't quite measure up. How can you improve them? Whether or not a sentence presents your ideas effectively depends largely on its structure. So you can often improve weak sentences by revising their structure.

There are several rewriting techniques you can use in revising the structure of your sentences. Perhaps the most useful is combining several sentences into one. A short, simple sentence—even a group of short, simple sentences—can be very effective. But if your writing consists only of short, simple sentences, it will probably be jerky, flat, and uninteresting. More important, such writing separates ideas that belong together. And so it fails to give your readers a clear understanding of the relationships between your ideas and of the relative importance of your ideas. To improve such sentences, you will need to combine some of them. You can do this in two ways—by compounding sentences and by embedding sentences.

Other important rewriting techniques include rearranging sentence parts and eliminating incomplete sentences.

Compounding sentences   One way to make one sentence from two is by compounding—joining two related sentences with a comma and a connecting word like *and, but,* or *or.* Which connecting word you use depends on the relationship of the ideas you are bringing together. *And* shows that one idea is added to another. *But* shows a contrast between ideas. *Or* shows a choice between ideas.

> The houselights dimmed, and the curtain began to rise. I enjoyed the show, but Randy thought it was silly. You must be in the theater by 8:15, or the ushers will not seat you.

Sometimes a semicolon can be used instead of a comma and a connecting word. A semicolon simply shows a connection between ideas—it may be one of addition, contrast, or choice.

> I can't tell you what to do; you'll have to decide for yourself.

Compounding, like other sentence-rewriting techniques, can be used to make the intended effect of some sentences more clear. As you read the following paragraph, consider which sentences might be improved by compounding:

> We waited for another two hours. No news came. The silence was disturbing. We had expected to hear something—good or bad—long ago. Pat began to express the doubts we all felt. Maybe the lines were down. Maybe our plan had been discovered. Maybe one of our runners had been sighted. Maybe one of our runners had even been captured. The rest of us just listened, discouraged. Then, when we no longer expected it, we heard the signal. All our doubts were forgotten. We had succeeded.

If you were revising that paragraph, you would probably want to join some of the sentences by compounding. Do two sentences express closely related ideas? Perhaps those ideas belong in a single sentence. Do you want to point up the contrast between the events described in two sentences? Maybe you should join them with a comma and *but*. You might rewrite the paragraph like this:

> We waited for another two hours, but no news came. The silence was disturbing; we had expected to hear something—good or bad—long ago. Pat began to express the doubts we all felt. Maybe the lines were down. Maybe our plan had been discovered. Maybe one of our runners had been sighted or even captured. The rest of us just listened, discouraged. Then, when we no longer expected it, we heard the signal, and all our doubts were forgotten. We had succeeded.

If you compare the two paragraphs, you will find that the rewritten version is clearer and easier to read. With some of the sentences joined by compounding, the paragraph no longer seems choppy. Because they are preceded by longer sentences, the short sentences beginning with *maybe* take on an added sense of urgency and suspense. And because there is some variety in the length and structure of the sentences, the short, direct sentence at the end—"We had succeeded"—has more force.

You may have noticed that one of the sentences in the rewritten paragraph resulted from something more than compounding. If two of the sentences from the first paragraph had been simply joined, the new sentence would have been this:

> Maybe one of our runners had been sighted, or maybe one of our runners had even been captured.

Because the two parts of that sentence are alike in so many ways, the repeated words can be deleted:

> Maybe one of our runners had been sighted or even captured.

You may sometimes want to use this rewriting technique of compounding and deleting as you revise your draft. It can help you make some sentences smoother and easier to understand.

You can use compounding to add depth and interest to your writing. But don't overuse it. A continuous compounding of sentences results in something like this:

> We waited for another two hours, but no news came, and the silence was disturbing, and we had expected to hear something—good or bad—long ago, and Pat began to express the doubts we all felt; maybe the lines were down. . . .

That long, rambling sentence needs to be broken down. You might find, as you reread your draft, that you've written one like it. If so, separate some of the sentence parts. You may want to keep some of the connecting words—but not all of them. Your rewritten passage should include a balanced mixture of compounded sentences and short, simple sentences.

Embedding sentences   As you reread your first draft, you may find two sentences expressing closely related ideas that belong together:

> Ms. Dabney is my French teacher. She used to live in Paris.

If you were to combine these sentences by compounding, the ideas they express would be more closely linked:

> Ms. Dabney is my French teacher, and she used to live in Paris.

But if you used this structure, you would be giving each idea equal weight. Maybe the fact that Ms. Dabney is your French teacher is more important than the fact that she used to live in Paris. Or maybe it's the other way around. The two ideas belong together, but not on the same level.

So how can you combine these ideas and yet give one idea more emphasis than the other? You can do this by embedding. Instead of simply connecting the sentences, you can reduce one sentence and make it part of another sentence. In other words, you can insert—or embed—one sentence in another.

If you want to join two sentences by embedding, you first have to choose one of the sentences to serve as the main structure. Then you can embed the other sentence in the main one. For example, if you were writing about Ms. Dabney and your French class, you would probably use the first sentence as the main structure and embed the second sentence:

> Ms. Dabney, who used to live in Paris, is my French teacher.

But if you were writing about Ms. Dabney's living in Paris, you would probably choose the second sentence as your main structure:

> Ms. Dabney, who is my French teacher, used to live in Paris.

In many cases, you can further reduce an embedded sentence to a phrase or even a single word. In the previous sentence, for example, you might shorten *who is my French teacher* to simply *my French teacher*. The new sentence would have the same meaning, but its structure would place even greater emphasis on the main idea:

> Ms. Dabney, my French teacher, used to live in Paris.

You can use embedding in many different ways. You will probably use it most often to add details to the sentence you select as your main structure:

> The bike is mine. The bike is green. → The bike that is green is mine. *or* The green bike is mine.

> The presents are beneath the tree. They are for my cousins. → The presents that are beneath the tree are for my cousins. *or* The presents beneath the tree are for my cousins.

> We were nearly exhausted from the long climb. We finally reached the cabin. It was ten o'clock. → Nearly exhausted from the long climb, we finally reached the cabin at ten o'clock.

You can use embedding to show conditions and causes:

> The cost of eggs has gone up. We have had to raise the price of our Breakfast Special. → Because the cost of eggs has gone up, we have had to raise the price of our Breakfast Special.

> You walk quickly. You can reach the lake in half an hour. → If you walk quickly, you can reach the lake in half an hour. or Walking quickly, you can reach the lake in half an hour.

> Mr. Bojarski avoided hitting the pedestrian. He swerved off the road. → In order to avoid hitting the pedestrian, Mr. Bojarski swerved off the road.

You can use embedding to show relationships of time:

> We finally found Piedmont High. The basketball game was over. → When we finally found Piedmont High, the basketball game was over.

You can also use embedding to replace indefinite words like *it* and *that* with specific information:

> Barbara was declared the winner. I was glad about it. → I was glad that Barbara was declared the winner.

> Duncan hates football. Everyone knows that. → Everyone knows that Duncan hates football.

Of course, the fact that you *can* use embedding doesn't mean you will always want to. Whether you embed and how you embed will depend on the effect you want your sentences to have. Two related ideas that deserve equal emphasis might be best expressed in two short, emphatic sentences. For example, here one sentence states a fact; the other makes an equally important comment about that fact:

>Duncan hates football. Everyone knows that.

Whether you use embedding to join two particular sentences will also depend on the other sentences in your writing. Consider the length, emphasis, and meaning of the surrounding sentences. Remember that embedding, like compounding, is a technique for making your meaning and your emphasis clear to your readers.

TRY IT   Rewrite the following paragraph. Use compounding and embedding to make the paragraph less disjointed and flat. Some sentences may be effective as they are.

>It was last summer. I first met Johanna. We were at the beach. Everyone else was soaking up the sun. Everyone else was swimming in the ocean. Everyone else was playing volleyball. Not Johanna. She was wearing jeans. She was wearing a grey sweatshirt. She was sitting on a towel. It was under a huge beach umbrella. The umbrella was green. Johanna didn't notice all the other people. She was reading. I walked by her. I wanted to see what she was reading. I saw the cover of the book. I smiled. It was one of my favorite books. It was *Catch 22*.

Rearranging sentence parts   As you reread your draft, you may find a sentence that doesn't need to be joined with another and that doesn't need to be broken into smaller parts. Still, it doesn't quite say what you want. Your general meaning may be there, but the emphasis you want is missing. The most important part of the sentence doesn't stand out the way it should; a less important part takes over. You can improve that sentence—and others like it—by rearranging its parts.

You can often change the emphasis of a sentence by moving a single word or phrase. In general, the sentence positions that convey the greatest emphasis are the beginning and the end. For example, notice the differences between these sentences:

> The mood of the crowd gradually changed.
> The mood of the crowd changed gradually.
> Gradually, the mood of the crowd changed.

The emphasis on the idea of *gradually* changes with the position of the word in the sentence. The idea receives the least weight when *gradually* comes in the middle of the sentence, somewhat more when it comes last, and most when it comes first.

There are several different ways you can change the order— and emphasis—of a sentence. Compare these sentences. How does the emphasis change from one sentence to the other?

> Dr. Jekyll made an important discovery.
> An important discovery was made by Dr. Jekyll.

In both sentences, the beginning is most important. The first sentence emphasizes Dr. Jekyll; the second emphasizes the discovery.

Occasionally you may invert the word order of a sentence for particular emphasis. In the following pair of sentences, the first sentence is in the normal word order. The second, however, has been rewritten in inverted order to give special emphasis to *wealth* and *fame*.

> I could accept wealth, but I would reject fame.
> Wealth I could accept, but fame I would reject.

Often the best order and emphasis for a particular sentence will depend on the sentences around it. For that reason, you can't judge your sentences in isolation. You have to see how each one fits into its context. For example, the sentence in color fits well between the sentence before it and the one after it. If this were its context, you would probably leave it in this order:

> Roscoe was apparently hypnotized by the sound of his own voice. He continued lecturing enthusiastically, even though no one was listening. He seemed not to notice that his audience had disappeared almost completely.

But if you used the same sentence in a different context, you would want to reverse the order of its main parts:

> Roscoe seemed unaware that he had lost his audience. **Even though no one was listening, he continued lecturing enthusiastically.** His voice grew louder and more authoritative, and his face began to redden with excitement.

Revising incomplete sentences   As you reread your first draft, look for sentence fragments—sentences you unintentionally left unfinished. If you find part of a sentence carelessly punctuated as a complete sentence, fill it out. Either add its missing parts or join it with another sentence. For example, suppose you find a sentence fragment like this:

> Standing stiffly in the lobby, the sweat breaking out under his too-tight collar.

You could make this fragment into a complete sentence by adding two words:

> Standing stiffly in the lobby, **Josh felt** the sweat breaking out under his too-tight collar.

Sometimes it is easier to fix a sentence fragment by making it part of another sentence. The following complete sentence is followed by a fragment:

> Trisha manages to be absent. Whenever we have a surprise quiz.

The fragment can be rewritten as part of the sentence:

> Trisha manages to be absent whenever we have a surprise quiz.

Incomplete sentences, however, do not necessarily need to be rewritten. In certain cases, an incomplete sentence can make good sense. If it does, and if it is intentionally incomplete, then it is an elliptical sentence, not a fragment.

You may want to use an elliptical sentence occasionally in dialogue or in informal writing. But be sure you know what you're doing. Be aware that the sentence is incomplete. And be sure that the sentence is absolutely clear.

Read the following passage. Notice especially the second and third sentences, which are elliptical. The writing is informal, and the elliptical sentences fit in.

> . . . I slammed the closet door shut and whirled around, and there was Bo Jo standing in the bedroom door. For real. Him. He was carrying the same old beat-up suitcase of his father's that he'd used to move his things into the apartment and a big cardboard cartoon. —ANN HEAD

If your elliptical sentences have the smooth, clear effect that Ann Head's have, leave them in your writing. If they don't serve a specific purpose, however, treat them as sentence fragments and rewrite them.

Your words

Paragraphs, sentences, and words—each need to be checked as you revise your first draft. You've seen how to check paragraphs and sentences. But how do you check words? First, make sure you haven't used too many. Could something be said with fewer words? Then, sure that the words you have used express your meaning accurately. Have you written exactly what you meant? Finally, make sure your words are "right" for your subject, your purpose, and your audience. And in all phases of checking your words, keep your dictionary handy.

Word choice: economy   If you've written three words where one would do, go back and cross out the unnecessary words. Be easy on your readers. There's no reason to write *loud in volume* instead of simply *loud* or *orange in color* instead of simply *orange*. And there's no reason to fill your writing with extra words like *really* and *you know what I mean* that add nothing to your readers' understanding. The following sentence, for example, is loaded with extra words:

> It was two hours later that the people who were really going to help us arrived.

That sentence needs to be cut drastically; its idea is lost in meaningless words. You might rewrite it like this:

Two hours later, help arrived.

Often, knowing the exact word will help you express your meaning clearly and directly in a minimum of space. There is no reason to write a long sentence like this:

> The shoemaker used a tool with a heavy wooden handle and a sharp metal point to go through the leather and make holes in it.

The tool described in that sentence has a name: *awl.* And *to go through and make holes in* can be said more simply and more accurately: *to pierce holes.* So you can rewrite the sentence like this:

> The shoemaker used an awl to pierce holes in the leather.

You may be afraid that taking out extra words will make your writing too short. But it's the meaning, not the length, that counts. And extra words can only add length. If you feel you must make your paper longer, develop your ideas. Expand your thoughts, not your words.

TRY IT Rewrite the following sentences to eliminate unnecessary words:

1. The first thing that happened was that the alarm clock failed to go off.
2. It was while she was practicing playing her tuba that Jan heard a strange noise.
3. The really rather unusual looking object was eight feet tall in height and nearly twelve feet around in circumference.
4. There was a loud buzzing sound coming from the room that was the kitchen.
5. A ripe tomato is usually soft feeling and bright red in color.

Word choice: accuracy The words you choose should express your meaning accurately. This means, first, that you should be sure you've written the word you had in mind. It's easy to mix up words that look or sound alike. For example, suppose you have written a sentence like this:

Emmy Noether was an imminent mathematician.

Imminent means "likely to happen soon"—which doesn't make much sense in that sentence. The word you want is *eminent*, "outstanding." As you reread your first draft, look for the words that you're not positive about. Is the spelling right? Is the meaning exact? If you're not sure, use your dictionary.

Secondly, you should check for "rubber stamp" words and expressions. That is, look for overused words like *nice, interesting*, and *lovely*. Look for euphemisms, like *memory garden* instead of *cemetery* and *underprivileged* instead of *poor*. And look for clichés, like *grin and bear it, with bated breath*, and *part and parcel*. The cure for "rubber stamp" writing is to be as specific as you can. For example, the following sentence with the overused word *bad* doesn't say much:

The stew was bad.

But it can be rewritten to describe—in specific terms—what the problem with the stew was:

The stew had too much salt, not enough meat, and a pasty gravy.

Word choice: appropriateness   Choosing the right word is not only a matter of getting the exact meaning and being as direct and concrete as possible. It's also a matter of deciding what word is right for your subject, for your purpose, for your audience, and for you.

Your subject, of course, will make an obvious difference in your choice of words. Telling about a trip to the desert, explaining the meaning of a poem, or describing the difference between electrical energy and mechanical energy—each subject will call for special words. You'll want to know and use the specialized vocabulary your subject demands.

Your purpose, too, will affect your choice of words. If you

are writing an objective medical description of the effects of polio, certain words will be appropriate.

A patient may develop paralysis of the lower limbs.

But if you're telling what happened to your best friend when she had polio, your words will be different—more personal, more emotional.

Sandy couldn't move her legs.

Your audience will also help determine which words you use. If you're writing a story for second graders, you will want to choose words they can understand.

They had a hard job.

If you're writing the same story for your classmates, you will choose more sophisticated words. But don't be stuffy.

They faced a difficult task.

Finally, you, the writer, enter into your choice of words. You'll always want to use words you're comfortable with. Your attitude toward what you're writing will help you decide what's comfortable. If you consider your writing serious and important, you'll be most comfortable with serious, important words. But if you're writing something you think is light and funny, you'll be most comfortable with light, funny words.

So subject, purpose, audience, and attitude will all affect your word choice. You have already thought about these rough things in the prewriting stage, so most of the words in your rough draft will be appropriate. That means the inappropriate words will probably stick out if you read your draft carefully. Each of the following sentences, for example, includes a noticeably inappropriate word:

On one end of the leash stood a heavy, scowling man; on the other stood a small, timid canine.

Miss Otterness is our biology educator this year.

In today's inflated economy, consumers have to spend most of their bread for necessities.

Those sentences should be rewritten so that each word is appropriate:

On one end of the leash stood a heavy, scowling man; on the other stood a small, timid **dog.**

Miss Otterness is our biology **teacher** this year.

In today's inflated economy, consumers have to spend most of their **income** for necessities.

You'll find it helpful to read your draft aloud. As you do, be aware of the impression you want your writing to make. Watch for words that might disturb that impression, and replace them with more appropriate choices.

EDITING FOR MECHANICS

You've revised your writing to make it clear, interesting, well organized. Your major concern has been the effective expression of ideas. Now, one final step needs your attention before you can safely send your work out to meet its public.

Before you make a final copy of what you have written, you need to check it for mechanics—for spelling, capitalization, punctuation, and any earlier copying mistakes. This checking involves proofreading, a special kind of reading. Proofreading means slowing down and looking carefully at the words and punctuation marks. It means reading what is there, not what you expect to be there. In doing this, you may want to read aloud. And while you are checking, keep a dictionary and this handbook nearby.

Proofreading for punctuation

Remember that some punctuation marks, like a period at the end of a statement, are required by convention or custom. Such punctuation marks are always included in careful writing. Your reader expects them and will be distracted from what you are trying to say if they are not there.

Other punctuation marks, however, offer you some choice, depending on your audience and the tone of your writing. You might, for example, enclose an interrupting element in a sentence with commas or parentheses or dashes. And sometimes you will want to add a comma just to be sure that your reader sees clearly the separation that it signals in the sentence. Think of punctuation as visual aids to your reader, signals that link, separate, enclose, or show omission. And check to be sure that you have used punctuation accurately to make your meaning as clear as possible.

Punctuation to link   If you want to link sentence structures, you have a choice of punctuation. Check to see if you have used a comma before connecting words like *and, but, for,* and *or.* If there is no connecting word, have you used a semicolon or punctuated the structures as two sentences?

> Dad washed the dishes, and we dried them.
> Dad washed the dishes; we dried them.
> Dad washed the dishes. We dried them.

If you are linking a list, a formal quotation, or an explanation to the main sentence structure, have you used a colon?

> We found the following: two paper clips, an empty match box, and a ball-point pen.

If you are providing an example or showing a sudden change in thought, have you used a dash?

> There at the top of the stairs stood the cause of all the confusion—a very frightened puppy.

If you have used compound words or phrases, do you need a hyphen to link the parts? Is it *paper-back, paperback,* or *paper back?* Remember, sometimes the placement of a compound phrase affects its punctuation—it's *a well-written report,* but *the report is well written.* You will find your dictionary helpful in these matters of hyphenation.

If you have linked words in contractions like *shouldn't,* have you used an apostrophe to indicate missing letters? Do you need an apostrophe, either alone or with an *s,* to show possession? If so, have you used it correctly to show singular or plural possession? Finally, do you need an apostrophe to link a plural *s* to a certain word, symbol, or numeral?

> We've noticed that Joe's conversation is full of *like*'s and *you know*'s.

Punctuation to separate   Check to see that end punctuation is present—periods, question marks, or exclamation points. Also, be sure that the first word of each sentence begins with a capital letter. Keep separate things separate.

Within the sentence, check the places where you might need punctuation to separate parts. If you are separating the parts in a series, have you used a comma between them?

> Sara bought nails, paint thinner, and sandpaper.

If you have an introductory element before the main sentence structure, do you need a comma? Would the sentence be confusing without it?

> As we continued playing, the game became more exciting.

And if you are dividing a word that won't fit at the end of a line, have you used a hyphen? Have you checked the dictionary to be sure where the word may be divided? Should it be *refer-ring* or *referr-ing? occup-y* or *occu-py?*

Punctuation to enclose   Words or phrases that are not part of the main sentence structure are usually set off by dashes, parentheses, or commas. And you have some choice here, especially in informal writing. For example, you might use any of these punctuation marks in a sentence like this:

> Mom always felt, and we agreed, that caring for our pets was our responsibility.
> Mom always felt (and we agreed) that caring for our pets was our responsibility.
> Mom always felt—and we agreed—that caring for our pets was our responsibility.

Usually, parentheses tend to separate the added element more completely, and dashes, more informally.

But these kinds of punctuation marks are not always interchangeable. In some situations, only one is appropriate: for reference information, you need parentheses; for explanations or additions, you need dashes; and for phrases in apposition, commas.

> In completing the second problem (page 24), be sure to indicate both possible solutions. [reference]
> Everyone expected—and everyone was right—that Rita and Nick would elope. [addition]
> "The Waltons," an award-winning TV show, describes rural family life during the 1930's. [apposition]

If you have used nonrestrictive modifiers, are they set off by commas? Remember, nonrestrictive words or phrases provide added information but are not essential to the meaning of the main sentence structure. Notice the difference in punctuation in the following sentences. The second sentence contains a restrictive modifier, which is not set off by commas.

> Bicycles, which are becoming more and more numerous, are creating a traffic problem.
> Bicycles which have no license plates will be ticketed.

Watch for transitional words and phrases like *therefore, of course,* and *nevertheless* within the main sentence structure. These are normally set off by commas.

If you are quoting someone's exact words, be sure you have enclosed these words in quotation marks. But if you are reporting someone's words indirectly, remember that no quotation marks are needed.

> Sally said, "I'll drive."
> Sally said that she would drive.

Check also to be sure that other marks of punctuation used with quotation marks are in their proper places.

> "Now," she suggested, "let's eat lunch."
> "Are you ready?" the children called.
> Did you say, "I'm not going"?
> Max insisted, "I didn't do it"; we believed him.

If there is quoted material inside quoted material, have you used single quotation marks around the inner quotation?

> "I don't see," Bill complained, "why I can't use 'To Build a Fire' for my book report."

Have you added to a quotation some words that are not part of the quotation? Then, be sure the added words are set off with brackets.

> "My long-range plans [about the project] are not yet complete," the mayor added.

Punctuation to show omission   If you have left out words to avoid repeating them, have you shown the omission by using a comma?

> My brother enjoys soccer; my sister enjoys baseball.
> My brother enjoys soccer; my sister, baseball.

And if you have left out words within a quotation, be sure you show the omission by using points of ellipsis.

> Martha replied, "The other reason . . . is a secret."

Open and close styles   There are two general styles of punctuation. The open style uses the minimum of punctuation necessary for clarity and is often found in informal writing. The close style (*close* rhymes with *gross*) tends to use more punctuation—especially commas, colons, parentheses—and is more often found in formal writing.

The following pairs of sentences illustrate some of the differences between these two styles of punctuation. In each pair, a sentence representing the open style is followed by one representing the close style.

> Sandy ordered chop suey, fried rice and egg rolls.
> Sandy ordered chop suey, fried rice, and egg rolls.
>
> At first we were pleased at the invitation.
> At first, we were pleased at the invitation.
>
> You may of course decide not to go.
> You may, of course, decide not to go.
>
> We found an unfortunate situation—half the group had missed the last train.
> We found an unfortunate situation: half the group had missed the last train.

Using an open style doesn't mean you can omit punctuation where it is needed to prevent confusion. Without the comma, the following sentence might cause readers to stumble:

> Dad sat on the sofa with Mom, and Diane stretched out
> on the floor by the TV.

Most modern writers use a style that is neither fully open nor fully close, but somewhere in between. You will want to choose a style that seems appropriate to your writing and your audience and that is, of course, acceptable to your teacher. But whichever way you decide to punctuate, you should try to be consistent within a composition.

Proofreading for spelling and copying errors

You will find it helpful to read your paper aloud as you proofread for spelling and copying errors. If you've written *do* instead of *to,* the word will "look" right, but it won't "sound" right. Listening as well as looking will help you find this kind of copying mistake.

Check for letters or words that have been transposed, like *clibm* for *climb* or *see to* for *to see.* And watch for words with syllables left out, like *traing* for *training.* Check also that words have not been repeated or omitted because of the break at the end of a line. Make sure there are no larger omissions—sometimes a sentence or a paragraph will be lost in copying from a rough draft.

When you check words for spelling, pay attention to capitalization at the beginning of sentences, including sentences in direct quotation. Have you used proper nouns and titles that should be capitalized?

If a word is not one you use often or if you think it looks strange, take time to check the spelling in the dictionary. Be on the lookout for endings like *–ible* and *–able, –ence* and *–ance* or doubled consonants before endings, as in *submitted, rebelled,* and *occurring.*

Do you need to underscore or use quotation marks around certain titles, words, or letters?

> In Sports Illustrated Al read the article on lacrosse and
> the one on women gymnasts, "Mixing Satin and Steel."
> Does Mississippi have four i's?

TRY IT   Here is part of an essay on transportation in Alaska. Edit these paragraphs for mechanics, including spelling, punctuation, hyphenation, and copying mistakes.

```
The Alaska Railroad links four cities. Exten-
ding from Fairbanks in the center of the State
south to Anchorage, whittier and Seward on the
the coast. But there is no passanger service on this
railroad, it is used for frieght only.
    The only link to major road systems outside the
State is the Alaska Highway, build during world
war II as a militery supply route. Parts of the
road are not paved and the summer months are the
best for travelling on it
    In addition air travel is widely used because
the lack of roads. Most small towns have an air-
field to accomodate planes carrying passengers
supplys, and messages.
```

Conventions of manuscript form

When you have checked your paper for content and mechanics and have made needed changes, you are ready to prepare a final copy. You should ask your teacher for specific instructions, such as using a title page or including the name of the course. But here are some general rules—conventions of manuscript form—for you to follow:

Type your paper or write it neatly in ink.

Use standard-size paper, 8½ x 11 inches.

Use only one side of a sheet of paper; if you type your paper, double-space it.

Leave margins of at least one inch at all four edges.

Number each page.

Include your name, the date, and the title of the paper.

Of course, you will need to check the final copy. Look for the kinds of mistakes discussed throughout this section, especially for any that may have occurred during the final copying process. Your aim is to have a neat paper that is easy to read. In this way the ideas you have put into words will reach your reader clearly and effectively.

The Research Paper

For many of your courses, you'll have to write a research paper. This means you'll have to locate information, record it, and adapt it to fit your special purpose. The research paper, which may run three to six typewritten pages, is also called a term paper, a library paper, and a reference paper. It is the kind of paper that explains something—the causes of air pollution, the different kinds of rock music, the formation of hurricanes. At times a research paper may persuade, but its overriding purpose is to inform in clear, impersonal, concise language.

USING THE LIBRARY

In collecting information for your research paper, you will have to consult a number of sources. Most of these you'll find in the library. Learning to use the library—knowing where and how to look things up—is probably the biggest benefit you'll gain from writing such a paper.

Even before going to the library, you'll probably have a general idea of what to write about. Perhaps your teacher has suggested a subject. The first thing you need to do is find out where material on your subject is located in the library.

The card catalog

The card catalog tells what books the library owns and where they are. It consists of cabinets containing drawers of cards arranged alphabetically. There is at least one card for each book in the library. Most books have three—an author card, a title card, and a subject card. In other words, you have three ways to find a particular book in the card catalog: by author, by title, and by subject.

At this stage in your research, you probably aren't familiar with the authors or titles of books on your subject. So you'll have to begin with your subject. Simply look it up in the card catalog. If you're going to write a paper on skydiving, look under that subject. What you'll probably find in a drawer of S-cards is a divider card marked "Skydiving." Behind that card will be all the books the library has on that subject, arranged alphabetically according to the last name of the authors. You may also find another card marked "Skydiving, *see also* Parachuting." This card directs you to another place in the catalog where you will find more cards relating to your subject.

Here is a subject card. The labels in color explain the different kinds of information you'll find on such a card.

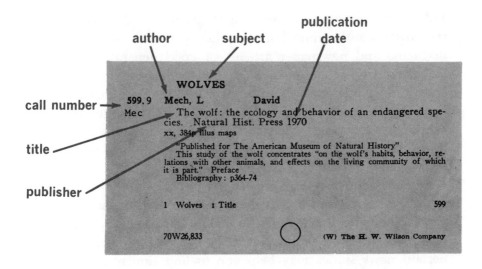

Notice the *call number*, the number listed on the upper left-hand corner of the card. This number will enable you or the librarian to find the book on the shelves.

Reference materials

Not all materials in the library can be checked out. Many books and most magazines must be used in the library. They are for reference only and usually carry the letter *R* before the call number. If you don't know where the reference books are kept in your library, ask the librarian.

General reference books. A good place to get an overall view of your topic is in an encyclopedia. There are encyclopedias with many volumes, like the *World Book Encyclopedia* and the *Encyclopaedia Britannica.* Other encyclopedias consist of a single volume, like the *Columbia Encyclopedia.* There are also encyclopedias devoted entirely to specific subjects, such as literature, art, music, and social sciences.

An almanac is a one-volume reference book, published yearly, that contains up-to-date information on a number of subjects. *The World Almanac and Book of Facts,* for example, gives facts about subjects like sports, labor, weather, and government.

Indexes to magazine and newspaper articles. If your topic requires up-to-the-minute information, you will want to use magazine and newspaper articles. A good general index to magazine articles is the *Readers' Guide to Periodical Literature.* This guide lists articles in over two hundred magazines by author, title, and subject. After each entry is a series of abbreviations that tells when and where the article was published. Along with the card catalog, this guide will be your most valuable resource.

A good index to newspaper articles is *The New York Times Index,* which, of course, lists the articles printed in that newspaper. The index lists the articles mainly by subject, giving the date of each article. Using this index to find the dates of important news stories may help you to find similar stories in other newspapers.

NARROWING YOUR SUBJECT

More often than not, the subject you begin with will be too broad to handle in a short paper. Suppose, for example, your subject is "endangered animal species." To treat this subject adequately, you would need to write volumes, not pages. So you have to narrow the subject to a size you can handle. How do you do this?

Your first step might be to go to the card catalog. Look up

"endangered species" there. In some libraries you might find a single card which reads: "Endangered Species, *see* Rare Animals." Look through the cards you find there, pick a book that you think might be helpful, and check it out. You don't have to read the entire book, but thumb through it to get an idea of the scope of your subject. You might find that there are many endangered species—the tiger, the gorilla, the buffalo, the crocodile, the wolf. It would make sense in writing your paper to concentrate on one of those animals rather than try to write about all of them. You might write about the wolf simply because it interests you—you've heard and read stories about wolves. So you have found a narrow focus within a general subject; "endangered species" has become "the wolf."

PREPARING A WORKING BIBLIOGRAPHY

Once you've narrowed your subject, you're ready to prepare a working bibliography—a list of books and articles containing information about your subject. The place to begin is the card catalog. If, for example, you're going to report on the wolf, look up "Wolves." Thumb through the cards you find there and list on a sheet of paper any books you think might prove helpful. Be sure to number each book. Here's an illustration of the kind of information you should write down for each book. The last item is the book's call number.

> 3. Jerome Hellmuth, *A Wolf in the Family,*
> New York, The New American Library, 1964.
> 599 h.

Before you leave the card catalog, check the cards under such related subjects as "Animals," "Wildlife," "Endangered Species," and "Rare Animals." If you are in doubt about a particular book, list it anyway. It's better to have too many than too few books in your working bibliography.

Next, find out what encyclopedias the library has. Look up your subject in each and list and number each article in your bibliography. Here's what you should put down for such an article:

4. William O. Pruitt, Jr., "Wolf," *The World Book Encyclopedia*, 1974, volume 21, pages 312-13.

In some encyclopedias, you may have to consult another volume to determine the author's name.

You will also wish to consult the indexes to magazine and newspaper articles, especially the *Readers' Guide to Periodical Literature*. First, check to see what magazines the library has. (Every library displays a list of magazines it keeps on file.) Then, check through the *Readers' Guide* for your subject. List useful articles from the magazines the library has. Here's the information you put down for a magazine article:

5. L. D. Mech, "That Valuable Villain, the Wolf," *National Wildlife*, volume 6, Feb, 1968, pages 2-7.

It's important to number each listing in your bibliography. Later, when you take notes, you can use the numbers to identify the sources. This saves having to write out the author and title for each note you take.

TAKING NOTES

When you've completed a working bibliography, you'll be ready to begin reading and note-taking. Whether it's a book or an article, you'll save time if you go directly to those parts that are about your subject. If you are reading a book, use the table of contents and the index to locate information. Perhaps only one or two chapters really bear on your subject. If it's an article, skim it rapidly to see what it contains. Then, give it a second, slower reading and take notes.

Keeping track of your notes is fairly easy if you use cards— either 3 x 5 or 4 x 6 inches. Use a separate card for each idea or group of facts that relates to a single idea. Here's a typical note card:

> *Cruelty of Wolves* ③
>
> *Even museums of natural history portray the wolf as "a slinking ruthless killer, like a popular Hollywood villain." page 15*

At the top of the card is a subject label. This tells briefly what the note is about. Subject labels help to organize your notes. Later, they will help in preparing an outline.

Next to the subject label is a number that corresponds to the number of a particular source listed in your working bibliography. Using the number from the bibliography saves you from having to write out again the author, title, and other information about the source.

Most of the card is devoted to the note itself. And this will usually be in the form of a summary. If you include a writer's exact words, even just a phrase, be sure to put them in quotation marks. Then, if you use the quotation in your research paper, you can give the author proper credit.

Finally, there is the number identifying the page from which the information has been taken.

PLANNING THE PAPER

Once you start reading and taking notes, you'll be able to see your subject more clearly. A general plan for the paper will begin to take shape in your mind. Putting this plan in the form of an outline will help you to organize your thinking.

As you prepare your outline, you may discover that you've strayed fairly far from your original intention. Suppose, for example, you began with the idea of writing about wolves as an endangered species. But in researching your subject, you hit upon a new idea. You found that there is a big difference between the wolf of legend and the wolf of reality. This difference becomes the new topic of your paper.

Once you've found a subject you think you can handle, your next step is to frame a statement of intent—a single-sentence description of how you mean to handle the central idea of your paper. Your statement might read like this:

    I will describe two myths about wolves and then
    show why these myths are false.

This statement will not appear in your paper. It's a guide. Knowing exactly what your paper will be about will keep you from including unnecessary information. It will also help you to find logical divisions for your material. For example, the statement above strongly suggests this division: two myths and two realities about wolves. So once you've written your statement of intent, you're ready to use it to make a topic outline like this one:

    The Wolf: Two Myths and Two Realities

    I. Wolves versus people
        A. The popular belief about wolves
            1. Forming packs to attack people
            2. Making wilderness unsafe
        B. The scientific studies of wolves
            1. Afraid of people
            2. Gentle under most circumstances

II. Wolves versus the environment
    A. The popular belief about wolves
       1. Dangerous to domestic animals
       2. Destructive to valuable wild animals
    B. The scientific studies of wolves
       1. Killing mostly old or sick animals
          a. Prevents overcrowding
          b. Prevents famine due to overcrowding
       2. Keeping down populations of rodents and
          pests

In a topic outline such as this, the items are expressed in words and phrases rather than in complete sentences. Note the form of the outline—the indentions, the capitalization, the numerals and letters of the headings. Note also that each division in this outline has at least two parts. If there's a *I.*, then there's a *II.* If there's an *A.*, then there's a *B.* What's more, parallel parts of the outline are expressed in parallel ways— for example, "I. Wolves versus people" and "II. Wolves versus the environment." When you put together your working outline, don't worry too much about putting the ideas in parallel form. Your primary aim is to organize your material logically.

Another type of outline you may wish to use is a sentence outline, one in which each item is expressed in a complete sentence. Compare the first part of the topic outline given earlier with this part of a sentence outline. Note that since each item is a sentence, it is followed by end punctuation.

The Wolf: Two Myths and Two Realities

I. Are wolves really dangerous to people?
   A. Popular belief holds that wolves will attack
      and kill people without reason.
      1. Wolves gather together in packs to hunt
         people down.
      2. Wolves perform no useful function but only
         make the wilderness unsafe.
   B. Scientific studies show that wolves go to
      great lengths to avoid people.
      1. Wolves are instinctively afraid of people.
      2. Wolves often behave gently even when sur-
         prised by people.

WRITING A FIRST DRAFT

Basically, you should assume that the readers of your research paper are not specialists in the subject you are reporting on. This means that you must explain and clarify technical terms and difficult concepts for them.

You should also assume that your audience is more interested in the subject of your report than in your opinions about it. Since you are not dealing in personal experiences, the tone of your writing will be more formal and objective than usual, but not stuffy or dull.

In writing your first draft, don't worry too much about style or mechanics. The important thing is to get your ideas in a logical sequence and to find the places in your paper where the information you've collected best fits in. As you write, you may discover new slants on your subject, new ways to organize your material and express your ideas. Writing is nearly always a process of discovery. So, be flexible. If you find a better way to say something, don't worry about following your original outline. Instead, change the outline.

The first draft is the place to give credit to the sources you have used. At this stage you don't need to put your credits in the form of footnotes. Simply write the identifying number from your working bibliography and the page number of the source in parentheses after the information you are using. Remember, you should credit not only a person's exact words but also his ideas and facts.

In writing a first draft, don't spend too much time on the introductory paragraph. If it doesn't come easily, go on to the body of the paper. Very likely, you'll write a better introduction after you know exactly what you'll say in the paper. In your introductory paragraph, avoid a long, elaborate statement about what your paper will accomplish. Instead, you might gain your reader's interest by starting with a question like this:

Is the wolf really a vicious, bloodthirsty killer?

Or you might start with a quotation like this:

"Beginning with the story of Little Red Riding Hood, children are taught to believe nothing good about the wolf." (9) *page* 37)

Or you might start with a quotation from a naturalist who claims that many legends about wolves are false.

In writing the body of your paper, follow your outline. First, sort your notes by their subject labels into stacks that correspond to the headings of your outline. Then collect the notes for the first heading on your outline and begin writing. But remember, while the research paper is a report on what you found out about a certain subject, it is more than a string of quotations and facts copied from note cards. The note cards record other people's words and ideas. But how you organize and present this information depends on your own judgment and creativity. Two people using the same set of note cards will write two very different papers.

In writing your concluding paragraph, you might use a summary, a quotation, or even a question. If you summarize your main points, do so briefly and concisely. Long, detailed summaries are awkward and unnecessary.

PREPARING THE FINAL DRAFT

There's much "fine tuning" to be done between the first draft and the final version of your research paper. Words and phrases will have to be scratched out and new and better ones added. Some paragraphs will have to be reordered, others rewritten, and still others discarded. Your aim is to prepare a final draft that is as nearly perfect as you can make it—right down to the spelling and punctuation. For help in revising your first draft, see pages 190–221 of this text.

Mechanics

Your final draft should be typed or written in ink on one side only of standard-sized, unlined paper. Leave margins of 1 to 1½ inches at the top, bottom, and sides. If you type your paper, double-space everything except quotations that run longer than three lines. Set these off from the body of the paper by indenting from both margins, by single-spacing, and by omitting quotation marks.

Begin numbering your paper on page two. End on the page on which the bibliography appears.

When you've finished the final draft of your research paper, you will have four main sections:

1. The title page, on which appears the title of the paper, the name of the course, the teacher's name, your name, and the date due

2. The final outline headed by the title of your paper

3. The body of the paper

4. The final bibliography headed by the word *Bibliography*

Your paper could have more sections. For example, you might place all your footnotes together on a single page. This fifth section would be inserted after the body of the paper. Also, if you wish to include maps or pictures, you could have a special appendix after the final bibliography.

Footnotes

An important part of preparing the final draft involves giving formal credit to the sources from which you drew your facts, ideas, and quotations. This credit is usually given in a footnote. For the sake of illustration, suppose that these sentences appeared in your first draft:

> To survive, a wolf needs about forty miles of wilderness in which to roam. Today, however, "a wolf is fortunate to have 10 square miles of uninterrupted forest." (6) page 5)

In your final version, these sentences might look like this:

To survive, a wolf needs about forty miles of wilder-

ness in which to roam. Today, however, "a wolf is for-

tunate to have 10 square miles of uninterrupted

forest."[8]

The number at the end of the sentence refers to a footnote with the same number at the bottom of the page:

[8] Timothy Harpen, "Northerners Howling—For and Against Wolves," Chicago Tribune, September 29, 1974, sec. 1, p. 5.

This footnote tells the reader the source of the quotation you used. The number 8 means that it is the eighth footnote in your paper. (Footnotes are numbered consecutively.)

Strictly speaking, a footnote should appear at the bottom of a page. In practice, however, footnotes are often grouped together on a separate page at the end of the paper. This is the easiest way to handle them.

The form of a footnote depends upon the source being credited. You have just seen the form for crediting a signed newspaper article. Here is the form for crediting a book:

[1] Lois Crisler, Arctic Wild, p. 97.

This is the form for an unsigned magazine article:

[2] "Archaic Bounty System," National Parks Magazine, February, 1966, p. 21.

For a signed magazine article, this is the form:

[3] L. D. Mech, "That Valuable Villain, the Wolf," National Wildlife, February, 1968, p. 2.

This is the form for an unsigned encyclopedia article:

[4] "Wolf," <u>Encyclopaedia</u> <u>Britannica,</u> Vol. 23, p. 696.

This is the form for a signed encyclopedia article:

[5] William O. Pruitt, Jr., "Wolf," <u>The</u> <u>World</u> <u>Book</u> <u>Encyclopedia,</u> Vol. 21, p. 312.

You may find that you have to refer to the same source more than once. But this does not mean that you have to repeat the entire footnote. If the second reference occurs right after the first reference, simply use *Ibid.* This is an abbreviation of the Latin *ibidem* and means "in the same place."

[1] Lois Crisler, <u>Arctic</u> <u>Wild,</u> p. 97.
[2] <u>Ibid.,</u> p. 98.

If the second reference is also to the same page as the first reference, then no page number is needed. If the second reference does not occur directly after the first one, you must use this form instead of *Ibid.*:

[7] Crisler, p. 106.

Final bibliography

Your working bibliography, with unused references crossed out, will form the base for the final bibliography that you submit with your research paper. The entries in your final bibliography—both books and articles—should be arranged alphabetically according to the author's last name. If an author is unknown, begin with the first important word in the title.

The form for typical bibliographical entries is shown in the following examples. Here is the form for a book with one author:

Crisler, Lois, <u>Arctic</u> <u>Wild,</u> New York, Harper and Row, 1958.

This is the form for a book by two or more authors:

Milne, Lorus J., and Margery Milne, <u>The</u> <u>Balance</u> <u>of</u> <u>Nature,</u> New York, Alfred A. Knopf, 1960.

This is the form for a book compiled by an editor:

Caras, Roger, ed., <u>Vanishing</u> <u>Wildlife,</u> Richmond, Westover Publishing Company, 1970.

This is the form for an unsigned magazine article:

"Archaic Bounty System," <u>National</u> <u>Parks</u> <u>Magazine,</u> Vol. 40, February, 1966, p. 21.

For a signed magazine article, this is the form:

Mech, L. D., "That Valuable Villain, the Wolf," <u>National</u> <u>Wildlife,</u> Vol. 6, February, 1968, pp. 2-7.

This is the form for an unsigned encyclopedia article:

"Wolf," <u>Encyclopaedia</u> <u>Britannica,</u> 1958 edition, Vol. 23, pp. 695-696.

This is the form for a signed encyclopedia article:

Pruitt, William O., Jr., "Wolf," <u>The</u> <u>World</u> <u>Book</u> <u>Encyclopedia,</u> 1974 edition, Vol. 21, pp. 312-313.

When two or more works by the same author are given, you should use the following form:

Crisler, Lois, <u>Arctic</u> <u>Wild,</u> New York, Harper and Row, 1958.

------, <u>Captive</u> <u>Wild,</u> New York, Harper and Row, 1968.

Practice

ambiguity

Revise each of the following ambiguous sentences so that it has a single, clear meaning.

1. Vanessa reminded her sister that she had an appointment.
2. Lydia and Cecilia were late because they couldn't find her keys.
3. Jim said yesterday he had called you.
4. Bernie helps his mother more than his father.
5. I thought during the game the pitcher was ill.
6. When the president of the company came into Mr. Mancilla's office, he was very surprised.
7. They decided in Reno they would call their parents.
8. Nikki said at the conference Jan was a good leader.
9. Cats get along better with dogs than rabbits.
10. Nora said last night nothing unusual happened.
11. Steve said on Tuesday we would meet after school.
12. The Phoenicians traded with the Greeks more than the Egyptians.
13. After you have taken all the suitcases out of the closets, clean them carefully.
14. Aunt Harriet gave me a nicer present than Mom.
15. When Jesse and Karl came on stage, he was wearing a long orange cape.
16. Angie invites Patty more frequently than Becky.
17. Dad and Dick just had a long discussion, and he looks upset.
18. Ms. Brodski told Rhoda her story would be published.
19. Did you realize during the test some people were cheating?
20. I enjoy being with Paul more than Jeff.

apostrophe

Rewrite each construction in parentheses, adding an apostrophe or an apostrophe and *s* to indicate either a possessive, a plural, or a contraction.

1. (Everyone) morale improved after the new rules went into effect.
2. There were (*oh*) and (*ah*) from the children when the puppet show began.
3. (Im) afraid (youre) not going to believe this.
4. How many (*g*) are there in *exaggerate?*
5. (Arent) they ready yet?
6. No, they (havent) even had lunch.

7. The (Alveses) dog Dina is having puppies.
8. All night long the (ship) crew worked on the engine.
9. (Shouldnt) we taste the spaghetti before we serve it?
10. Next week the (girls) tennis team will travel to Springfield.
11. There are four (*sad*) in this paragraph; can you find some synonyms?
12. The (passengers) luggage will arrive on the next plane.
13. When Mr. Russo writes fast, his (*7*) look like (*1*).
14. (Werent) you planning to play softball today?
15. The outcome of the debate is (anyone) guess.
16. Leroy said (theyd) call us at noon.
17. Change each of the (+) and (−) to *plus* or *minus* when you retype your report.
18. Naomi just found (somebody) bicycle lock outside the gym.
19. Is the new wing of the library just for (children) books?
20. The (factories) joint pollution control program goes into effect next month.

capitalization

Rewrite each of the following sentences, using capital letters wherever needed.

1. next summer we hope to travel to the black hills, in south dakota and eastern wyoming.
2. my advisor doesn't think i should take biology 1 and chemistry 1 at the same time.
3. the environmental protection agency was established by the president in 1970.
4. ten-year-old tatum o'neill won an academy award for her role in *paper moon*.
5. uncle henry and aunt ruth usually drive to kentucky over the memorial day weekend.
6. in 1889 jane addams and ellen starr founded hull house to help immigrants settling in chicago.
7. both senator fong and congresswoman mink are from hawaii.
8. last august the national park service stopped charging fees for camping.
9. dad reads *sports illustrated* every week; so does mom.
10. one of the first textile mills in this country, built by samuel slater in 1793, is still standing in pawtucket, rhode island.
11. did you know that *julie of the wolves* was about alaska?
12. continue west until you reach the civic auditorium, at the intersection of jackson and taylor streets.

13. a 50-foot statue of chief black hawk overlooks the mississippi river near oregon, illinois.
14. in canada both french and english are official languages.
15. the 630-foot gateway arch in saint louis is the nation's tallest monument.
16. which do you like better, *all in the family* or *the waltons*?
17. over thirty thousand tennis fans attended the billie jean king-bobby riggs match in the houston astrodome in september.
18. has grandfather lived in the south ever since world war II?
19. the junior class at springfield high school is raising money for a trip to washington, d.c., in march.
20. in chiapas, mexico, we saw murals painted by maya indians in the eighth century.

collective nouns

Choose the verb form or pronoun that agrees with the collective noun in each of the following sentences. Assume that each collective noun refers to a single unit, not to its parts.

1. When will the committee hold (its, their) next meeting?
2. The band (is, are) traveling by bus to the tournament.
3. After four hours, the jury reached (its, their) decision.
4. A crowd of spectators (has, have) already gathered at the scene of the fire.
5. When did the army relax (its, their) ruling about long hair?
6. The audience always (seems, seem) to enjoy the informal atmosphere of the performance.
7. I understand that the club will vote on (its, their) new regulations tomorrow.
8. By the time we got to our seats, the orchestra (was, were) already warming up.
9. The public often (feels, feel) helpless about affecting government policy.
10. In the summer a dance troupe (gives, give) free performances in the city parks.
11. The panel (has, have) agreed to postpone the television debate until after the game.
12. The class voted to present (its, their) gift at the banquet.
13. A group of parents (is, are) still waiting to talk with the school board.
14. How long did the crew train for (its, their) flight?
15. When a hive becomes overcrowded, a bee swarm (leaves, leave) to form a new colony.

16. The team announced (its, their) decision not to play.
17. The night shift (has, have) drawn up a list of suggestions.
18. On Assateague Island, in Virginia, a herd of wild ponies still (roams, roam) freely.
19. The community (was, were) determined to preserve the public park along the river.
20. When (is, are) the legislature going to vote on that issue?

comma

Rewrite the following sentences, adding commas wherever they are needed.

1. The fare is $13.45 and the trip takes three and a half hours.
2. A group of noisy angry demonstrators filled the street.
3. Lucy Molly Roger and Aaron flew to Salt Lake City Utah.
4. No the reports aren't ready yet.
5. Will you be back before noon Toni?
6. If everyone's ready let's go.
7. The sign said "Please keep off the grass."
8. Nick ordered a bowl of vegetable soup a large salad and a glass of milk.
9. Darcy selected a large heavy box; Ted a small light one.
10. Jesse Jackson who was born in Greenville South Carolina is the director of PUSH.
11. When the phone finally rang everyone jumped.
12. That unfortunately is not the end of the story.
13. The winners have been announced but they have not received their trophies yet.
14. The papers are due on Friday March 27.
15. In fact her idea makes a lot of sense.
16. My mother who had been in New York came home last night.
17. The cold hard biscuits were particularly unappetizing.
18. Your decision will I am sure be approved.
19. Jeannie received the first prize; Lonny the second.
20. "Why" wondered Tina "is everything so complicated?"

compound subject

Choose the singular or the plural verb form to agree with the subject in each of the following sentences.

1. Neither the novel nor the movie (has, have) a happy ending.
2. Unfortunately, the history test and the track meet (is, are) on the same day.

3. Neither the blue jacket nor the plaid one (matches, match) the slacks.
4. A safety pin or some Scotch tape (is, are) strong enough.
5. Neither my grandparents nor my uncle (was, were) expecting us.
6. The geologist explained that both wind and water (is, are) wearing away the coastline.
7. Neither this solution nor that one (makes, make) sense to me.
8. Either lemon juice or melted butter (is, are) used to flavor fish.
9. Neither the subway nor the buses (was, were) running.
10. Either the coach or the manager (presents, present) the awards.
11. Tennis and soccer (has, have) always been my favorite sports.
12. Either the twins or their sister (feeds, feed) the animals.
13. The free-style race and the 50-meter race (was, were) the most exciting.
14. Either Betsy or Jack (is, are) going to baby-sit tonight.
15. Beef fat or seeds (makes, make) a good meal for birds.
16. Neither the train nor the bus (stops, stop) at Centerville.
17. Usually, either Diane or Steve (runs, run) the projector.
18. Too much water or too much sunlight (damages, damage) these plants.
19. Either ice cream or a hot shower (is, are) refreshing.
20. Neither Mom nor Dad (knows, know) about my award yet.

dangling modifier

Revise the following sentences to eliminate dangling modifiers.

1. Sitting in the last row, the stage was hardly visible.
2. After reading the book, a brief report should be prepared.
3. Looking for an exciting city to visit, New York seemed a natural choice.
4. Before taking a vote, the various options were discussed.
5. After running half a mile, his strength gave out.
6. While waiting for the bell to ring, the hands of the clock seem to stand still.
7. After swimming all morning, the hamburgers smelled good.
8. Running across the goal line, the ball slipped from Gene's hands.
9. While shopping downtown, Dwayne's wallet was stolen.
10. Looking down from the office window, the accident was witnessed by two people.
11. While rehearsing my song, our dog began to howl.

12. By practicing every day, her accuracy improved.
13. Huffing and puffing, the top of the stairs was finally reached.
14. Stuck between the back of the sofa and the wall, Barbara found the overdue library book.
15. Pacing back and forth in the cage, we watched the tiger.
16. While waiting in line for our tickets, the movie started.
17. Barking and wagging its tail, Tessa was greeted by the dog.
18. After giving a piece of the candy to everyone else, there was none left for me.
19. Thick, white, and puffy, Marvin watched the clouds.
20. Unable to telephone my grandmother, she received a long letter instead.

doesn't and don't

Choose either *doesn't* or *don't* to complete each of the following sentences.

1. __ this signature look authentic?
2. Brenda and Nina __ have parts in the play.
3. You __ have to wash the dishes right now.
4. The engine still __ run very smoothly.
5. I __ know how to play tennis.
6. This recording sounds better, __ it?
7. Randy still __ understand why the meeting was canceled.
8. It __ seem fair that only the boys get to play.
9. __ they have any new ideas?
10. That question __ seem important anymore.
11. These melons taste sweeter than the others, __ they?
12. __ you want to work on the committee?
13. That man __ look at all like Mr. Timmons.
14. Jenny said that she __ enjoy most concerts.
15. The opposing candidates __ seem to disagree about anything.
16. __ these two sides have to be equal in length?
17. My father usually cooks dinner, because my mother __ like to.
18. It __ matter if you are a few minutes late.
19. Most teachers __ expect you to be quiet all the time.
20. __ your sister have a bike?

double negative

Choose the appropriate word or words in parentheses to complete each of the following sentences.

1. Theresa (had, hadn't) never been to Arizona before.

2. We have hardly (no, any) milk left.
3. During the test there (should, shouldn't) be no interruptions.
4. Haven't you (ever, never) read *Madeline's Rescue?*
5. Matty doesn't like (none, any) of the choices.
6. There didn't seem to be (no, any) point in continuing.
7. Wasn't the spy Belle Boyd (never, ever) captured?
8. That store didn't have (any, no) strawberries.
9. Hasn't the Kentucky Derby ever been held (no place, any-place) else?
10. There were scarcely (any, no) cookies in the canister.
11. Max insists that he didn't have (anything, nothing) to do with it.
12. Japan couldn't be (a, no) member of the O.A.S.
13. Those beavers hardly (never, ever) rest.
14. Couldn't Jason find (nobody, anybody) to help him?
15. The audience (couldn't, could) hardly hear the speaker.
16. Roxanne felt she (had, hadn't) no alternative.
17. Didn't Mr. Rosas make (no, any) corrections?
18. There (is, isn't) scarcely enough material.
19. The police (had, hadn't) no reason to suspect him.
20. I (can, can't) hardly afford to miss class again today.

everyone, anything, and somebody

Choose the form of the pronoun that is appropriate to formal speaking and writing.

1. Each must do (her, their) share of the work.
2. Sombody was practicing (his, their) tuba at 6 A.M.
3. Did you give each (his, their) assignment?
4. Everyone should bring (his, their) lunch on Wednesday.
5. Did somebody bring (his, their) road map?
6. Everyone should fasten (his, their) seat belt.
7. Each must do (her, their) part to make this program succeed.
8. Everyone will do (his, their) best.
9. Each sang (her, their) favorite song.
10. Everyone should write (her, their) congressional representa-tive and give (her, their) opinion on this matter.
11. Sometimes nothing goes the way (it, they) should.
12. Has everyone learned (his, their) part in the play?
13. Each is going to give (her, their) report today.
14. Somebody should bring (his, their) guitar.
15. I asked each to give (his, their) opinion about the proposal.
16. Somebody has left (her, their) coat in the hallway.

17. Did you tell each to bring (her, their) notebook?
18. Somebody was singing at the top of (her, their) voice.
19. Has everyone finished (his, their) work on the project?
20. Did you ask everyone to bring (her, their) records?

good and well

A. Choose the word in parentheses that correctly completes each sentence.

1. The committee did its work (good, well).
2. Your children behave (good, well).
3. The movie received (good, well) reviews in the newspapers.
4. I don't feel (good, well) about my performance today.
5. My cactus is not doing (good, well) in this humidity.
6. She stayed home because she didn't feel (good, well).
7. It seems (good, well) to be back in school.
8. That filly runs (good, well) on a muddy track.
9. Ramona followed her shot and saw that it was (good, well).
10. Your temperature indicates that you are not (good, well).
11. My garden should grow (good, well) this summer.
12. If your engine is (good, well) tuned, your operating expenses will decrease.
13. Frank doesn't feel (good, well): his eyes are red; his cheeks are flushed.
14. The basic design is very (good, well).

B. Write the sentences below, filling in each blank space with *good* or *well*.

1. Stay in bed until you're feeling better; you should feel __ within ten days.
2. That's a __ book; it's one of the best I've read.
3. The team is playing better; in fact, they're playing __.
4. This is not just __ fudge—it's the best.
5. The second game was __ —a lot better than the first one.
6. The choir sings best before a large audience; it often doesn't sing __ when the audience is small.

his, her, and their

Choose the form of the pronoun that is appropriate to formal speaking and writing.

1. Each student who is going must bring (his, their) lunch.
2. Any professor can finish (her, their) lecture in time.

3. Each ecologist gave (his, their) opinion about the proposal.
4. Each student gave (his, their) report.
5. Every finalist read (her, their) poem to the English Club.
6. Each driver stopped (his, their) car at the red light.
7. None of the debaters has studied (his, their) notes.
8. No camper pitched (her, their) tent near the stream.
9. Each singer sang (her, their) part with enthusiasm.
10. Every actor must memorize (his, their) lines carefully.
11. Each student brought (her, their) notebook to class.
12. None of the chemists has finished (his, their) experiment.
13. Every player did (her, their) best to win.
14. Each musician must learn (his, their) part by next Tuesday.
15. No club member has paid (her, their) dues.
16. Every worker must follow (her, their) schedule.
17. Each member must cast (her, their) ballot by six o'clock.
18. None of them has remembered to bring (his, their) film.
19. Each committee member must make (her, their) report.
20. Each witness gave (his, their) version of what happened.

hyphen

A. Rewrite each of the following words, inserting a hyphen to indicate where each word could be divided at the end of a line. Use your dictionary.

1. climate	6. honor	11. bankrupt
2. number	7. fatal	12. ethics
3. forward	8. surface	13. dictate
4. fraction	9. neutral	14. revise
5. pattern	10. foreign	15. persist

B. Rewrite each word group in italics, adding hyphens where appropriate. Not all the italicized word groups require hyphens.

1. The runner ran a *four minute* mile.
2. The *newly hatched* chickens followed their mother.
3. The politician made some *spur of the moment* remarks.
4. The *closely kept* secret was finally revealed.
5. The professor gave a *forty minute* lecture.

C. Decide whether the following words should be joined by a hyphen, written as one word, or written as two or more separate words. Use your dictionary.

book + store   bookstore
twenty + two   twenty-two

1. self + reliance
2. vice + president
3. master + piece
4. dime + store
5. post + Depression
6. text + book
7. grand + uncle
8. thirty + seven
9. sister + in + law
10. blue + print
11. tape + deck
12. high + octane
13. sweet + and + sour
14. earth + quake
15. news + magazine
16. surf + board
17. scale + down
18. long + jump
19. ski + pole
20. new + math

its and it's

Choose the correct form from the choices given in parentheses.

1. (Its, It's) almost two o'clock.
2. The oak tree doesn't shed (its, it's) leaves until spring.
3. (Its, It's) been raining all week.
4. That Ford has lost (its, it's) muffler.
5. The ginger cat and (its, it's) kittens are on the back porch.
6. (Its, It's) been a long time since I've seen you.
7. (Its, It's) hard to work when you're tired.
8. The groundhog saw (its, it's) shadow.
9. (Its, It's) almost spring.
10. The hurricane left fallen trees, damaged houses, and floods in (its, it's) wake.
11. The monkey was annoying (its, it's) owner.
12. (Its, It's) time to leave for the movie.
13. The crow cawed (its, it's) warning as the farmer approached.
14. (Its, It's) been a windy spring afternoon..
15. That robin builds (its, it's) nest in that old maple every·year.
16. (Its, It's) past time for that bus to arrive.
17. (Its, It's) time for the football season.
18. The snake sheds (its, it's) old skin several times a year.
19. (Its, It's) fun to make model airplanes.
20. That Mustang has lost (its, it's) front license plate.

like and as

A. Choose the word in parentheses that completes each sentence according to formal usage.

1. Do (as, like) I do.
2. I did it exactly (as, like) you told me to.
3. She swims (as, like) a champion.

4. Clark won the race, just (as, like) he does every year.
5. Roll up your sleeping bag (as, like) I have demonstrated.
6. It looked (as, like) another squall line approaching.
7. The glass sparkled (as, like) jewelry.
8. He is tall, (as, like) me.
9. The plan worked (as, like) a charm.
10. My teacher spoke (as, like) a doctor would about health.
11. Plan your moves carefully (as, like) a strategist.
12. Her hat looked (as, like) a fallen soufflé.
13. There goes a unicycle (as, like) mine!
14. Have you ever heard anything (as, like) that?
15. The horns on that bull were shaved (as, like) they should be.

B. Rewrite the following sentences, inserting the words *the way* in place of *like* or *as* only where appropriate.

1. The furnace is working as it used to.
2. The chairperson, like her predecessor, appointed a press agent.
3. I know him like I know my own brother.
4. We will proceed as we should—with caution.
5. The moon hung in the sky like a pendant.

parallelism in sentences

Revise the following sentences to eliminate unparallel and needlessly shifted constructions.

1. Greg and Chuck spent most of the summer playing chess on the porch, swimming in the pool, and sailed on the lake.
2. After one has greased and floured the pans, you should preheat the oven.
3. The movie was long, boring, and had no point.
4. You will have to choose between going to the movie tonight, or you can go to the basketball game tomorrow.
5. Before the miller's daughter had a chance to say anything, Rumpelstiltskin disappears.
6. The director reminded us to keep calm, to speak clearly, and that we should move quickly after the curtain closed.
7. Catholics, Jews, and Protestant people attended the Ecumenical Council.
8. Jennifer is a good student, a good leader, and athletic.
9. If one is really worried about it, you could talk to your parents.
10. Before the test begins, everyone seemed very nervous.
11. Bareback riding, bull riding, and how to rope a calf were the main events at the rodeo.

12. The furniture is comfortable, sturdy, and has bright colors.
13. Ginny has to decide between going to camp for the summer, and she could get a job here in town.
14. After one has a nightmare, I cannot get back to sleep.
15. Nell likes playing tennis, riding her bicycle, and magazines.
16. Just as my favorite TV program was about to begin, the electricity goes off.
17. Both the twins are tall, brown-eyed, and have blond hair.
18. We considered setting up our own department, working with an existing department, or we could drop the project.
19. Miguel is a person with talent and who has a will to win.
20. Mr. Wing asked Lilla to come forward, and she was given the award by him.

pronouns and nouns before *ing* verb forms

Choose the form of the pronoun or noun in parentheses that is appropriate to formal speaking and writing.

1. I wish I understood (him, his) thinking on that question.
2. (Them, Their) washing the dishes helped us finish on time.
3. The (dog, dog's) barking may have frightened the children.
4. Graceful movements, fine shooting ability, and excellent team-work mark (Kareem Abdul-Jabbar, Kareem Abdul-Jabbar's) basketball playing.
5. (Mom, Mom's) working until five means we all help cook.
6. Sometimes the (cat, cat's) purring sounds like a motorboat.
7. (Sharon, Sharon's) clenching her fist revealed her anger.
8. (Us, Our) cleaning out the garage turned into a day's work.
9. We are getting tired of (you, your) boasting.
10. (Jo, Jo's) discussing the problem with Danny made them both feel better.
11. (Kevin, Kevin's) studying for the test consisted of a half-hour review with the radio on.
12. What upset us was (Martha, Martha's) pretending to care.
13. Marcela felt cheered by (Jo, Jo's) understanding.
14. (Us, Our) protesting about the dress code made the principal reevaluate its usefulness.
15. (Me, My) finishing last in the race disqualified me.
16. My (brother, brother's) talking all the time annoys me.
17. (Them, Their) accepting Roberto's poem for publication was no surprise.
18. The most exciting part of the meet was (Kathy, Kathy's) swimming the free style.

19. (Me, My) repairing the motor took almost an hour.
20. (Marion Anderson, Marion Anderson's) singing in public began in church choirs when she was eight years old.

quotation marks

Rewrite the following sentences, adding quotation marks wherever they are needed.

1. Grey Cohoe wrote a story, The Promised Visit, while he was a student at the Institute of American Indian Arts.
2. Where, asked Joan, could you have left the keys?
3. The entire crowd was shouting, We want George!
4. Nora recited two poems by Langston Hughes: Dream Variation and I, Too, Sing America.
5. The best chapter in the book was Western Ways.
6. Dina asked, Aren't we all forgetting something?
7. We read The Street of the Cañon by Josephina Niggli.
8. Bob submitted an essay entitled Confused and Condemned.
9. One of John Coltrane's recordings was My Favorite Things.
10. Who said, I regret that I have but one life to give for my country?
11. Dotty reported on The Brown House, a story by Hisaye Yamamoto.
12. If everyone is finally ready, said Ms. Rodriguez, we can begin.
13. Melvin B. Tolson's poem, Dark Symphony, was published in *The Atlantic Monthly.*
14. "Piece of My Heart was Janis Joplin's best song," said Annette.
15. Carrie did a modern dance interpretation of Go Down, Moses.
16. "Did your mother say, I was young once, too?" asked Roger.
17. A Good Long Sidewalk appears in *Dancers on the Shore,* a collection of short stories by William Melvin Kelley.
18. Wouldn't that be a lot easier? asked Stella.
19. My favorite song is Roberta Flack's version of Let It Be Me.
20. "Tomorrow we'll discuss Richard Olivas' poem The Immigrant Experience," announced Miss Dryjanski.

run-on sentence

Correct each of the following run-on sentences.

1. We went to see a movie, afterward we stopped for pizza.
2. Rita has an extra pair of skis, you might be able to borrow them.
3. Manny wants to go to the game, I want to watch TV.

4. The magazine came out in April, I didn't have a chance to read it until July.
5. Snow fell all night, the roads were impassable in the morning.
6. The Yamaguchis have gone on vacation, they are driving to Carmel and Big Sur.
7. The plaintiff did not appear, therefore the judge dismissed the case.
8. Dave and Liz don't want to come, they have seen the movie.
9. The alarm is ringing, it must be 7:15.
10. We have decided, now we must act.
11. Lenny was pleased, his brother's team won the tournament.
12. Nina understands these math problems, maybe she can help us.
13. Max claims the fire was an accident, I doubt it.
14. Lori read about John Adams, he was our second President.
15. I enjoy Emily Dickinson's poems, some of them are in our literature anthology.
16. Our leader is Ms. Vasquez, she is the recreation director.
17. Mindy has a job at the drive-in, she is earning money for college.
18. Rick plays the piano, Randy plays the violin.
19. I am going to Camp Lone Tree, it's in Michigan.
20. The first conference proved very helpful, therefore we have scheduled another for next Tuesday.

sentence fragment

Revise the following examples to eliminate sentence fragments.

1. Mary Lyon founded Mount Holyoke. And served as its president.
2. After he finishes washing the dishes. Denny is going to the basketball game.
3. Gertrude Stein wrote *The Autobiography of Alice B. Toklas.* Which is really the story of Stein's own life.
4. Everyone enjoys picnics. Especially at the beach.
5. Flora, who was called Chloris by the Greeks. She was the Roman goddess of springtime and flowers.
6. As soon as the snow began to fall. All the children ran outside.
7. Lou wants to visit the Fountain of Trevi. Which is in Rome.
8. Dad is reading *Wonderland.* A novel by Joyce Carol Oates.
9. The first California mission was established by Father Junipero Serra. Near what is today the city of San Diego.
10. Marcus Garvey was born in Jamaica. And moved to the United States as an adult.

11. Richie jogged to the top of the mountain. And collapsed when he got there.
12. The Havasupai Indians live in a section of the Grand Canyon. Called Havasu Canyon.
13. Geronimo's Indian name was *Goyathlay*. Which means *one who yawns*.
14. Virginia lives in Winnipeg. Which is the capital of Manitoba.
15. We want to go swimming in the Pacific. And hiking in the Sierras.
16. Whenever someone comes to the door. Brutus growls and whines.
17. Gloria Steinem helped establish the National Women's Political Caucus in 1971. And founded *Ms.* magazine in 1972.
18. Mom went to visit her father. Who lives in South Dakota.
19. We went to see *The Great Gatsby*. Based on the book by F. Scott Fitzgerald.
20. Our humanities class is studying Mary Cassatt. Who was an American painter who settled in Paris.

several, each, and some

Choose the singular or the plural form in parentheses to match the singular or plural word italicized in each sentence.

1. *Many* of the flights (have, has) been cancelled.
2. *Both* the boy and his father (are, is) working in the garden.
3. *Neither* of the rings (were, was) expensive.
4. *Everybody* (have, has) an assignment.
5. Only a *few* (are, is) missing.
6. *Either* of the plans (meet, meets) her specifications.
7. (Do, Does) *anyone* have a set of jumper cables?
8. *Each* of the titles (are, is) appropriate.
9. *Some* of the money (were, was) missing.
10. *Most* of the field (were, was) plowed.
11. *Some* of the pencils (are, is) broken.
12. *All* of the audience (are, is) calling for an encore.
13. The *rest* of the seeds (are, is) to be planted in the fall.
14. *Part* of the renovation (have, has) been completed.
15. *Most* of the tennis courts (are, is) asphalt.
16. (Have, Has) *all* of the votes been counted?
17. *Anyone* who (wish, wishes) may enter the contest.
18. *Either* of the girls (are, is) eligible to play on the team.
19. We looked for a seat, but *many* (were, was) already taken.
20. *Several*, however, (were, was) still vacant.

subject-verb agreement

Choose the verb in parentheses that agrees in number with the subject of each sentence.

1. His chief support (is, are) his mother and father.
2. The winning quartet (was, were) the Semi-precious Tones.
3. The judge, as well as the jury, (was, were) impressed by the witness.
4. Physics (is, are) Rita's favorite subject.
5. Tigers and leopards (is, are) dangerous game.
6. Sam, with Martin and Ivan, (is, are) taking music lessons.
7. There (is, are) the skid marks.
8. Beyond the horizon (waits, wait) the fleet.
9. The barrels that (sits, sit) on the dock should be loaded.
10. The women in the office (is, are) in the majority.
11. Sixteen feet (is, are) the maximum length.
12. The recurrence of similar sounds (heightens, heighten) the poem's appeal.
13. Linda, together with Joyce and Louella, (was, were) going to enlist in the navy.
14. It (is, are) the children who suffer.
15. The bridge over the railroad tracks (needs, need) repair.
16. Measles (is, are) usually a childhood disease.
17. My favorite breakfast (includes, include) eggs and muffins.
18. The chief attraction (was, were) the kudu and the wildebeest.
19. The sound of the drums (is, are) terrifying.
20. Two dollars (is, are) all that I have.

them and those

Choose *them* or *those* to complete each of the following sentences.

1. Would you hand me __ paintbrushes, please?
2. __ last two games were the most important ones in the series.
3. Mother and Dad moved __ old chairs out of the attic.
4. I hope the judges give __ gymnasts an award.
5. Did you put sugar on __ pancakes?
6. I can hear the children outside; ask __ to come in now.
7. __ reports should be made available to the public immediately.
8. Beavers built that dam and left __ tree stumps.
9. __ look like Jeanne's books; maybe she's still here.
10. If you see Al and Chuck, will you tell __ I've gone?
11. Save __ bread crumbs for the birds!
12. Just put these new books next to __ old ones.

13. __ problems at the end of the test were really hard.
14. My cousins are teaching me to swim; I'm going to the pool with __ tomorrow.
15. __ are the ones I want.
16. As soon as Martha and Dan arrive, give __ this message.
17. Do you think __ tracks could have been made by a rabbit?
18. __ cookies should be done by now.
19. Lisa learned to use __ tools in her woodworking class.
20. Have you put __ reflecting strips on your bike yet?

underlining

Rewrite the following sentences, adding underlines wherever necessary.

1. We were all sad when we had to say arivederci to Rome.
2. There are three 6's in our phone number.
3. Pearl S. Buck received the Pulitzer prize for her novel The Good Earth.
4. Dr. Garcia lent me this issue of the American Heart Journal.
5. Should this word be illusion or allusion?
6. This book, Black Elk Speaks, was illustrated by Standing Bear.
7. My parents gave me a subscription to Ms. magazine.
8. The German philosopher Friedrich Nietzsche developed the concept of the Übermensch, or superman.
9. "Lady Lazarus" is one of the poems in Sylvia Plath's collection Ariel.
10. The members of the French Club dress, eat, and think à la française.
11. Katharine Hepburn won Academy Awards for her roles in Morning Glory, Guess Who's Coming to Dinner, and The Lion in Winter.
12. Is the third digit a 7 or a 9?
13. Ben Shahn painted The Passion of Sacco and Vanzetti to protest the execution of Nicola Sacco and Bartolomeo Vanzetti.
14. All the vowels in dependent are e's.
15. The largest wooden ship ever built, the Great Republic, was launched in 1853.
16. Catalogue may be spelled without the final ue.
17. Katherine Graham is the publisher of The Washington Post.
18. Michelangelo's Pietà is now protected by bulletproof glass.
19. They are members of the monde, or fashionable society.
20. I frequently confuse the words eminent and imminent.

(ACKNOWLEDGMENTS continued from page 2.)

SOULSCRIPT: AFRO-AMERICAN POETRY, edited by June Jordan. Published by Doubleday & Company, Inc.; copyright © 1970 by June Meyer Jordan./ From "Fixing Things: A Guide for the Bewildered" by Bill Elisburg in *Esquire Magazine*, September 1974. Reprinted by permission of *Esquire Magazine* © 1974 by Esquire, Inc./ "The Rebel" in I AM A BLACK WOMAN by Mari Evans. Published by William Morrow & Company, Inc.; copyright 1970 Mari Evans and used by permission./ "Stopping by Woods on a Snowy Evening" by Robert Frost from THE POETRY OF ROBERT FROST edited by Edward Connery Lathem. Copyright 1923, © 1969 by Holt, Rinehart and Winston, Inc. Copyright 1951 by Robert Frost. Reprinted by permission of Holt, Rinehart and Winston, Publishers./ "two words" by Sarah Gallagher in ANTHOLOGY OF CONCRETE POETRY, edited by Lavonne Mueller. Used by permission of Lavonne Mueller./ From "Among My People" by Jovita González in TONE THE BELL EASY, edited by J. Frank Dobie. Published by the Texas Folklore Society; copyright 1932 by the Texas Folklore Society./ From "How to Recognize LIBRA" in SUN SIGNS by Linda Goodman. Copyright © 1968 by Linda Goodman; published by Taplinger Publishing Co., Inc., New York./ From "Robin Sails Home" by Robin Lee Graham in *National Geographic*, October, 1970; copyright 1970 National Geographic Society./ From A RAISIN IN THE SUN by Lorraine Hansberry. Published by Random House, Inc.; copyright 1959 by Lorraine Hansberry./ From "The Girls Who Taught Lane Tech a Lesson" by Rochelle Harris in the *Chicago Tribune*, May 19, 1974; reprinted, courtesy of the *Chicago Tribune*./ From MR. & MRS. BO JO JONES by Ann Head. Published by The New American Library, Inc., by arrangement with G. P. Putnam's Sons; copyright 1967 by Ann Head./ From "On the Road" in LAUGHING TO KEEP FROM CRYING by Langston Hughes. Reprinted by permission of Harold Ober Associates Incorporated; copyright 1952 by Langston Hughes./ From "Where Do We Go from Here in Education?" by Robert M. Hutchins. Reprinted by permission of the Author and his Agent, James Brown Associates, Inc.; copyright © 1953 by Robert M. Hutchins./ From "The Lottery" with the permission of Farrar, Straus & Giroux, Inc. from THE LOTTERY by Shirley Jackson; Copyright 1948, 1949 by Shirley Jackson./ From "Baseball" by Pat Jordan in *Sports Illustrated*, July 29, 1974. Copyright © 1947 by Pat Jordan; reprinted by permission of The Sterling Lord Agency, Inc./ From "Sports" by Roger Kahn in *Esquire Magazine*, October, 1973. Reprinted by permission of *Esquire Magazine* © 1973 by Esquire, Inc./ From "Communes for All Reasons" by Rosabeth Moss Kanter in *Ms.*, August, 1974; copyright 1974 Rosabeth Moss Kanter./ From TENNIS TO WIN by Billie Jean King with Kim Chapin; copyright © 1970 by Harper & Row, Publishers, Inc. By permission of Harper & Row, Publishers, Inc./ From FOUR WAYS OF BEING HUMAN by Gene Lisitzky. Copyright © 1956 by Gene Lisitzky; reprinted by permission of The Viking Press, Inc./ Copyright © 1968 by Jean McCord. From DEEP WHERE THE OCTOPI LIE. Used by permission of Atheneum Publishers./ From "The Way We Talk" by Raven I. McDavid, Jr. in *The New York Times Magazine*, April 23, 1950; © 1950 by The New York Times Company. Reprinted by permission./ "A Choice of Weapons" from TIMES THREE by Phyllis McGinley; copyright 1954 by Phyllis McGinley. Originally appeared in *The New Yorker;* reprinted by permission of The Viking Press, Inc./ From DON'T FALL OFF THE MOUNTAIN by Shirley MacLaine. By permission of W. W. Norton & Company, Inc. Copyright © 1970 by Shirley MacLaine./ From "Becoming a spokesperson" by Stephen Marshall in *The Chicago Guide*, June, 1974; copyright 1974 by WFMT, Inc./ From DEATH OF A SALESMAN by Arthur Miller. Copyright 1949 by Arthur Miller; reprinted by permission of The Viking Press, Inc./ "Gone Forever" by Barriss Mills is from DOMESTIC FABLES, © 1971 Barriss Mills, and reprinted by permission of The Elizabeth Press./ From "Exploring America Underground" by Charles E. Mohr in *National Geographic*, June, 1964; copyright 1964 National Geographic Society./ From THE WAY TO RAINY MOUNTAIN by N. Scott Momaday. Published by The University of New Mexico Press; copyright 1969 The University of New Mexico Press./ From DO WITH ME WHAT YOU WILL by Joyce Carol Oates by permission of the publisher, Vanguard Press, Inc. Copyright, © 1973 by Joyce Carol Oates./ From EXPENSIVE PEOPLE by Joyce Carol Oates by permission of the publisher, Vanguard Press, Inc. Copyright, © 1968 by Joyce Carol Oates./ "Clock" by Beth Oderkirk in ANTHOLOGY OF CON-

255

CRETE POETRY, edited by Lavonne Mueller. Used by permission of Lavonne Mueller./ From "The 1974 Oldsmobile 98 Regency" advertisement, courtesy of Oldsmobile Division of General Motors Corporation and General Motors of Canada Limited./ From "Wells, Hitler and the World State" in THE COLLECTED ESSAYS, JOURNALISM AND LETTERS OF GEORGE ORWELL, Volume 2, edited by Sonia Orwell and Clair Angus; copyright 1968 Harcourt Brace Jovanovich, Inc./ From "The Bending of a Twig" by Alfredo Otero y Herrera in *Arizona Quarterly*, Vol. XXV, No. 1, Spring, 1969. Published by the University of Arizona; copyright 1969 the *Arizona Quarterly*./ From "In Darkness and Confusion" by Ann Petry in CROSS-SECTION 1947, edited by Edwin Seaver. Published by Simon & Schuster, Inc.; copyright 1947 by Edwin Seaver./ From "The Nutrition Dilemma" by Clara Pierre in *Saturday Review/World*, May 18, 1974; copyright 1974 *Saturday Review/World*./ From THE BELL JAR by Sylvia Plath. Copyright © 1971 by Harper & Row, Publishers, Inc.; by permission of Harper & Row, Publishers, Inc. Canadian rights by permission of the Estate of Sylvia Plath; copyright Sylvia Plath, 1963; published by Faber and Faber, London./ From OUT OF MY LEAGUE by George Plimpton. By permission of Harper & Row, Publishers, Inc./ From "Anyone for Burger Builder?" by Geraldine Pluenneke in *Saturday Review/World*, December 18, 1973; copyright 1973 *Saturday Review/World*./ From "An Effective Approach to Paper Recycling" by Philip W. Quigg in *Saturday Review/World*, June 15, 1974; copyright 1974 Philip W. Quigg./ "On Watching the Construction of a Skyscraper" by Burton Raffel; copyright © 1961 by The Antioch Press. First published in THE ANTIOCH REVIEW, vol. 20, no. 4; reprinted by permission of the editors./ From MOMENT IN THE SUN by Robert and Leona T. Rienow. Published by The Dial Press; copyright 1967 by Robert Rienow and Leona Train Rienow./ From "Spinnaker Flying" by Frank Rohr in *Travel & Leisure*, July, 1974; copyright 1974 by American Express Publishing Corporation./ From "We *Must* Subsidize Mass Transit" by William J. Ronan in *Reader's Digest*, April, 1974./ "War" by Dan Roth. Reprinted by permission from *Literary Cavalcade*, © 1963 by Scholastic Magazines, Inc./ From "School Spirit" by David Royce in WRITER'S ADVISER by Irwin Griggs and David Webster, published by American Book Company./ From "How to Play Second Base" by Laurence Sheehan in *The Atlantic Monthly*, September, 1974. Copyright © 1974, by The Atlantic Monthly Company, Boston, Mass. Reprinted with permission./ From "The Dark Glasses" in VOICES AT PLAY by Muriel Spark. Copyright © 1961 by Muriel Spark. Reprinted by permission of J. B. Lippincott Company./ From THE WEB OF LIFE by John H. Storer. Published by the Devin-Adair Company; © 1953 by John Storer./ From BLESS THE BEASTS AND CHILDREN by Glendon Swarthout. Published by Doubleday & Company, Inc.; copyright 1970 by Glendon Swarthout./ From OF MEN AND MUSIC by Deems Taylor. Published by Simon & Schuster, Inc.; copyright 1937 by Deems Taylor./ From GENERAL CHEMISTRY by John Arend Timm. Copyright 1944 McGraw-Hill Book Company. Used with permission of McGraw-Hill Book Company./ From "Remembering D-Day" by TRB in THE NEW REPUBLIC, vol. 170, no. 23. Reprinted by Permission of THE NEW REPUBLIC, © 1974 The New Republic, Inc./ From "An olive branch for the polar bear" by Savva M. Uspenskij; copyright B932440 by the National Wildlife Federation. Reprinted from the May–June, 1974, issue of *International Wildlife* Magazine./ From INNOCENT KILLERS by Hugo and Jane van Lawick-Goodall. Published by Houghton Mifflin Company; copyright 1970 by Hugo and Jane van Lawick-Goodall. Canadian rights by permission of Wm. Collins Sons & Co. Ltd./ From THE FEMININE FIX-IT HANDBOOK by Kay B. Ward. Published by Grosset & Dunlap, Inc.; copyright 1972 by Kay B. Ward./ From "The Patented Gate and the Mean Hamburger" in THE CIRCUS IN THE ATTIC AND OTHER STORIES by Robert Penn Warren. Published by Harcourt Brace Jovanovich, Inc.; copyright 1947 Robert Penn Warren./ From "A Memory" in A CURTAIN OF GREEN AND OTHER STORIES by Eudora Welty. Published by Harcourt Brace Jovanovich, Inc.; copyright 1943 by Eudora Welty./ From "Freedom" in ONE MAN'S MEAT by E. B. White. Copyright 1940 by E. B. White; by permission of Harper & Row, Publishers, Inc./ From FOXFIRE 2, edited with an introduction by Eliot Wigginton. Published by Doubleday & Company, Inc.; copyright 1973 by the Southern Highlands Literary Fund, Inc. and Brooks Eliot Wigginton./ From WRITERS AT WORK: The Paris Review Interviews, Third Series; copyright © 1967 by the Paris Review, Inc. All rights reserved; reprinted by permission of the Viking Press, Inc./From "Mending Wall" from THE POETRY OF ROBERT FROST, edited by Edward Connery Lathem. Copyright 1930, 1939, © 1969 by Holt, Rinehart and Winston, Inc. Copyright © 1958 by Robert Frost. Copyright © 1967 by Lesley Frost Ballantine. Reprinted by permission of Holt, Rinehart and Winston, Publishers.